Addison-Wesley
Science

Authors

Charles Barman, Ed.D.
Associate Professor of Science Education
Indiana University, Indianapolis

Michael DiSpezio, M.A.
Science Department Chairman
Cape Cod Academy, Massachusetts

Vallie Guthrie, Ph.D.
Director, Greensboro Area Math
and Science Education Center
North Carolina Agricultural and Technical
State University

Michael B. Leyden, Ed.D.
Professor of Education
Eastern Illinois University

Sheryl Mercier, M.A.
Elementary Science Specialist
Fresno Unified School District,
California

Karen Ostlund, Ph.D.
Associate Professor of Education
Southwest Texas State University

Reading Consultant

Bonnie Armbruster, Ph.D.
Associate Professor
Center for the Study of Reading and
Department of Elementary and Early
Childhood Education
University of Illinois

▲ **Addison-Wesley Publishing Company**

Menlo Park, California • Reading, Massachusetts • New York
Don Mills, Ontario • Wokingham, England • Amsterdam • Bonn
Sydney • Singapore • Tokyo • Madrid • Bogotá • Santiago • San Juan

Content Consultants

Thomas H. Callen II, Ph.D.
Program Resource Manager
Albert Einstein Planetarium
National Air and Space Museum
Smithsonian Institution

Jym Ganahl
Chief Meteorologist
WCMH-TV, Columbus, Ohio

Edwin Harper, Ph.D.
Associate Professor of Biochemistry
Indiana University School of Medicine

Robert W. Hinds, Ph.D.
Professor of Geology
Slippery Rock University, Pennsylvania

Chelcie Liu, Ph.D.
Physics Instructor
City College of San Francisco

Luis A. Martinez-Perez, Ph.D.
Associate Professor of Science Education
Florida International University

Linda Medleau, D.V.M., M.S.
Assistant Professor
Department of Small Animal Medicine
University of Georgia

Larry K. Pickering, M.D.
Professor of Pediatrics and Director of
Pediatric Infectious Diseases
University of Texas Medical School at Houston

Linda Sanford
Curator of Youth Education
Morton Arboretum, Lisle, Illinois

Lydia Young, Ph.D.
Senior Engineer
Perkin-Elmer Electron Beam Technology
Hayward, California

Critical Thinking Consultant
Robert Swartz, Ph.D.
Director of Critical and Creative Thinking Program
University of Massachusetts, Boston

Safety Consultant
Jay A. Young, Ph.D.
Chemical Consultant
Silver Spring, Maryland

Testing Consultant
David P. Butts, Ph.D.
Aderhold Distinguished Professor
College of Education
University of Georgia

Getting to Know
Addison-Wesley Science

This book has been made to help you learn science. It has many features to make learning science exciting. It will answer some questions you have and probably start you thinking about some new ones. Explore your book. See what features you can find.

To make the most of *Addison-Wesley Science,* take some time to learn how it is organized. That will make science easier to understand. Find the table of contents. Notice that this book is divided into four units. Each unit focuses on a certain kind of science: life, physical, earth, or health science. Each unit consists of several chapters. Each chapter is made up of a few lessons.

Pick a chapter that sounds interesting. What unit is it a part of? Turn to the beginning of that unit. Each unit begins with a preview of the chapters in it. Read what your chapter is about.

Now turn to the chapter. At the beginning of each chapter, you will find a yellow box. It tells you what you will learn in the chapter. What can you look forward to learning when your class studies your chapter?

Contents

Reading Science   6
Thinking About Science   8
Doing What Scientists Do   10
Safety in Science   12

Unit 1   Life Science   14

Chapter 1
Animals Without Backbones   16
1   The Simplest Animals   18
2   Shell and Spiny Animals   24
3   Joint-Legged Animals   28

Chapter 2
Animals with Backbones   40
1   Fish   42
2   Amphibians and Reptiles   46
3   Birds and Mammals   52

Chapter 3   Food from Plants   64
1   Plants Make Food   66
2   Energy from Food   74

Chapter 4   Ecosystems   82
1   Living in an Environment   84
2   Cycles in Ecosystems   90
3   Changing Ecosystems   94

Chapter 5   The Earth's Biomes   102
1   Climate and Life   104
2   Biomes on Earth   110
3   Water Ecosystems   120

Ask a Scientist   130
Careers & Science   131
Thinking Critically   132

Unit 2   Physical Science   134

Chapter 6
The Structure of Matter   **136**
1 Matter   138
2 Combining Elements   144
3 Different Mixtures   150

Chapter 7 Sound   **160**
1 How Sound Travels   162
2 Why Sounds Are Different   168
3 Making and Hearing Sounds   174

Chapter 8 Motion   **184**
1 Speed of Motion   186
2 Laws of Motion   190
3 Gravity and Friction   196

Chapter 9 Energy Resources   **206**
1 Today's Energy Resources   208
2 Future Energy Resources   216
3 Energy Conservation   222

Ask a Scientist   230
Careers & Science   231
Thinking Critically   232

Unit 3   Earth Science   234

Chapter 10
The Earth's History   **236**
1 Reading the Rock Record   238
2 Millions of Years Ago   246

Chapter 11
Oceans of the Earth   **258**
1 The Ocean Water   260
2 The Ocean Bottom   268
3 Ocean Resources   276

Chapter 12
The Changing Weather   **284**
1 The Causes of Weather   286
2 Storms   292

Chapter 13 Motion in Space   **306**
1 Movements of the Earth   308
2 Movements of the Moon   316

Ask a Scientist   328
Careers & Science   329
Thinking Critically   330

Unit 4   Health Science   332

Chapter 14 Transport Systems   **334**
1 The Circulatory System   336
2 The Respiratory System   344
3 Care of Transport Systems   348

Chapter 15
Drugs and Your Health   **356**
1 Helpful Drugs   358
2 Harmful Drugs   364
3 Drug Choice and Health   370

Ask a Scientist   378
Careers & Science   379
Thinking Critically   380

Data Bank   382
Science Fair   386
Double Check   388
Glossary   403
Index   410

Reading Science

Reading a science textbook is not like reading a story. You may not need to work hard to understand a story. You may not need to remember a story for a long time, either. But when you read science, you are reading to learn something new. You will need to think about what you read. You will also need to remember as much as you can. You may just *read* a story. But you will need to *study* your science textbook.

Here is a way to help you study. Following these steps will help you understand science.

 Skim

Skim means look over. Read all the titles in the chapter. Notice the science words. Look at the pictures. These things will tell you what the chapter is about.

Take just a few minutes to skim. Then, think of what you already know about the topic.

Each lesson begins with a purpose question in the margin. After you read the lesson, you should be able to answer the question.

A lesson is divided into sections. Each section begins with a title in dark print.

Within a section, important science words are in dark print. You need to remember what each science word means.

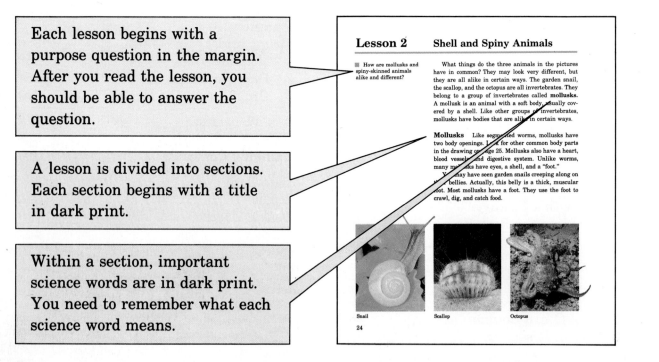

Lesson 2   Shell and Spiny Animals

■ How are mollusks and spiny-skinned animals alike and different?

What things do the three animals in the pictures have in common? They may look very different, but they are all alike in certain ways. The garden snail, the scallop, and the octopus are all invertebrates. They belong to a group of invertebrates called **mollusks**. A mollusk is an animal with a soft body, usually covered by a shell. Like other groups of invertebrates, mollusks have bodies that are alike in certain ways.

Mollusks   Like segmented worms, mollusks have two body openings. Look for other common body parts in the drawing on page 25. Mollusks also have a heart, blood vessels, and digestive system. Unlike worms, many mollusks have eyes, a shell, and a "foot." You may have seen garden snails creeping along on their bellies. Actually, this belly is a thick, muscular foot. Most mollusks have a foot. They use the foot to crawl, dig, and catch food.

Snail
Scallop
Octopus

24

6

2 Read

Carefully read one section at a time. Try to find the main ideas. Learn what the science words mean. Try to pronounce the new words that are respelled. Look at all the pictures. Read the labels and captions.

If you do not understand what you are reading, try this. Read the confusing part plus what came right before it again. If that does not help, read on a little. If you still do not understand, ask for help.

3 Review

Review means look back over. Read all the section titles again. Look at the pictures again, too. Make sure you can define all the science words in your own words.

Review the chapter at least twice. First, review each lesson right after you finish reading it. Then review the whole chapter a day or two later. The more times you review, the more you will remember.

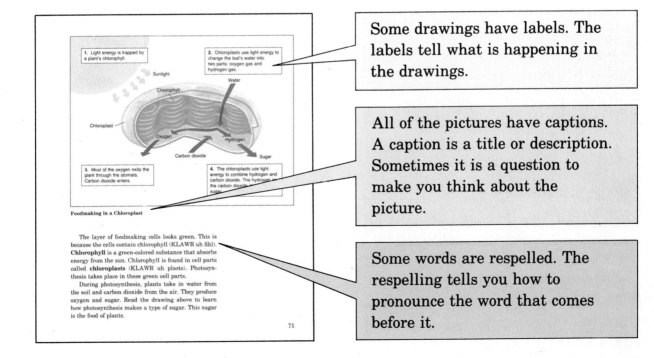

Some drawings have labels. The labels tell what is happening in the drawings.

All of the pictures have captions. A caption is a title or description. Sometimes it is a question to make you think about the picture.

Some words are respelled. The respelling tells you how to pronounce the word that comes before it.

Thinking About Science

As you study science, you will probably ask a lot of questions. You will have to answer a lot of questions, too. You will run into some questions as you read. When you do, you should stop and think about the answers. Some captions are questions. You should think about the answers when you look at the pictures.

Knowing more about questions will help you be a better question answerer. Here is one way to look at questions. Think about where you will find the answers.

You may find the answers in this book. Two kinds of questions in *Addison-Wesley Science* are answered in the book.

1. **Purpose question** Read the question in the margin before you read a lesson. It tells you the purpose of the lesson. Read the question again after you have read the lesson. If you cannot answer the question, you should read the lesson again.

2. **Checkup questions** You will find these questions at the end of each lesson and each chapter. They will help you review what you read. After reading, you should be able to answer the questions, but if you cannot, you can find the answers by reviewing the lessons. There are extra checkup questions for each lesson on the Double Check pages at the end of your book.

Four other kinds of questions in *Addison-Wesley Science* are not answered entirely in this book.

T H I N K

Do you think the oxygen you are breathing now may once have been breathed by a dinosaur? Explain.

Z O N E

1. **Think Zone** appears once in each lesson. It is always in the margin.

2. **Think Critically!** always appears at the end of each lesson.

3. **Think About It** appears in the Technology Today at the end of each chapter.

4. **Problem Solving** always appears at the end of each chapter.

You will need to use some information from the lesson to answer these questions. But you will also have to think about what you know. These questions may not have only one right answer. So do not worry about whether your answer is right. Just say what you think.

As you come across questions in *Addison-Wesley Science,* think about where you will find the answers. Remember that you may find some answers in this book and a lot in your head! Always answer questions in your own words. That will help you remember what you have learned.

Doing What Scientists Do

Scientists ask a lot of questions. Sometimes the answers are not in any book. There may not be anyone who knows the answers. Then scientists use scientific methods to find answers.

A factory wants to dump waste water into a nearby bay. The waste water is clean, but it is hot. Two scientists were asked, "Will the factory's waste water harm living things in a bay?" The pictures show the scientific methods they used to find the answer.

Before the experiment, the scientists measured the temperatures of the bay and waste water. Then they collected several samples of each. They counted the living things in each sample.

The scientists set up their experiment with a variable and a control group. A **variable** is some factor that is changed during the experiment. A **control** group is not changed by the variable. With a control group, scientists can tell

1 **Problem**

Will the factory's waste water harm living things in the bay? The scientists guessed that it would. This guess is called a hypothesis.

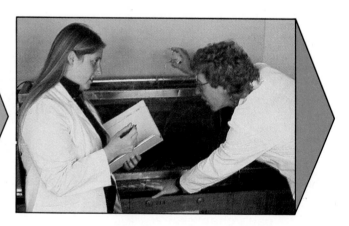

2 **Experimenting**

The scientists added waste water to three bay samples and nothing to three others. This last group was the control. The variable was waste water.

whether the variable caused the results or if the results would have happened anyway. In this experiment, the scientists could not conclude that the hot waste water was harmful to fish if fish had died in the control group, too.

Sometimes finding the answer to a question brings up other questions. For example, how hot does the water have to be to harm fish? How would you solve this problem? What would your variable be?

You probably wonder about many things. You are like a scientist. You may have questions that are not answered in your textbook. You may find the answers in other books. Sometimes your teacher will know the answers. Or you might ask a scientist. Sometimes you can use scientific methods to find the answers.

Whenever you think about science, do not be afraid to ask questions. Then think about where you can find the answers.

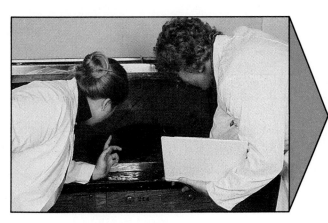 

3 | Recording Data

The scientists counted the living things in each sample every day for a week after the experiment. They kept track of all this data.

4 | Drawing Conclusions

The scientists found no changes to the control group but a few dead fish in the other group. They concluded that the waste water was harmful to fish.

Safety in Science

Scientists are careful when they work. You need to be careful in science, too. Here are some safety tips to remember.

WEAR GOGGLES!

1. Before you do an activity, make sure your teacher says it is okay to do it.

2. Read all the directions before you start. If you do not understand them, ask your teacher for help.

3. As you do the activity, follow the directions carefully. Tell your teacher if you make a mistake.

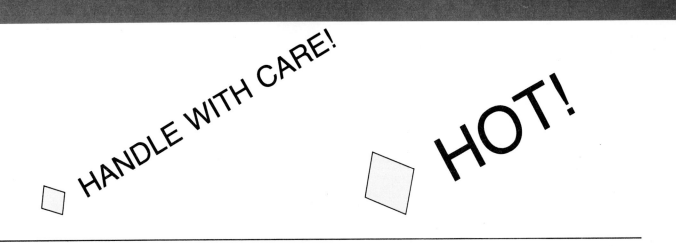

4. Obey the safety notes where you see a ◇. Wear goggles or an apron when needed.

5. Never taste anything unless your teacher says it is okay. Do not touch your eyes or mouth while you are working with plants, animals, or chemicals.

6. After you have done the activity, clean up and put things back where they belong. Then wash your hands.

13

Unit One
Life Science

Chapter 1
Animals Without Backbones

The animal world can be divided into animals with backbones and animals without backbones. Most animals on earth do not have backbones.

Chapter 2
Animals with Backbones

Animals with backbones are found everywhere. Each type of animal has particular body parts that make it different from other animals.

Chapter 3
Food from Plants

Plants use the sun's energy, plus water and air, to make food and give off oxygen. Animals depend on plants for both food and oxygen.

Chapter 4
Ecosystems

Organisms interact with nonliving resources in the environment. The living and nonliving resources in an ecosystem often change with time.

Chapter 5
The Earth's Biomes

Plants and animals live in areas that meet their needs. The plant community in a certain area determines the animal life.

Chapter 1
Animals Without Backbones

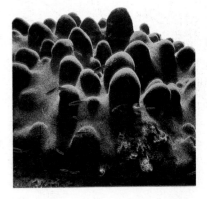

In this chapter, you will learn

- how scientists group animals
- how animals without backbones can be classified into eight groups
- what features are common to all joint-legged animals
- how to tell one joint-legged animal from another

Jeremy's family lives near the seashore. He likes to walk along the beach with his older sister, Janice. On the beach and on the rocks, they find many plants and animals. Jeremy and Janice often find shells of animals or pieces of seaweed.

Sometimes Jeremy sees starfish. The starfish gets its name from its arms, which make it look like a star. Jeremy finds starfish clinging to rocks. Sometimes the starfish cling to coral, like the starfish in the picture.

Yesterday, Jeremy and Janice found a starfish and a piece of coral. Janice said that both the starfish and the coral are living things. Jeremy knew the starfish was an animal. He asked if the coral was an animal or a plant.

With Janice's help, he compared the two. They discussed how the starfish and coral differed from one another. As you read the chapter, think about the ways animals are alike. Think, too, about the ways they are different.

Lesson 1   The Simplest Animals

■ How do scientists group animals?

Scientists classify living things, or organisms, according to the ways organisms are alike. The animal kingdom is divided into two large groups, vertebrates (VER tuh brihts) and invertebrates.

All animals with backbones are **vertebrates.** You are a vertebrate. You can feel your backbone if you rub your hand up and down the center of your back. The fish shown below are also vertebrates.

Most animals do not have backbones. The other group in the animal kingdom contains animals without backbones, or **invertebrates.** The coral animals and sponges in the picture are two invertebrates found in the ocean.

In this chapter, you will learn about invertebrate animals. Scientists classify invertebrates into many groups.

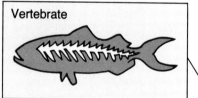

Fish, coral, and sponges

Orange sponge

Sponges   The simplest kinds of invertebrates are sponges. Sponges live in water. The bodies of sponges are like sacks. Sponges have no heads, mouths, or other separate body parts. However, they do have cells that do different jobs.

A sponge draws water into its body through small openings. Look at these openings in the drawing. Cells called collar cells are found inside the sponge. Hairlike parts on these cells whip back and forth, moving water through the sponge. The collar cells remove oxygen and tiny food particles from the water. The water then leaves the sponge's body through one or two large openings.

Sponges can have different shapes and colors. You can see the orange sponge above is shaped like a fan. Like most sponges, the orange sponge lives in the sea. It may look like a plant, but it is not. It is an animal. It cannot make its own food like plants can.

Sponges do not have a backbone. But sponges do have skeletons that can be either hard or soft. The orange sponge has a skeleton of soft material. Other sponges have hard skeletons of rock or glass. People sometimes use a sponge's soft skeleton for cleaning. But most sponges used in homes today are artificial.

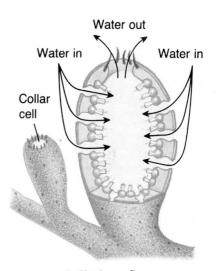

Collar Cells in a Sponge

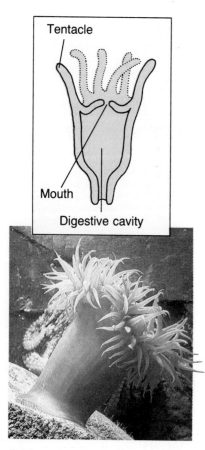

Sea anemone

Hollow-Bodied Animals

Hollow-Bodied Animals   Another simple invertebrate group is hollow-bodied animals. Most of these animals live in the sea. Their body parts differ from sponges. Hollow-bodied animals have a hollow center lined with digestive cells. They have one opening, the mouth. In addition, they have muscle cells and a simple system of nerves.

All hollow-bodied animals have movable fingerlike parts called **tentacles** (TEHN tuh kuhlz). Inside the tentacles are stinging cells. When a small sea animal brushes a tentacle, the stinging cells dart out. They inject poison in the animal so it cannot move. Then the hollow-bodied animal can eat the small animal.

Hollow-bodied animals may have two body forms. Coral animals and sea anemones (uh NEHM uh neez) are examples of one form. Look at the tentacles and mouth on the sea anemone. Its tentacles and mouth are usually above its digestive cavity. Sea anemones stay in one place for most of their lives.

Jellyfish are an example of the other body form. The tentacles and mouth of the jellyfish hang below its digestive cavity. Also unlike sea anemones, jellyfish move around for most of their lives.

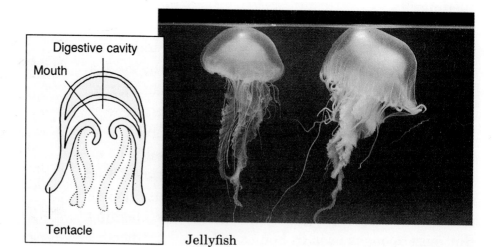

Jellyfish

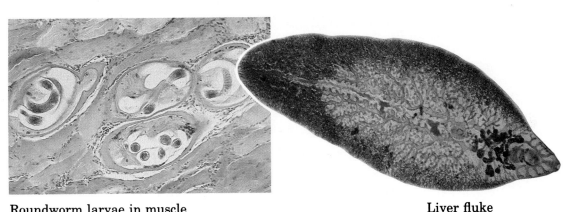

Roundworm larvae in muscle   Liver fluke

Flatworms and Roundworms   Like sponges and hollow-bodied animals, worms are invertebrates. Scientists divide worms into three groups—flatworms, roundworms, and segmented worms. The groups are named according to the shapes of the worms' bodies.

Flatworms and roundworms are the simplest worms. They are found in many places. Flatworms are found in fresh water and salt water. Most roundworms live in soil. Both can also live in plants and animals.

Flatworms and roundworms have simple digestive systems. The flatworm's system has one opening. Food enters and wastes leave through the same opening. The roundworm has two openings.

Many flatworms and roundworms are **parasites.** A parasite feeds and lives on another plant or animal. This plant or animal is called a host. Cattle, dogs, even people, can be hosts. By taking food from the host, a parasite may harm it.

A fluke is one kind of flatworm that is a parasite. The fluke shown in the picture above may live in the intestine, liver, lungs, or blood of other animals.

The roundworm shown above is a parasite. It is found in humans and other animals. This roundworm develops in muscles. Then it moves to the intestines and absorbs digested food.

T H I N K

Most invertebrates are small, like worms, and live in water, like hollow-bodied animals. Why?

Z O N E

Inside an Earthworm

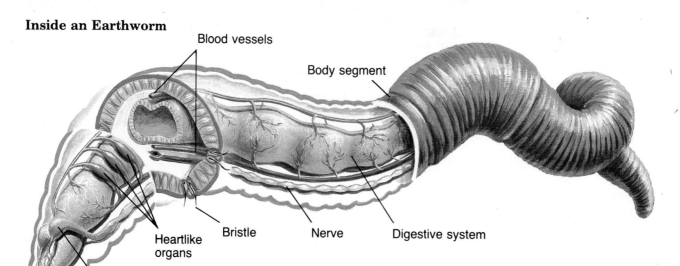

Blood vessels

Body segment

Mouth

Brain

Heartlike organs

Bristle

Nerve

Digestive system

Segmented Worms   If you dug a hole in the ground, you might find an earthworm. The earthworm is one kind of segmented worm. Like other worms, segmented worms are found in many places. Segmented worms live in soil, lakes, ponds, and salt water.

Segmented worms are more complex than flatworms and roundworms. A segmented worm has a digestive system with an opening at each end. It also has a nervous system with a simple brain. Unlike flatworms and roundworms, it has heartlike organs that pump fluid through its circulatory system.

The earthworm's body is divided into ringlike segments. Look at the segments on the earthworm above. Each segment, except the first and the last, has four pairs of bristles. Bristles help the earthworm move through the ground.

As an earthworm moves through the ground, it swallows soil. The worm's digestive system removes bits of plant and animal matter and tiny living things from the soil. These are the worm's food. The soil then passes out as waste. Soil that has been through an earthworm's body is good fertilizer. Burrowing earthworms mix soil and let air and water into it. This soil is better for growing plants.

Earthworm

Building Skills: Predicting

How does an earthworm mix soil?

Steps

1. Put a layer of dark soil about 2 cm thick in the bottom of each jar. Cover the soil with a layer of light sand. Add dark and light layers until the jars are almost full. Moisten the soil.

2. ◇ **HANDLE WITH CARE!** Put the earthworms in one of the jars on top of the soil. Add the carrot scraps. Wash your hands with soap and water after handling the worms.

3. Cover each jar with a lid. Wrap both jars with a dark piece of paper. Put the jars aside.

4. Write down what you think will happen in the jars.

5. After three days, unwrap the jars.

Questions

1. How can you tell which jar contained the earthworms? Describe the soil and sand in the jars.

2. Which of the jars do you think would be a better place for a plant to grow? Why?

Materials

2 jars
lids with holes
dark soil
light-colored sand
2 earthworms
carrot scraps
dark paper
masking tape
water

Step 1

✓ Lesson Checkup

1. Into what two groups do scientists classify animals?

2. What body features make a sponge different from a worm?

3. **Think Critically!** Why do you think earthworms are sometimes called "farmers' friends"?

Lesson 2   Shell and Spiny Animals

■ How are mollusks and spiny-skinned animals alike and different?

What things do the three animals in the pictures have in common? They may look very different, but they are all alike in certain ways. The garden snail, the scallop, and the octopus are all invertebrates. They belong to a group of invertebrates called **mollusks.** A mollusk is an animal with a soft body, usually covered by a shell. Like other groups of invertebrates, mollusks have bodies that are alike in certain ways.

Mollusks   Like segmented worms, mollusks have two body openings. Look for other common body parts in the drawing on page 25. Mollusks also have a heart, blood vessels, and digestive system. Unlike worms, many mollusks have eyes, a shell, and a "foot."

You may have seen garden snails creeping along on their bellies. Actually, this belly is a thick, muscular foot. Most mollusks have a foot. They use the foot to crawl, dig, and catch food.

Snail

Scallop

Octopus

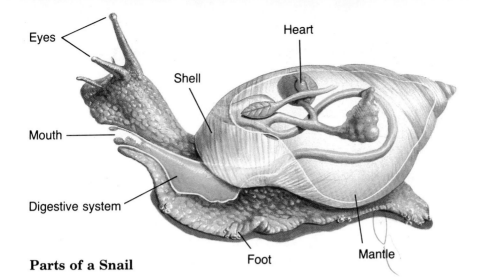

Eyes

Heart

Shell

Mouth

Digestive system

Parts of a Snail

Foot

Mantle

Mollusks have soft bodies just as worms do. A tough outer covering called the **mantle** protects the soft bodies of mollusks. In many mollusks, this mantle makes a hard shell. You can see the shells on the snail and the scallop on page 24.

Mollusks can be put into three groups according to differences in their shells and feet. The garden snail is an example of one kind of mollusk. It has a single foot on its lower body. Many mollusks in this group have single, spiral shells.

The scallop is an example of a mollusk with two shells hinged together. Scallops live in shallow or deep ocean waters. By opening and closing its shells, a scallop can swim rapidly. When on the ocean bottom, a scallop draws water into and out of its body through tubes. The scallop can then remove bits of food from the water. Featherlike feelers help the scallop sense changes in the water around it.

An octopus is a third kind of mollusk. This mollusk does not have a shell. And instead of a single foot, an octopus has tentacles. An octopus swims through the sea, using its tentacles to catch food. These tentacles do not have stinging cells, as the tentacles of hollow-bodied animals do.

T H I N K

Are spiny-skinned
animals likely to move
slowly or quickly?
Explain your answer.

Z O N E

Spiny-Skinned Animals

Starfish and sea urchins are common spiny-skinned animals. Spiny-skinned animals are another group of invertebrates.

Unlike mollusks, spiny-skinned animals have firm bodies. They get their name from the spines that cover their bodies. Can you see the spines on the starfish? These spines can be short like a starfish's or they can be long like a sea urchin's.

Spiny-skinned animals have mouths and digestive systems. The starfish, like all spiny-skinned animals, has a circulatory system and a nervous system.

Most starfish have five arms. Under each arm are rows of hollow, water-filled tubes called tube feet. All spiny-skinned animals have tube feet. Each tube foot is tipped with a suction cup. Hundreds of these tube feet help the starfish to move and get food.

A starfish, like all spiny-skinned animals, lives in the sea. It uses its arms to capture food. Using the suction from its tube feet, the starfish can pull open a scallop and eat the soft animal inside.

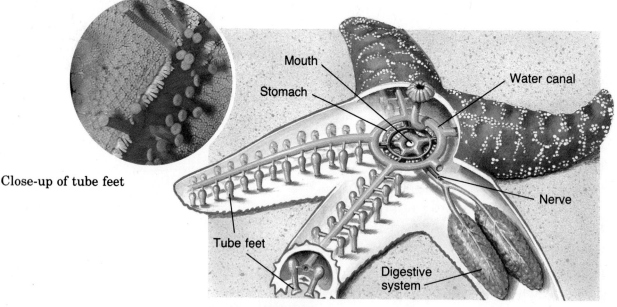

Close-up of tube feet

Mouth

Stomach

Water canal

Nerve

Tube feet

Digestive
system

Inside a Starfish

Building Skills: Observing

What type of food does a pond snail eat?

Steps

1. ◇ **HANDLE WITH CARE!** Add pond water to the dish. Place the pond snail in the dish.

2. Tear little squares off each of the leaves. Measure each square with your ruler. Record the type and size of each leaf square.

3. Place the leaf squares in the water with the snail. Place the dish in a safe place overnight.

4. The next day, note which leaf squares have been nibbled and how much was eaten.

5. Compare your results with your classmates.

Questions

1. How much of each leaf was eaten? What was the favorite food of the snail?

2. Did the snails of your classmates prefer the same vegetable as your snail? Explain why you think this was so.

Materials

shallow dish

pond water

pond snail

ruler

celery, lettuce, and
 spinach leaves

Step 3

✓ Lesson Checkup

1. What two body structures are used to group mollusks? What are the three groups of mollusks?

2. How does a starfish use its feet?

3. **Think Critically!** In what ways are mollusks like segmented worms?

Lesson 3   Joint-Legged Animals

■ What are four things all arthropods have in common?

Pretend that all the different kinds of animals in the world are 100 marbles. Of these 100 marbles, 95 would be invertebrate animals. Imagine 90 of those marbles painted red. The red marbles would be joint-legged animals, or **arthropods** (AHR thruh pahdz). Arthropods are the largest group of animals and the largest group of invertebrates. They live in air, on land, and in water.

Arthropods   Like other invertebrate groups, all arthropods have certain body features that are alike. For one thing, they all have a segmented body. Look for the body segments on the animals in the pictures. Each segment is very different.

Look at the legs on each arthropod in the pictures. Arthropods usually have pairs of jointed legs attached to the body segments. Different legs often do different

Ladybug beetle

Shrimp

jobs. Some may be used for walking, while others may help the arthropod capture food.

The bodies of arthropods are protected by a hard outer covering called an **exoskeleton** (EHK soh SKEHL uh tuhn). The exoskeleton cannot change size. For this reason arthropods must **molt,** or shed their exoskeletons, as they grow. The cicada (suh KAY duh), like most arthropods, must molt several times as it grows. It can only grow just after molting, when the new exoskeleton is still soft.

Arthropods have well-developed sense organs. Most have eyes, and feelers called **antennas.** Antennas help the animals smell and feel. Some antennas are used to sense sound and light.

Arthropods have a well-developed nervous system with a brain. They have a circulatory system with a heart and a complex digestive system with different organs.

You can compare the features of arthropods with other invertebrates in the table on the next page.

Molting cicada

Scorpion

Grasshopper

Invertebrates

Type	Body structures	Where found	Examples
Sponge	Sacklike body, one large body opening	Fresh or salt water	Sea sponge
Hollow-bodied animals	Hollow body with tentacles surrounding mouth	Fresh or salt water	Jellyfish, Sea anemone
Flatworms	Long, flat body, one body opening	Fresh or salt water, inside animals or plants	Tapeworm, Fluke
Roundworms	Rounded body, two body openings	Fresh or salt water, inside animals or plants, soil	Pinworm, Hookworm
Segmented worms	Body divided into many segments, two body openings	Fresh or salt water, soil	Earthworm
Mollusks	Soft bodies with large muscular foot, mantle, most protected by a shell	Fresh or salt water, land	Snail, Octopus
Spiny-skinned animals	Protective spines cover soft body parts, tube feet	Oceans	Sea urchin, Sand dollar
Arthropods	Segmented bodies, jointed legs, antennas, exoskeleton	Fresh or salt water, land	Lobster, Butterfly, Spider

Hard-Covered Arthropods Arthropods can be classified by the number of legs, body segments, and antennas they have. There are five main groups of arthropod animals.

The first group is the hard-covered arthropods, or **crustaceans** (KRUHS TAY shuhnz). Shrimp, crayfish, and lobsters belong to this group.

Crustaceans have four or more pairs of legs. Look for the lobster's ten main legs. The front two legs have huge claws. Crustaceans have two main body parts. They also have two pairs of antennas.

The lobster is one kind of crustacean that people like to eat. It lives in the sea. A lobster crawls along the bottom of the sea and captures small animals to eat. Strong muscles let it bend its rear part back and forth. This helps the lobster swim backward and escape enemies. These muscles are usually the part of the lobster that people eat.

Lobster

Wolf spider
American house spider
Daddy-longlegs
Black widow

A Variety of Spiderlike Animals

Spiders Have you ever seen one of these creatures crawling around your house or garden? Spiders and spiderlike animals make up another group of arthropods. You probably have seen a garden spider. Like other animals in this group, the garden spider has eight legs. The garden spider and other spiderlike animals have no antennas. These animals have two main body parts, just as crustaceans do.

31

Garden spider capturing food

The garden spider and most other spiders have poison glands. Fangs inject the poison into the insects the spiders eat. The poison of the garden spider and most other spiders cannot harm people. However, some spiders, such as the black widow, do have poison strong enough to be harmful to people.

The garden spider has six silk-making organs at the rear end of its body. It uses the silk to make a sticky web that captures insects. The garden spider's web is spiral-shaped. Other spiders spin webs of different shapes or do not spin webs at all.

Insects   The largest group of arthropods is insects. There are more different kinds of insects than of all other animals combined. Each insect, though, has three things in common—the number of body segments, legs, and antennas.

Count the number of body segments on each of the insects in the drawing on the next page. How many legs do you see on each? Does the butterfly have the same number of antennas as the beetle?

Butterflies are common insects. Like other insects, they have six legs. They also have three body segments. A butterfly has two antennas. It also has two pairs of wings for flying. Not all insects have or use wings.

The shape of an insect's mouth depends on the food it eats. A butterfly has a long, coiled tonguelike tube for sucking nectar (sugar water) from flowers. Other insects have mouthparts that pierce or chew. What might the insects in the pictures eat?

Like all insects, the butterfly begins life as an egg. Most insects, and most other invertebrates as well, produce large numbers of eggs. They need to do this because the young usually get no care from their parents once the eggs are laid. Many of the young do not survive.

A wormlike larva hatches out of the butterfly's egg. The butterfly larva, a caterpillar, does not look at all like an adult butterfly. Later it goes through a pupa stage, during which its body changes greatly. It emerges as an adult butterfly. Many insects, but not all, undergo these stages in their life cycles.

Some Common Insects

Butterfly mouthpart

Grasshopper mouthpart

Mosquito mouthpart

THINK

Why is the larva stage of a butterfly more damaging to plants than the adult stage?

ZONE

The larvae (LAHR vee) of some butterflies and other insects cause great damage to crop plants. Some adult insects are harmful, too. Others, however, help crops by spreading pollen from plant to plant. What kinds of insects do this?

Centipedes and Millipedes Centipedes and millipedes are two other groups of arthropods. Both have a head and many similar body parts.

Centipedes have two legs on each body part, while millipedes have four. The word centipede means hundred feet. *Centi* means hundred and *pede* means feet. *Mille* means thousand. What does the word millipede mean? It is not true, as their names suggest, that centipedes have a hundred feet and millipedes have a thousand feet.

Most centipedes and millipedes live in dark, damp places. However, they do not compete with each other for food. Centipedes have poison claws, which they use to kill insects and other small animals. The poison of most centipedes does not harm people. Millipedes, on the other hand, eat dead plants.

Centipede

Millipede

Building Skills: Making Models

What kind of arthropod can you build?

Steps

1. Review the body parts of an arthropod.

2. Use the materials and your imagination to build an arthropod. Beads could be your arthropod's eyes. A twist tie could form a mouthpart or antenna. Your model does not have to look like a real arthropod, but it must have the correct body parts.

3. Look carefully at your model when you are finished. Study its legs, antennas, body regions, and other features.

Questions

1. Is your model a crustacean, spider, insect, centipede, or millipede?

2. Why did you classify your arthropod as a crustacean, spider, insect, centipede, or millipede?

Materials

plastic foam balls
pipe cleaners
twist ties
colored paper
beads
buttons
glue
scissors

Step 2

Lesson Checkup

1. What three body parts are used to classify arthropods into the different groups?

2. Why is a spider not considered an insect?

3. **Think Critically!** Look at the table on page 30. Many invertebrate types live in water, while many arthropod types live on land. How do the body parts of an arthropod help it to live on land?

Technology Today

Controlling Insect Pests

Many kinds of insects harm farm crops. Fruit flies, moths, grasshoppers, and other insects feed on plants. Farmers can lose entire crops to insects.

About 50 years ago, scientists discovered that many harmful insects could be controlled by pesticides (PEHS tuh sydz). Pesticides are chemicals that kill insects and other harmful pests. These pesticides have helped farmers grow more food than was ever possible before.

However, pesticides also cause problems. Many kill insects that help crops as well as those that harm crops. Often pesticides kill birds and other wildlife, too. Pesticides can build up in the bodies of people, perhaps making them sick.

Some farmers are finding that they can use less pesticide by putting nature to work. Animals that naturally gobble up pests are also used. For example, some California farmers use a beetle to eat an insect harmful to orange trees. Ladybugs, garter snakes, and birds are other animals used to eat harmful insects. Farmers are learning different ways to control pests.

Praying mantis eating a grasshopper

Think About It

Many people would like farmers to stop using pesticides. Some farmers say they would lose far too much of their crops if they did not use pesticides. These crops are necessary to feed the growing number of people in the world. How can the problems caused by pesticides be solved? Do you think farmers should use pesticides? Why or why not? What more would you want to know in order to decide?

Ladybug beetle eating an aphid

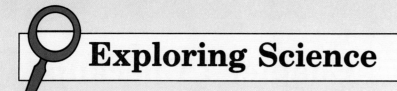

Exploring Science

Observing Pill Bugs

Problem: What environment do pill bugs prefer?

Experimenting

1. ◇**HANDLE WITH CARE!** Gather some pill bugs in a jar.

2. Line a shoe box with the foil. Put a paper towel in each half of the box. Tape down the two paper towels as shown. Dampen one paper towel.

3. Put the pill bugs on the masking tape, then close the lid of the box. Wait three minutes.

4. Open the box. Count the number of pill bugs on the dry paper, on the damp paper, and on the masking tape. Record your observations in a data table like the one shown.

5. Repeat steps 3 and 4 two more times.

6. Wash your hands after you are finished.

Materials

jar
pill bugs
shoe box with lid
foil
2 paper towels
water
masking tape
clock or watch

Step 4

Recording Data

Trial	Number of pill bugs		
	Wet paper	Dry paper	Tape
1			
2			
3			

Drawing Conclusions

1. Where did most of the pill bugs crawl?

2. What kind of environment do you think pill bugs prefer? Did you find your pill bugs in this type of environment?

37

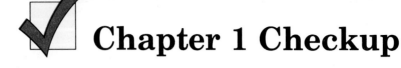

Chapter 1 Checkup

Summary

- Scientists group animals as vertebrates or invertebrates according to ways they are alike.

- Invertebrates can be classified as sponges, hollow-bodied animals, flatworms, roundworms, segmented worms, mollusks, spiny-skinned animals, or arthropods.

- Arthropods are classified according to the number of legs, body segments, and antennas they have.

Science Words

Copy the words. Define each word in a sentence.

antenna
arthropod
crustacean
exoskeleton
invertebrate
mantle
mollusk
molt
parasite
tentacle
vertebrate

Science Ideas

1. Letter your paper from a to e. Write the word that best completes each sentence.

   a. (Mollusks, Arthropods, Crustaceans) are the largest group of invertebrates.

   b. (Parasites, Invertebrates, Arthropods) eat and live in or on plants and animals.

   c. The fingerlike parts with stinging cells on all hollow-bodied animals are called (antennas, mantles, tentacles).

   d. The feelers on arthropods are called (tentacles, vertebrates, antennas).

   e. Arthropods can only grow after molting, when the (exoskeleton, invertebrate, mantle) is still soft.

Hollow-bodied animals	Worms	Mollusks	Spiny-skinned animals	Arthropods

2. Make a table like the one shown above. Classify the following organisms.

pinworm   earthworm   lobster
scallop   fluke   octopus
starfish   jellyfish   sea anemone
millipede   snail   black widow

3. Look at the picture. Write a short story about the coral and starfish. In the story, describe what they are and where they can be found.

Data Bank

Use the circle graph on page 383 to answer the following questions.

1. There are estimated to be one million different kinds of animals. What percent of these are invertebrates? Vertebrates? Insects?

2. Which group in the animal kingdom is the largest? The smallest?

Science Ideas, Question 3

Problem Solving

Imagine you are on a scientific field trip studying the animal and plant life in a forest. You find an organism that lives on land, eats dead plant matter, has 14 body segments, 2 antennas, and 56 legs. How would you classify this animal? Why?

Chapter 2
Animals with Backbones

A little creek ran behind Rayna's house. She liked to visit it and look at the plants and animals that lived there. All spring she saw frogs sitting on rocks in the creek. She thought they were funny, with their big eyes and wide mouths. She was amazed at how far they could jump with their long back legs.

In midspring, Rayna noticed what looked like little blobs of jelly on some water plants. The "jelly" was clear except for lots of little black dots. A few weeks later, she saw small, fishlike things swimming in the creek. They had round heads and long tails.

When summer came, the fishlike things began to change. One day Rayna saw one that had grown two back legs! It still had a tail, too. Later, she saw one with both back and front legs. It was trying to climb out of the water.

Rayna wondered what the fishlike things were. She wondered how they were like and unlike the frogs. She even wondered if they might be anything like her! As you read the chapter, look for the answers to Rayna's questions.

Lesson 1   Fish

■ What are some features of fish?

As you know, scientists divide animals into two large groups, invertebrates and vertebrates. A vertebrate gets its shape from an **endoskeleton** (EHN doh SKEHL uh tuhn), which is a skeleton inside its body. A backbone is always part of this skeleton.

Vertebrates are classified into five groups. These groups are fish, amphibians (am FIHB ee uhnz), reptiles (REHP tuhlz), birds, and mammals. In this lesson, you will learn about fish.

Features of Fish   Most of the earth is covered with water. The most common vertebrates in this environment are fish. The bodies of fish are covered with scales. Scales protect fish. Most fish also have fins. Fins help fish move through the water. Even the tail is a fin.

Backbone

Fish are the most common vertebrates in water.

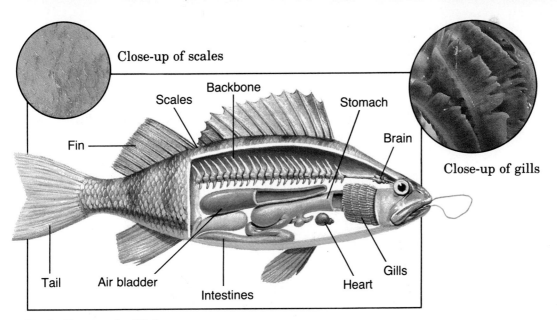

Close-up of scales

Close-up of gills

Body Parts of a Fish

Fish need oxygen just as you do. Fish get their oxygen from water. When a fish appears to be swallowing water, it is usually taking in oxygen. Fish have featherlike structures called **gills**. Find the gills behind the fish's mouth in the drawing above. The gills are filled with blood vessels. As a fish opens and closes its mouth, water passes through the gills. Oxygen in the water is absorbed by the blood.

All fish are **cold-blooded** animals. This means that their body temperatures are the same as the temperatures of their surroundings. They do not really have cold blood. Cold-blooded animals have changing body temperatures. If the water temperature turns cold, a fish's body temperature drops to the temperature of the water. Cold-blooded animals become less active when temperatures are too low or too high.

Most fish lay eggs. Others give birth to live young. Often hundreds or even thousands of young are born at once. Most fish do not take care of their young. Of the many that are born, only a few survive.

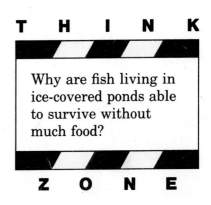

T H I N K

Why are fish living in ice-covered ponds able to survive without much food?

Z O N E

Kinds of Fish   Fish are classified into two groups: fish with skeletons of cartilage (KAHR tl ihj) and fish with skeletons of bone. Hold your ear and move it back and forth. Your ear is made mostly of cartilage. Cartilage is hard, but it is not as hard as bone.

A tiger shark is one kind of fish that has a skeleton of cartilage. Like most fish with cartilage, this shark lives in warm seas around the world. The tiger shark wiggles its body to swim and keep afloat. A tiger shark eats smaller fish and other sea animals.

Bony fish are heavier than fish with cartilage. Therefore, most bony fish have a special organ to help them float. This baglike organ, called an air bladder, lies below the fish's backbone.

A salmon is one kind of fish with a bony skeleton. Salmon hatch in freshwater streams. Adult salmon, though, spend most of their lives in the ocean. Unlike salmon, however, most bony fish spend their entire lives either in salt water or in fresh water.

Tiger shark

Salmon have bony skeletons.

44

Building Skills: Classifying

How do the scales of fish differ?

Steps

1. Use the plastic knife to scrape off the fish scales.

2. Using a hand lens, look at the scales. Draw what you see.

3. Compare your drawings with the drawings below. Classify the kind of scales you drew.

Materials

fish
hand lens
plastic knife

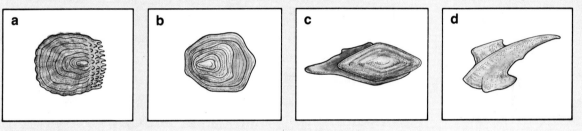

Fish scales

Questions

1. What kind of scales were found on your fish?

2. Fish can be classified by their skeletons. What other features can be used to classify fish?

 **Lesson Checkup**

1. What characteristics do fish have in common?

2. How are fish adapted to living in water?

3. **Think Critically!**   Why is "temperature-changing" a better name for fish than "cold-blooded"?

Lesson 2   Amphibians and Reptiles

■ How do amphibians and reptiles differ from each other?

Amphibians and reptiles are two other groups of cold-blooded vertebrates. **Amphibians** live part of their lives in water and part of their lives on land. They have moist skin. Amphibians breathe with gills as well as with lungs. Frogs and toads are amphibians. Most **reptiles** can live on land. They have dry, scaly skin and breathe with lungs. Lizards, snakes, and turtles are reptiles. In this lesson, you will learn about amphibians and reptiles.

Features of Amphibians   Look at the pictures below. Amphibian eggs have jellylike shells. The eggs can dry out easily. For this reason, amphibians must lay their eggs in water or damp places. Like the tadpole in the picture, the young of many amphibians live in water. These young amphibians have gills, like fish.

Eggs

Tadpoles

Adult frog

The different stages of a frog's life cycle

As the young grow up, their bodies change. The tadpole will lose its gills and tail, grow lungs and legs, and become a frog. It will return to water as an adult to lay eggs.

The outside of an amphibian's body is moist and slimy. Amphibians do not have scales. Most adult amphibians breathe with lungs and can spend part of their lives on land. However, a few amphibians, like mud puppies, spend almost their entire lives in water. Instead of lungs, these amphibians have gills outside their bodies. Some amphibians, such as red-backed salamanders, can breathe oxygen through their skins.

Body Parts of a Salamander

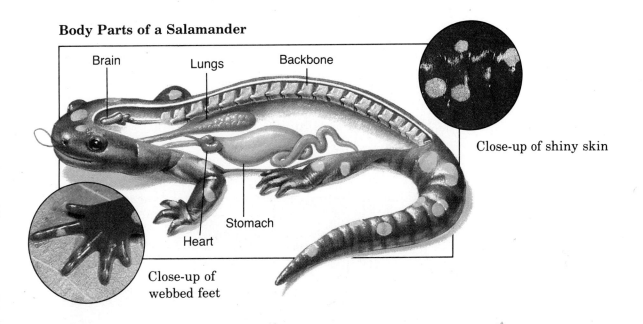

Brain   Lungs   Backbone

Close-up of shiny skin

Stomach

Heart

Close-up of
webbed feet

Kinds of Amphibians   Amphibians are placed in two main groups: amphibians with tails and amphibians without tails.

A salamander is one kind of amphibian with a tail. A salamander has a smooth, slender body with moist, thin skin. Its webbed feet are adapted for moving both on land and in water.

Toads are amphibians.

Frogs and toads are examples of amphibians without tails. Both have four legs, no tail, and large eyes. However, frogs usually have smooth, moist skins while toads have rough, dry skins.

Frogs live in or near water. Toads usually spend more time on land. However, both lay their eggs in water. The eggs may be laid in large puddles as well as in ponds, lakes, and streams. Desert toads lay eggs in water left by a rainstorm. Their young must develop lungs before this water dries.

Features of Reptiles   A third large group of vertebrates is reptiles. Reptiles are like amphibians in several ways. Both have skeletons and lungs, and are cold-blooded. But most reptiles spend all or most of their time on land. Reptiles differ from amphibians in important ways that help the reptiles live on land. For example, the tough, dry reptile skins do not dry out easily, as most amphibian skins do. Reptile skins are also protected by scales.

Close-up of snake scales

Eggs

Snakes are reptiles.

Most reptiles lay eggs. These eggs usually have tough, leathery shells. Liquid inside the eggs protects the young reptiles as they develop. Unlike amphibians, reptiles do not have to lay their eggs in water or wet places. In fact, even reptiles that spend time in water lay their eggs on land.

Like other cold-blooded vertebrates, a reptile's body temperature changes with its surroundings. To keep warm, a reptile might sun itself on a rock. To keep cool, it might crawl under the rock.

Kinds of Reptiles   There are four groups of reptiles: 1) lizards, 2) snakes, 3) turtles, and 4) alligators and crocodiles.

Most lizards have tails and four legs with clawed feet. The collared lizard is an example of a lizard. Look at the picture below. The collared lizard lives in the dry, desert regions of the southwestern United States. Like all lizards, it has dry, scaly skin. This skin helps keep valuable water inside the collared lizard's body.

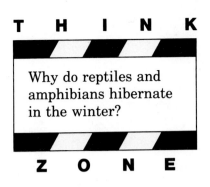

T H I N K

Why do reptiles and amphibians hibernate in the winter?

Z O N E

How are lizards and salamanders alike?

Prairie rattlesnake

Green sea turtle

American alligator

Snakes are a second group of reptiles. Snakes have long, slender bodies and no legs. They crawl on their ribs. Snakes have scales to protect the insides of their bodies from injury. Scales also help keep snakes from drying out. Many snakes are very important. They eat animals that people consider pests. Mice, rats, and insects are meals for these snakes. The rattlesnake shown above has poison fangs, though most other snakes do not.

The third group of reptiles is turtles. Turtles live in water. They walk or swim with flipperlike legs. Turtles have hard shells above and below their bodies. A turtle pulls its head and legs into the shell to protect itself. The green turtle shown above lives in the sea.

Alligators and crocodiles are the last group of reptiles. Their bodies are long and slender, with long, flat tails. Alligators and crocodiles have long mouths full of sharp teeth. These reptiles spend much of their time in the water. Their nostrils and eyes are on top of their heads. How does this help them catch food?

50

Building Skills: Measuring

What kind of environment is easier for a cold-blooded animal to live in?

Steps

1. Put a label on each jar. Number the jars.

2. Fill jars 2 and 4 halfway with water.

3. Place a thermometer in each jar. Measure and record the temperatures in a data table.

4. ◇ **HANDLE WITH CARE!** Place jars 1 and 2 near a sunny window. Place the other jars in a pan filled with ice.

5. Wait five minutes. Measure and record the temperatures of all four jars.

Questions

1. Did the jars filled with water or air have a more constant temperature?

2. In which environment would it be easier for a cold-blooded animal to live?

Materials

4 thermometers

4 jars

labels

water

pan

ice

Step 3

Lesson Checkup

1. Why must amphibians spend part of their lives in or near water?

2. How do reptiles differ from amphibians?

3. **Think Critically!** In some deserts, days are hot and nights are cold. Predict the behavior of snakes or lizards living in a desert.

51

Lesson 3   Birds and Mammals

How are birds and mammals alike?

Few animals live in the cold, cold environment of the South Pole. Imagine swimming about in the icy waters or sunning yourself on the rocky shoreline. The penguins and seals in the picture below live in this harsh environment.

Penguins are birds with feathers and wings, but they do not fly. Seals are mammals covered with fur. Both animals are **warm-blooded.** Warm-blooded animals keep steady body temperatures. They can remain warm even when the outside temperature becomes cold.

Unlike cold-blooded animals, most warm-blooded animals usually can be active in both cold and warm environments. In this lesson, you will learn about warm-blooded vertebrates.

How can these animals survive the cold South Pole?

Features of Birds   Birds live on land, in trees, and on water. They are vertebrates and have skeletons adapted to their needs. Instead of front legs, birds have wings. Most birds use their wings to fly. But some, like the penguin, do not fly. Look at the bones in the bird below. The bones are hollow, which make them light-weight. This helps birds fly.

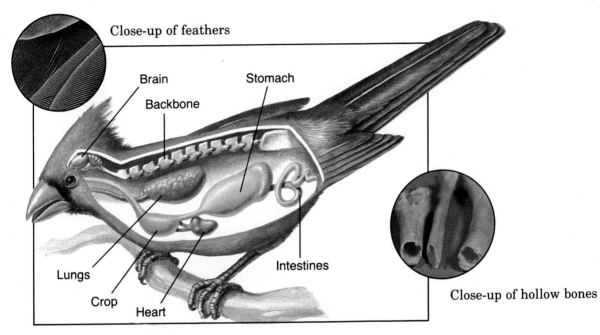

Close-up of feathers

Brain

Stomach

Backbone

Lungs

Crop

Heart

Intestines

Close-up of hollow bones

Body Parts of a Bird

Birds' bodies are covered with feathers instead of scales. No other animal has feathers. A bird's large outer feathers help it fly. Short, soft feathers, called down, lie close to a bird's skin. Fluffing these feathers helps keep a bird warm.

Like reptiles, birds lay eggs. However, birds lay hard-shelled eggs. Two to six eggs are laid at a time. Most birds sit on their eggs to keep them warm until they hatch. Since birds lay few eggs, the parents feed and care for the young birds. Because of this care, the babies' chances of becoming adults are good.

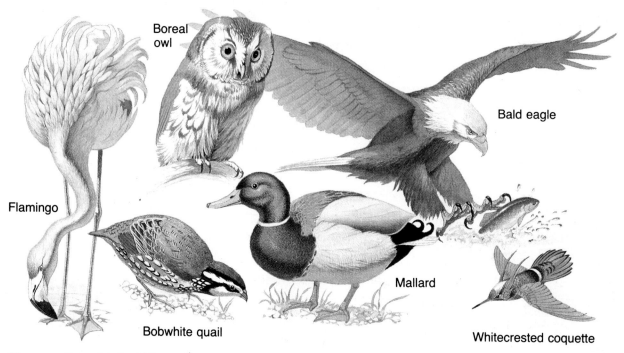

Boreal owl

Bald eagle

Flamingo

Mallard

Bobwhite quail

Whitecrested coquette

How are these birds different?

Differences Among Birds There are more than 8,500 different kinds of birds. One way in which birds differ is their beaks. Each type of beak is adapted for getting a certain kind of food. A bird may use its beak for catching insects, cracking seeds, pecking into wood, or sipping nectar.

Birds also have differently shaped legs and feet. Some legs and feet help birds perch on branches, wade in deep water, swim, run, or grasp prey. Look at the drawings above. Birds of prey, like bald eagles, have sharp beaks and strong claws. These beaks and claws help to rip meat apart. These birds catch snakes, mice, rabbits, and smaller birds for food.

Wading birds, such as the flamingo, have long legs. The flamingo feeds on tiny plants and animals in muddy water. It filters mud and water with its beak to get food. How might the beaks and feet of the other birds in the drawing help them to feed and move?

54

Features of Mammals   You are a mammal. While you and other mammals are different, you have many things in common. For one thing, all **mammals** are warm-blooded vertebrates. Only mammals have hair or fur. Cats are mammals with thick fur covering most of their bodies. Other mammals, such as whales, have only a few coarse hairs. Fur helps some mammals stay warm in cold temperatures. Most mammals that do not have fur have a thick layer of fat to keep them warm.

Mammals, even those that live in water, have lungs. Their skeletons usually have four limbs. Mammals living in water have flippers instead of legs and arms. Unlike birds, most mammals have teeth.

Most mammals give birth to only a few young. Female mammals nurse their young with milk from milk glands. The zebra in the picture is feeding her young this way. Since young mammals need their mother's milk, they receive care for a long time after they are born. This care helps young mammals survive.

Body Parts of a Mammal

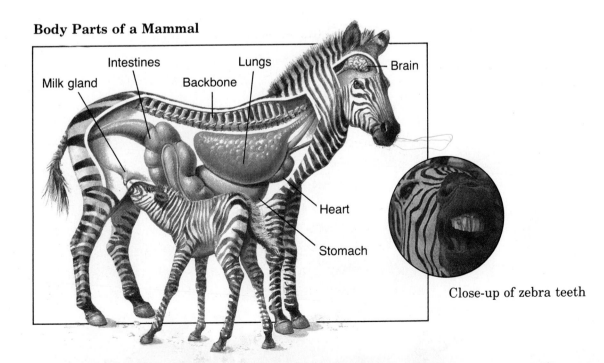

Milk gland

Intestines

Backbone

Lungs

Brain

Heart

Stomach

Close-up of zebra teeth

T H I N K

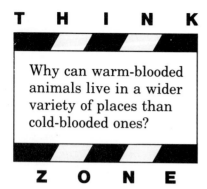

Why can warm-blooded animals live in a wider variety of places than cold-blooded ones?

Z O N E

Kinds of Mammals Mammals can be grouped in three ways according to how their young develop. The first group lays eggs. There are very few of these kinds of mammals. The duckbilled platypus (PLAT uh puhs) is an example of an egg-laying mammal. It lives in water and has a soft bill and webbed feet like a duck. However, its body is covered with fur. The female nurses its young.

A second group of mammals has pouches. The pouch is like a pocket on the front of the animal's body. These mammals raise their young in the pouch. The kangaroo is a pouched mammal. Baby kangaroos are very tiny and helpless when they are born. Immediately after birth, they crawl into the female's pouch. The young nurse on the female's milk and continue to develop inside the pouch.

The third group of mammals gives birth to fully-developed young. The young stay inside the female's body until they are developed. After birth, the young nurse on milk from the mother's milk glands. Most

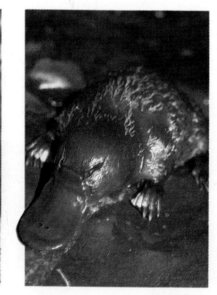

Mammals raise their young in different ways.

mammals belong to this group. Cats, dogs, mice, and elephants are just a few of these kinds of mammals.

Mammals are also grouped according to what they eat. Some mammals, like lions and tigers, eat other animals. They are called meat eaters, or **carnivores** (KAHR nuh vawrz). Their teeth are sharp and pointed for cutting and tearing. You can see the tiger's pointed teeth in the picture below.

Other mammals, like sheep, cows, and rabbits, eat plants. They are called plant eaters, or **herbivores** (HER buh vawrz). Their teeth are flat to help them grind up plants. The moose below is using its teeth to grind pond plants for food.

Still other mammals eat both plants and animals. These mammals are called **omnivores** (AHM nih vawrz). Many of these mammals eat fruits, nuts, and berries as well as meat. Omnivores have sharp teeth for tearing meat as well as flat teeth for grinding. You are an omnivore. Bears, skunks, and raccoons are also omnivores.

Are these mammals carnivores, herbivores, or omnivores?

Mammals are alike in many ways. However, they are different from other vertebrates. You can compare the features of mammals with other vertebrates in the table below.

Vertebrates			
Group	Features	Where found	Examples
Fish	Skeleton, cold-blooded, scales, fins, gills, lay eggs	Fresh water or salt water	Shark Salmon
Amphibians	Skeleton, cold-blooded, moist skin, gills as young, lungs as adults, lay jellylike eggs in water	In or near water, on land	Frog Salamander Toad
Reptiles	Skeleton, cold-blooded, dry skin, scales, lungs, lay leathery eggs on land	Land or water	Snake Turtle Lizard Alligator
Birds	Skeleton, warm-blooded, feathers, hollow bones, wings, lay hard-shelled eggs	On land, on water	Hummingbird Mallard Penguin
Mammals	Skeleton, warm-blooded, milk glands, hair or fur, teeth	On land, in water	Kangaroo Platypus Dog

Building Skills: Inferring

Does your body temperature change when the outside temperature is lowered?

Steps

1. ◇ **HANDLE WITH CARE!** Use the alcohol thermometer to measure the temperature of the ice water. Use the forehead thermometer to take your temperature. Record the temperatures.

2. Place your elbow in the water. After five minutes, remove your elbow from the dishpan. Quickly dry an area on your elbow. Use the alcohol thermometer to take the temperature of your skin. Record.

3. Repeat step 1. Compare your internal body temperature with your skin temperature.

Questions

1. Did the cold temperature of the ice water cause a change in your internal temperature?

2. When you go outside on a cold day, what do you think happens to your body temperature? Why?

Materials

dishpan of ice water
alcohol thermometer
forehead thermometer
towel

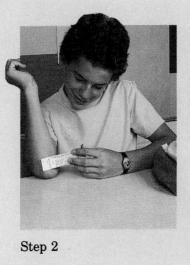

Step 2

✓ Lesson Checkup

1. What features of a bird's body help it fly?

2. Would a bear's teeth be more like a cat's or a cow's? Explain.

3. **Think Critically!** A penguin cannot fly but is classified as a bird. A bat can fly but is classified as a mammal. Explain why each is classified as it is.

59

Krill

Baleen

Krill: A Food Source

Krill are tiny, shrimplike crustaceans. Millions of krill swarm in the icy waters around the South Pole. They are the main food of whales that come to these waters. Other water-feeding animals of the area, such as seals and penguins, also depend on krill for food.

Whales that eat krill do not have teeth. Instead, they have baleen (buh LEEN). Baleen are sheets of horn, feathered at the edges, that hang down from the roof of a whale's mouth. When the whale feeds, it takes a huge mouthful of water. Then the whale presses out the water through the baleen. The krill remain in the mouth and are swallowed. Blue whales and humpback whales eat this way.

People, too, use krill. Fishing boats from Japan and the Soviet Union net thousands of tons of krill each year. Krill are used to feed farm animals such as pigs and chickens. Even fish in fish farms eat krill. Krill are high in protein and vitamins.

Other countries might soon start catching krill. Krill might help to feed the world's hungry people. With food scarce in many places, the demand for krill is growing.

Think About It

At this time, no one knows how many krill the seas hold. No one is sure how many can be taken by people without harming other animals. If too many krill are taken, the whales and other vertebrates that feed on them might starve. How might krill harvesting be managed to meet the needs of both people and ocean animals?

 **Exploring Science**

Observing Fish

Problem: How does water temperature affect the breathing rate of a fish?

Experimenting

1. Add water to the jar. Let it sit overnight.

2. ◇ **HANDLE WITH CARE!** Gently put your goldfish in the water.

3. Measure and record the water temperature.

4. Observe the fish closely. Count and record the number of times the fish opens and closes its mouth in one minute.

5. Carefully add three ice cubes to the jar. Stir the water gently. Repeat steps 3 and 4.

6. After three minutes, repeat steps 3 and 4.

Materials

goldfish
fish net
water
jar
ice
spoon
thermometer
clock or watch

Recording Data

	Start	After adding ice	After 3 minutes
Water temperature			
Fish's breathing rate			

Drawing Conclusions

1. How did the water temperature affect the fish's breathing rate?

2. Predict what would happen if the water temperature increased. How would you change this experiment to test your idea?

Step 4

Chapter 2 Checkup

Summary

- Fish, amphibians, reptiles, birds, and mammals are classified as vertebrates, or animals with backbones.

- Cold-blooded animals such as fish, amphibians, and reptiles have body temperatures that change with their surroundings.

- Warm-blooded animals such as birds and mammals remain warm even when outside temperatures drop.

- People are mammals. Mammals are warm-blooded and have hair or fur. The females nurse their young.

Science Words

Draw a picture to represent each word.

amphibian
carnivore
cold-blooded
endoskeleton
gill
herbivore
mammal
omnivore
reptile
warm-blooded

Science Ideas

1. Letter your paper from a to e. Write the correct word to answer each question.

   a. What kind of animal has gills when it is young and has lungs as an adult?

   b. What body parts do fish use to get oxygen?

   c. What kind of animal keeps a steady body temperature even when the surroundings are cold?

   d. What kind of animal has a body temperature that changes?

   e. Fish, amphibians, reptiles, birds, and mammals are classified into what group?

2. Letter your paper a and b. Write the name of the animal in each group that does not belong. Tell why.

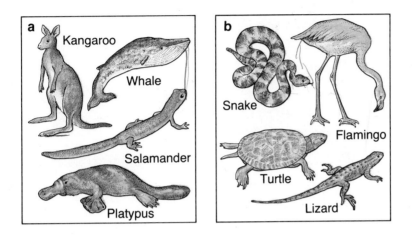

3. Look at the picture. Is the frog anything like Rayna? Explain.

Data Bank

Use the table on page 383 to answer the following questions.

1. Which snake is the shortest? What is its length?

2. Which two snakes are the longest?

Problem Solving

A scientist wanted to know which animal could best learn to run a maze. The animals were a mouse, a turtle, a frog, and a rat. Each animal was trained the same for one week. Then, each animal ran through the maze three times. Their times in minutes were: mouse (5, 7, 4), turtle (30, 36, 30), frog (11, 10, 12), and rat (5, 4, 5). Study the data and draw conclusions.

Science Ideas, Question 3

63

Chapter 3
Food from Plants

In this chapter, you will learn

- what plants need to make food

- how plants make food

- how living things get energy from food

- the ways plants and animals depend on each other for food and energy

On a sunny fall day, Wayne enjoyed harvesting the plants he weeded, watered, and cared for all summer. He could not believe that the large, ripe vegetables were once the small, dry seeds that he had planted in spring.

Wayne scratched his head in wonder as he came upon a gigantic pumpkin. How could a seed that was smaller than a dime grow into such a large plant? He was even more amazed by the huge pumpkin the plant produced.

How did the pumpkin grow so big? Wayne planted the seed so that the plant would have plenty of sunshine while it grew. The label on the seed package told him to do that. He also made sure the plant got lots of water during the hot summer months. Yet he did not give food to the plant and the plant still grew.

Wayne wondered if the plant got its food from the soil. He knew that if he only drank water and did not eat food, he would eventually die. How do plants get food? After reading this chapter, you should be able to answer Wayne's questions.

Lesson 1   Plants Make Food

■ How does a plant produce its own food?

Did you know that the food you eat can be traced back to plants? You know fresh fruit and vegetables come from plants. Even the hamburger you eat can be traced back to plants. Hamburger comes from a cow, which eats grass. How do plants get their food?

Plants can make their own food. They need three things from their environment to make food: sunlight, water, and air. Foodmaking usually occurs in the leaf cells of plants. The things needed to make food must be transported to these leaf cells. Special cells in a plant's roots, stems, and leaves do this. In this lesson, you will learn how plants use sunlight, water, and air to make their own food.

Plants use sunlight, water, and air to make food.

Roots   Most roots anchor a plant in soil. The soil contains water and minerals that the plant needs. The minerals found in soil dissolve in water, like sugar dissolves when it is poured into water. The roots take in, or absorb, water containing dissolved minerals.

Tiny **root hairs** grow from the tip of a root. These root hairs soak up water and minerals. Notice the root hairs of the plant below. Root hairs absorb almost all the water taken in by a plant. There are billions of root hairs on most plant roots. These root hairs give a plant a large surface over which it can absorb water. The more root hairs a plant has, the more water and minerals the plant can absorb. The drawing shows how root hairs push between bits of soil to reach water.

Root — Root hair — Soil particle — Air — Water

Close-Up of Root Hairs

Root of a pea plant

Parts of a Stem

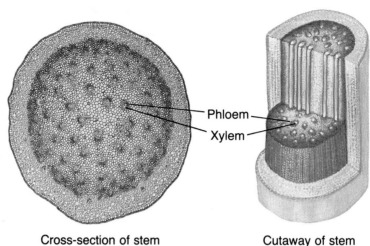

Cross-section of stem

Phloem
Xylem

Cutaway of stem

Stems and Leaves The water and minerals move from the roots through the stems to the leaves. Notice the stem in the drawing above. Two kinds of tubes in the stem help transport water and food within a plant. The water and minerals move through special tubes called **xylem** (ZY luhm). Xylem tubes carry water from the roots to the leaves. Tubes called **phloem** (FLOH ehm) carry food from the leaves to all parts of the plant.

To make food, leaf cells need carbon dioxide from the air as well as water from the soil. Tiny holes in a leaf allow carbon dioxide from the air to enter the leaf. These holes, called **stomata** (STOH muh tuh), are on the underside of a leaf. Stomata allow gases to enter and exit a leaf. Two guard cells are on the sides of the stomata. When these cells squeeze together, they keep gases from moving in and out. When the guard cells open wide, the gases then move in and out.

Plants make food from water and carbon dioxide. But this takes energy. Plants get energy from sunlight. Many plants have broad, flat leaves to absorb as much sunlight as possible.

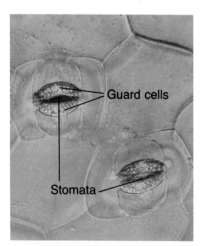

Guard cells

Stomata

Stomata and guard cells

Once all the materials are inside the leaf, foodmaking can take place. The drawing below shows how a plant gets the water, carbon dioxide, and energy it needs to make food.

Transporting Materials in a Plant

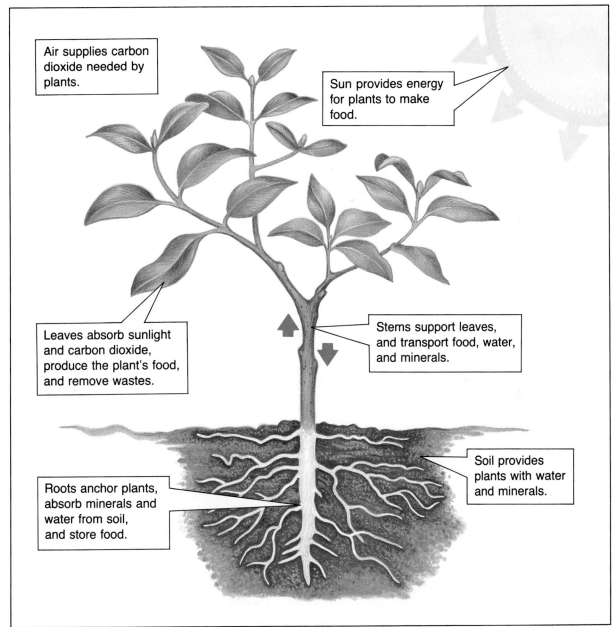

Air supplies carbon dioxide needed by plants.

Sun provides energy for plants to make food.

Leaves absorb sunlight and carbon dioxide, produce the plant's food, and remove wastes.

Stems support leaves, and transport food, water, and minerals.

Roots anchor plants, absorb minerals and water from soil, and store food.

Soil provides plants with water and minerals.

Foodmaking in the Leaf   The foodmaking process in a plant is called **photosynthesis** (FOH toh SIHN thuh sihs). The word comes from two Greek words. *Photo* means light. *Synthesis* means putting together. Leaf cells need light to put carbon dioxide and water together to make food.

As the drawing below shows, a leaf has several parts. The top and bottom layers protect the inside of the leaf in much the same way as a roof and a floor protect the inside of a building. The top layer of a leaf is clear to let in the sunshine. Beneath this is a layer of special foodmaking cells. There is also a spongy layer of cells where food is stored before it goes to the rest of the plant. Veins in the leaf connect the leaf with the stem.

Parts of a Leaf

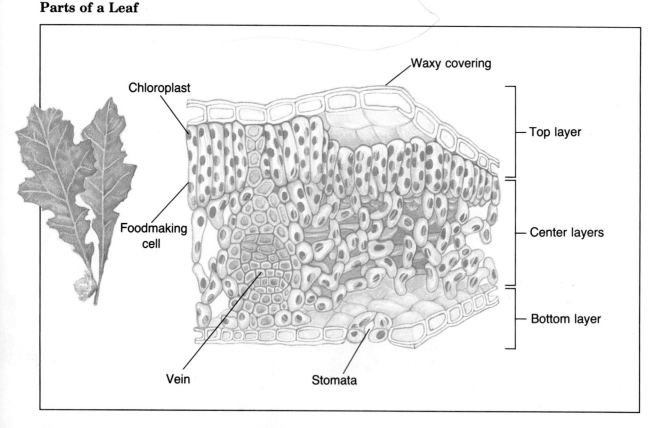

Chloroplast

Waxy covering

Top layer

Center layers

Bottom layer

Foodmaking cell

Vein

Stomata

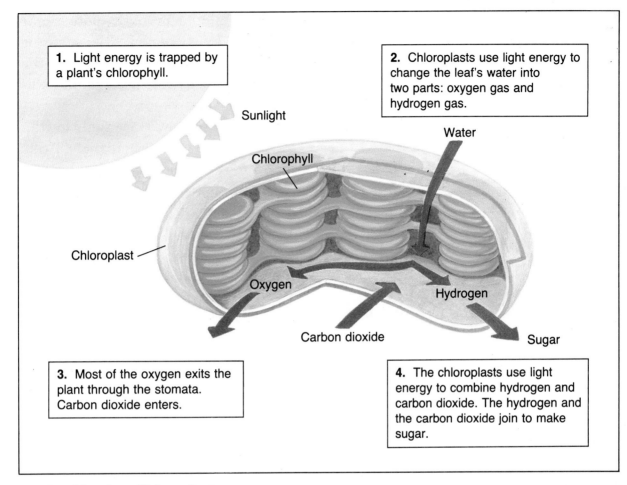

1. Light energy is trapped by a plant's chlorophyll.

2. Chloroplasts use light energy to change the leaf's water into two parts: oxygen gas and hydrogen gas.

Sunlight

Water

Chlorophyll

Chloroplast

Oxygen

Hydrogen

Carbon dioxide

Sugar

3. Most of the oxygen exits the plant through the stomata. Carbon dioxide enters.

4. The chloroplasts use light energy to combine hydrogen and carbon dioxide. The hydrogen and the carbon dioxide join to make sugar.

Foodmaking in a Chloroplast

The layer of foodmaking cells looks green. This is because the cells contain chlorophyll (KLAWR uh fihl). **Chlorophyll** is a green-colored substance that absorbs energy from the sun. Chlorophyll is found in cell parts called **chloroplasts** (KLAWR uh plasts). Photosynthesis takes place in these green cell parts.

During photosynthesis, plants take in water from the soil and carbon dioxide from the air. They produce oxygen and sugar. Read the drawing above to learn how photosynthesis makes a type of sugar. This sugar is the food of plants.

T H I N K

Plants that grow in water often have tiny bubbles sticking to them. What do you think these bubbles are? Explain your thinking.

Z O N E

Storing Food Most plants produce more sugar than they need right away. Some of this sugar is changed into starch. Sugar and starch are stored in the plants' roots, stems, fruits, or flowers. People and animals often eat these plant parts as food.

The plants in the pictures below store their food in different places. Carrots store food in their roots. Beets and turnips, also, store food in their roots. Other plants store starch in swollen stems called **tubers.** A potato stores food in tubers. Still other plants store sugar and starch in fruits. Bananas are an example of this kind of plant.

If you have ever eaten an artichoke, you have tasted the flower of the artichoke. Artichokes store some food in their flowers. In the tasty base of an artichoke petal is starch. This starch came from sugar made during photosynthesis.

When you eat a stew that contains potatoes and carrots, you are eating food that plants made during photosynthesis.

Where do these plants store food?

Building Skills: Inferring

Can you find the xylem tubes in a plant?

Steps

1. Put ten drops of red food coloring in half a cup of water. Stir the mixture.

2. Slice off part of the bottom of the celery stalk. Place the stalk in the colored water.

3. Let the celery stalk stand overnight in the colored water.

4. The next day, use the plastic knife to cut the celery stalk in half. Make the cut across the width of the celery as shown.

5. Look at the celery stalk carefully. Record what you observe.

Questions

1. Which parts of the plant have changed color?

2. Where do you think the xylem tubes are in the celery? Explain.

Materials

celery stalk with leaves attached

plastic knife

cup

water

red food coloring

Step 4

✓ Lesson Checkup

1. What do plants need to make food?

2. How does a plant get food to all its cells?

3. What is the green substance in plants called? What does it do?

4. **Think Critically!** Why can some plants live in shady places?

Lesson 2   Energy from Food

■ How do animals and plants get energy from food?

As you sit reading this lesson, you are breathing in oxygen from the air. Most living things need oxygen to live. During photosynthesis, plants not only make food, they also make oxygen. This is the oxygen you breathe every day. In this lesson, you will learn how living things use oxygen to get energy from food.

Getting Energy from Food   Living things need energy for their day-to-day activities. This energy comes from food. But the energy in food is stored energy. This energy must be released before it can be

Respiration in Plant Cells

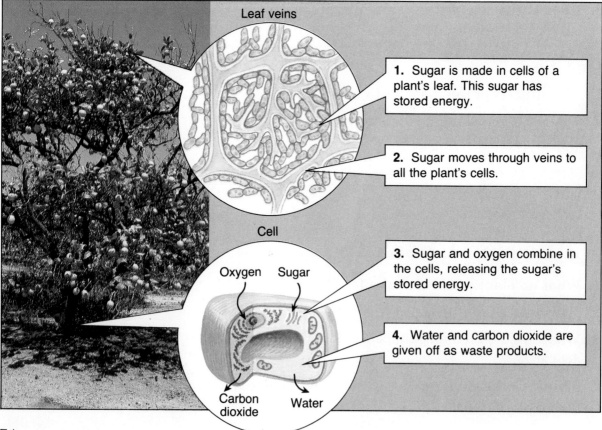

Leaf veins

1. Sugar is made in cells of a plant's leaf. This sugar has stored energy.

2. Sugar moves through veins to all the plant's cells.

Cell

Oxygen   Sugar

3. Sugar and oxygen combine in the cells, releasing the sugar's stored energy.

4. Water and carbon dioxide are given off as waste products.

Carbon dioxide   Water

Comparison of Photosynthesis and Respiration	
Photosynthesis	**Respiration**
Uses water	Gives off water
Uses carbon dioxide	Gives off carbon dioxide
Takes in the sun's energy	Gives off sugar's stored energy
Makes sugar	Breaks down sugar
Gives off oxygen	Uses oxygen
Needs sunlight	Does not need sunlight
Occurs only in cells with chlorophyll	Occurs in all cells

used by a plant or animal. **Respiration** (REHS puh RAY shuhn) is the process by which living things use oxygen to release energy stored in food.

During respiration, oxygen mixes with the sugar in a plant's or animal's cells. When oxygen and sugar combine, they give off energy. Plants or animals use this energy to grow, move, and do other activities.

Respiration produces more than just energy. It also produces waste. The waste products of respiration are carbon dioxide and water. All living things must remove these waste products. Plants get rid of the carbon dioxide and water through the stomata in their leaves.

Respiration is the opposite of photosynthesis. Read the table above to learn the differences between photosynthesis and respiration.

Even though photosynthesis and respiration are different, the two processes are very important to each other. Without photosynthesis, there would be no sugar for a plant to change into energy. Without respiration, the stored food in a plant would be useless.

Plants give off oxygen during photosynthesis.

Plants, animals, and other things use oxygen to release energy during respiration.

Plants use carbon dioxide during photosynthesis.

Living things give off carbon dioxide as a waste product during respiration.

Living things depend on each other for oxygen and carbon dioxide.

Oxygen–Carbon Dioxide Cycle You know that plants and animals use oxygen during respiration. The engines in cars also need oxygen to run. Fires need oxygen to burn. For millions of years, the earth's oxygen has been used in many ways.

Yet the earth has not run out of oxygen. The earth's supply is constantly being recycled, or used again. Plants are the earth's main source of oxygen. Notice how oxygen is recycled in the steps above. The cycle repeats itself. This repeating pattern is called the **oxygen–carbon dioxide cycle.**

In general, plants take in carbon dioxide from the air. And they give off oxygen. Because of this, plants and animals need each other. The oxygen–carbon dioxide cycle shows an important way in which plants and animals depend on each other.

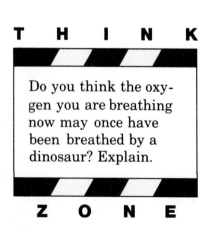

T H I N K

Do you think the oxygen you are breathing now may once have been breathed by a dinosaur? Explain.

Z O N E

Building Skills: Controlling Variables

Where are the stomata on a plant's leaves?

Steps

1. Place a geranium plant in a dark closet for three days.

2. After three days, take the plant out of the closet. Choose three leaves of the same size. Coat the top of one leaf with petroleum jelly. Coat the bottom of another leaf with the jelly. On a third leaf, do nothing. The third leaf is your control.

3. Set the plant in a sunny window for one week. Remember to water the plant if it gets dry. Each day record what you observe.

Questions

1. Describe the three leaves.

2. Where are the stomata on a leaf?

3. What do you think the petroleum jelly did to the leaf? On what do you base your conclusions?

Materials

geranium plant
petroleum jelly

Step 2

✓ Lesson Checkup

1. In what ways are photosynthesis and respiration opposites?

2. Where would more oxygen be used, in a busy city street or in a thick forest? Explain.

3. **Think Critically!** Explain how plants help people get energy from the sun.

Rising Carbon Dioxide Levels

Rain forests use up carbon dioxide.

Every year, forests are destroyed for firewood, lumber, cropland, and pastures. These forests give off huge amounts of oxygen into the air. They also use large amounts of carbon dioxide. Without the trees, carbon dioxide remains in the air. Thus, the amount of carbon dioxide in the air is increasing.

Fuels such as gas, oil, and coal give off carbon dioxide when they are burned. Burning these fuels also adds carbon dioxide to the air.

Scientists warn that too much carbon dioxide in the atmosphere can cause the earth to get warmer. The increased carbon dioxide in the atmosphere acts like a "glass shield" around the earth. Sunlight passes through this shield and changes to heat. The heat is then trapped beneath the carbon-dioxide shield. This causes temperatures to increase all over the earth.

The increased temperatures may melt the icecaps at the North and South Poles. Water released from glaciers has caused the sea level around the world to rise ten centimeters in the last 100 years. Warmer temperatures may cause the water level in the ocean to rise even more.

Think About It

People want to use the land where forests grow. As forests are lost, other people fear the change in the earth's atmosphere. Some even think that the cities on the coasts might be flooded with water! Is it important to keep the carbon dioxide levels from rising? If you lived in a town on the coast, would you feel differently? Explain your answers.

Cutting down forests increases carbon dioxide.

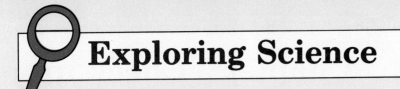

Exploring Science

Finding a Plant's Chlorophyll

Problem: Which areas of a leaf contain chlorophyll?

Experimenting

1. Observe the colors of a coleus leaf. Draw a picture of the leaf. Show the color patterns.

2. ◇ **HOT!** Put on your oven mitt. Boil the leaf in water for five minutes.

3. ◇ **HANDLE WITH CARE!** Use the spoon to remove the leaf from the water. Place in a beaker with warm diluted bleach until its color has been removed.

4. ◇ **WEAR SAFETY GOGGLES, APRON, AND GLOVES!** Float the bleached leaf in water in a bowl. Put two or three drops of iodine solution on the leaf. This will test for the presence of starch.

5. Observe the colors of the leaf. Compare the treated leaf to your drawing. Record the color changes in a table like the one shown below.

Materials

coleus leaves
pan
hot plate
water
diluted liquid bleach
beaker
bowl
iodine solution
spoon
oven mitt
apron
plastic gloves
paper towel
safety goggles

Step 2

Recording Data

	Coleus leaf colors
Before activity	
After activity	

Drawing Conclusions

1. What happened when you added the iodine solution to the leaf? What does this mean?

2. How can you tell where there was chlorophyll in the leaf? How do you know it was there?

✓ Chapter 3 Checkup

Summary

- Plants need sunlight, water, and carbon dioxide to make food.

- Photosynthesis is the process by which plants make food.

- Living things get energy from food through the process of respiration.

- Plants and animals depend on each other for food. They each play a role in the oxygen–carbon dioxide cycle.

Science Words

Copy the words below. Find each word in the glossary and write its definition.

chloroplast

chlorophyll

oxygen–carbon dioxide cycle

phloem

photosynthesis

respiration

root hair

stomata

tuber

xylem

Science Ideas

1. Letter your paper from a to h. Write the word in each list that does not belong.

   a. Photosynthesis: foodmaking, all cells, sunshine, uses water

   b. Respiration: all cells, uses oxygen, makes sugar, gives off water

   c. Stems: xylem, phloem, tubes, stomata

   d. Storing food: roots, wastes, flowers, stems

   e. Roots: anchor, absorb, guard cells, hairs

   f. Roots: banana, carrot, beet, turnip

   g. Leaves: anchor, stomata, guard cells, carbon dioxide

   h. Transporting materials: roots, flowers, stems, leaves

2. Letter your paper from a to d. Write whether the drawing is part of photosynthesis or respiration.

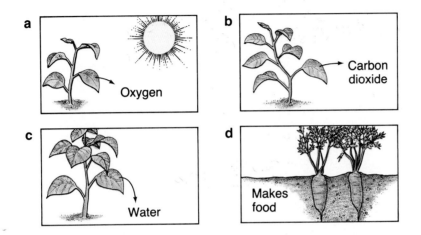

a
Oxygen

b
Carbon dioxide

c
Water

d
Makes food

3. Look at the picture. What did the pumpkin use to produce its food?

Data Bank

Use the table on page 384 to answer the following questions.

1. Which tree on the graph is tallest? How tall is it?

2. Which three trees reach the same height after fifteen years?

Science Ideas, Question 3

Problem Solving

How much sunshine does a plant need to achieve the best growth? Design an experiment to determine the effects of different amounts of sunlight on plant growth. It is important to keep the other variables the same (for example, soil, water, plant type). Make a hypothesis for your experiment.

Chapter 4
Ecosystems

In this chapter, you will learn

- what an ecosystem is
- how an energy pyramid works
- how the water, oxygen–carbon dioxide, and nitrogen cycles affect an ecosystem
- what causes changes to take place in an ecosystem

The brown bear cubs watch from shore as their mother catches a salmon. Then, oops! They see their dinner slip from their mother's jaws.

Though the stream is crowded with large fish, the cubs may be wondering if they will eat today. The salmon seem determined to make it upstream to lay their eggs. The mother bear is weak after a long winter's sleep. She is thin because she has not eaten for months. But with one last belly flop, the bear catches another salmon. This time, she grips it firmly in her teeth and heads for shore.

The cubs enjoy the taste of salmon! Then they try to catch a meal themselves. In the trees, birds watch the bears' every move. They are ready to swoop down and grab any fish that the bears drop.

In what ways do animals depend on one another? How is the water, air, and weather important to these animals? You will learn more about plants and animals interacting in their surroundings in this chapter.

Lesson 1   Living in an Environment

■ What are some examples of different ecosystems?

Where you live is important. In fact, the survival of all living things depends on where they live. The surroundings of a living thing are called its **environment.** Your environment includes all the living and nonliving things that affect your life.

Ecosystems   Notice the marsh drawing below. The marsh has several types of plants and animals. All of the same type of organisms living in a certain place make up a **population.** The marsh grass is one population. The heron, crab, and raccoon each belong to different animal populations. The populations may be large or small. For example, there may be 2 raccoons and 2,000 dragonflies in a marsh.

A Marsh Ecosystem

All of the different populations in a given area make up a **community.** The marsh community includes many kinds of plants, mammals, birds, fish, insects, amphibians, and mollusks.

The living things in a community depend on many nonliving things in their environment. Air, moisture, soil, and light are just a few nonliving things in an environment. Notice the smaller drawing below. It shows only the nonliving things in the marsh environment. What nonliving things can you find?

A community and its nonliving things are called an **ecosystem.** An ecosystem can be large or small. It can be as large as an ocean or as small as a puddle. The marsh shown below is an ecosystem.

Nonliving parts of a marsh

T H I N K

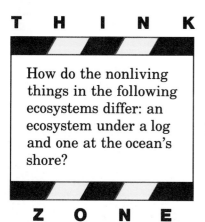

How do the nonliving things in the following ecosystems differ: an ecosystem under a log and one at the ocean's shore?

Z O N E

Nonliving Things Populations that live in the same ecosystem have certain needs. One common need may be water. Or a population may have a need for shade. You would not find a water lily growing in a desert. Nor would you find a cactus growing in a pond. These plants would live in ecosystems that fit their needs.

The nonliving things in an ecosystem often determine the ecosystem's community. These nonliving things can limit the type and size of a community. Because of this, nonliving things are often called limiting factors. Moisture, sunlight, soil type, and water are limiting factors. Even the amount of space can be a limiting factor for an ecosystem's community.

Notice the ecosystems in the pictures below. Each ecosystem is different. Yet each provides the basic needs of the community it supports. A community at the South Pole does well in cold temperatures. A desert community needs little rain and lots of sunlight. What nonliving things prevent a snake from living at the South Pole?

Different ecosystems support different communities.

Feeding Relationships The feeding relationships between living things in an ecosystem limit the size of populations. Food relationships begin with plants, since plants use energy from sunlight to produce their own food. For this reason, plants are known as producers.

Zebras are consumers of grass.

The food stored in grasses is eaten by animals, such as zebras. And these animals are eaten by other animals, such as lions. Therefore, both lions and zebras are consumers. A consumer is an organism that feeds on plants or animals. The zebra is a consumer of plants. The lion is a consumer of animals.

Although both zebras and lions are consumers, they have different roles. Animals that hunt, kill, and eat other animals are predators. Lions are predators. Animals that predators hunt are prey. Zebras are prey.

How can the feeding relationships limit the size of the populations? Suppose people kill many lions. With fewer lions to hunt zebras, the zebra population can increase rapidly. The zebras graze more, killing the grasses. With less grass to eat, many zebras die.

Lions are consumers of zebras.
Namibia

Grassland Food Chain

Energy in an Ecosystem   All ecosystems need energy. The main source of energy for an ecosystem is the sun. The sun provides the energy for green plants to make food. This energy passes from one living thing to another as one thing eats another. Look at the drawing of the food chain. Energy passes from the grasses to the prairie dog to the hawk.

The energy passing through an ecosystem can be drawn as an **energy pyramid**, as shown below. Plants, as food makers, are the bottom of the energy pyramid. This bottom level has the greatest stored energy. Going up the pyramid, available energy is lost. Organisms use energy to grow, reproduce, sleep, or do any life activity. This leaves less energy available for organisms on the next pyramid level. So, it takes a lot of producers to support a consumer at the top of the pyramid.

Grassland Energy Pyramid

Third-level consumers: meat-eating animals, such as hawks, that feed on other meat-eating animals

Second-level consumers: meat-eating animals, such as foxes, that feed on the plant-eating animals

First-level consumers: animals, such as rabbits, that feed on plants

Producers: grasses, which use the sun's energy to make food

Building Skills: Controlling Variables

Can you identify limiting factors?

Steps

1. Label one cup A and the other cup B.
2. Fill the cups with soil about two centimeters from the tops.
3. Plant five radish seeds in each cup. Make sure the seeds are not too deep in the soil.
4. Put three spoonfuls of water in cup A. Put three spoonfuls of salt solution in cup B.
5. Put the cups in a sunny spot. Check them daily. Add water to cup A or salt solution to cup B when the soil looks or feels dry.
6. Record any results you observe.

Questions

1. What were some limiting factors in this activity? Which factors did you control?
2. What plants live near the ocean's shore? What limiting factors must these plants adapt to?

Materials

2 plastic foam cups
10 radish seeds
soil
spoon
water
salt solution

Step 5

✓ Lesson Checkup

1. What is an ecosystem?
2. Why is it important for the lowest level of an energy pyramid to have the most energy?
3. **Think Critically!** How would an increase in the rabbit population affect a grassland community?

Lesson 2   Cycles in Ecosystems

■ Why are cycles important to an ecosystem?

Ecosystems get a constant supply of sunlight. There is no need to worry about replacing the sunlight that plants use to make food. The sun is always sending energy to the earth.

But other nonliving parts of the ecosystem, such as water, are in limited supply. Think of the earth as a big ecosystem. The earth must supply water and all the other nonliving things that organisms need. Therefore, some materials taken from the earth must be returned to it. Materials such as water are used over and over again. We say these things go through a cycle.

Look at the water cycle below. As water evaporates into water vapor and condenses into liquid, it moves in a constant cycle. In this lesson, you will learn how other materials in ecosystems move in cycles.

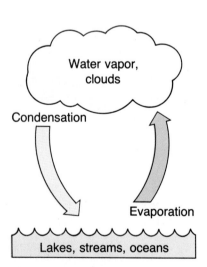

The Water Cycle

Storm clouds return water to the earth.

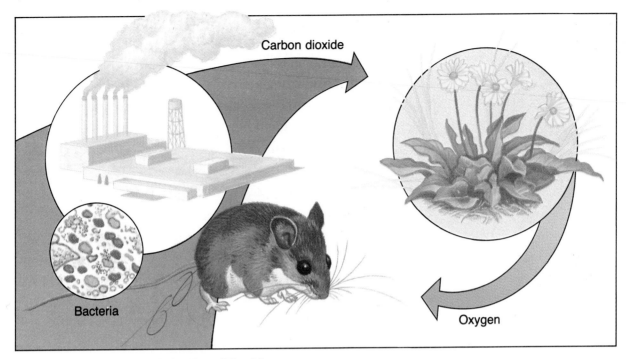

Recycling Oxygen and Carbon Dioxide

Oxygen–Carbon Dioxide Cycle

Water is not the only thing that moves in a cycle. Oxygen and carbon dioxide are two important gases in air. These gases are part of a cycle called the **oxygen–carbon dioxide cycle.**

You read about this cycle in Chapter 3. Oxygen and carbon dioxide are recycled during respiration and photosynthesis. Almost all living things need oxygen. Plants and animals use oxygen to break down the food stored in their cells. This process, called respiration, gives off energy. Living things need energy to live. During respiration, carbon dioxide is given off as a waste product.

Plants need carbon dioxide to make food. During photosynthesis, plants give off oxygen as a waste product. Oxygen enters the air to be used again during respiration. You can trace the flow of carbon dioxide and oxygen in the drawing above.

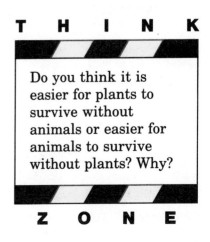

T H I N K

Do you think it is easier for plants to survive without animals or easier for animals to survive without plants? Why?

Z O N E

Nitrogen Cycle   Nitrogen is another gas found in air. It makes up four fifths of the air you breathe. Plants and animals need nitrogen to grow new cells. But plants and animals cannot use the nitrogen found in air. Before nitrogen can be used, the gas must be changed into nitrogen compounds.

The drawing below shows one way in which nitrogen compounds form. Tiny bacteria in the roots of certain plants change nitrogen gas into nitrogen compounds. These compounds are dissolved in water and then absorbed through a plant's roots. When plants die and decay, nitrogen returns to the soil and air. The movement of nitrogen is called the **nitrogen cycle.** Trace the steps of the nitrogen cycle.

Plants use the nitrogen compound to grow.

Animals get nitrogen by eating plants.

Plants and animals die. As they decay, nitrogen gas is released into the air and soil.

Special bacteria grow on the roots of peas, beans, and clovers. These bacteria change nitrogen gas into a nitrogen compound.

Recycling Nitrogen

Building Skills: Hypothesizing

Can limewater be used to test for oxygen and carbon dioxide?

Steps

1. Choose one of the following hypotheses:
   a. Limewater is used to test for oxygen.
   b. Limewater is used to test for carbon dioxide.

2. To test your hypothesis, fill one jar with limewater. Place the elodea in the jar.

3. Put the jar in a sunny place. Observe the jar carefully for several days. Record any changes in the limewater.

4. ◇ **WEAR GOGGLES!** Add limewater to the other jar. Using the soda straw, gently blow into the jar. Observe and record any changes in the limewater.

Questions

1. Which steps showed photosynthesis in action? Respiration in action? Explain your answers.

2. Did your results support your hypothesis?

Materials

elodea plant
2 jars
limewater
soda straw

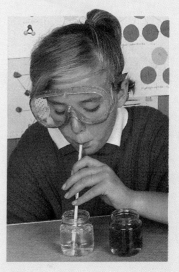

Step 4

 Lesson Checkup

1. How is oxygen returned to the air?

2. Why is it important to an ecosystem that its nonliving parts go through a cycle?

3. **Think Critically!** Why would farmers grow grain one year and clover the next year?

Lesson 3   Changing Ecosystems

■ How can a pond ecosystem change to a forest ecosystem?

Have you ever noticed plants growing in cracks in the sidewalk? These are a sign of a changing ecosystem. After the sidewalk splits, the crack slowly fills with soil. Seeds, carried by the wind, fall into the crack. With the first rainfall, the seeds take root. Tiny plants grow and produce seeds. Soon the plants make the sidewalk split more, and larger plants begin to grow in the cracks. These plants may later crowd out the smaller plants. The larger plants will then take over. This pattern is one way that one group of plants follows another in an ecosystem.

How are plants changing this ecosystem?

Succession Ecosystems are always changing. Sometimes changes happen suddenly. A natural disaster, such as a fire, flood, mudslide, or earthquake, may kill living things or change the environment. When this happens, a new community will replace the old community.

Mount St. Helens, before eruption (left), after eruption (center),
in 1985 (right), shows succession.

A volcanic eruption can cause a sudden change in
an ecosystem. Notice the pictures of the forest after the
eruption of Mount St. Helens in 1980. The forest was
destroyed in fifteen minutes by mud, volcanic ash, and
the force of the explosion. Five years later, small
plants began to grow where trees once stood. A new
ecosystem replaced the old. A change in the kind of
organisms that live in a place is called **succession.**

After many changes, one community may become
stable. A community with stable plant populations is
known as a **climax community.** Usually there is little
change once a climax community is established.

T H I N K

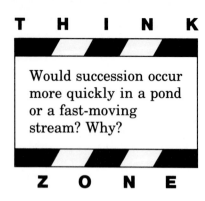

Would succession occur more quickly in a pond or a fast-moving stream? Why?

Z O N E

Slow Succession Volcanic eruption can cause violent change to an ecosystem. But succession is also a natural process that happens slowly. Though slow, it can change an ecosystem completely.

Notice the drawings of the pond below. They show how a water ecosystem can change to a land ecosystem. The pond plants are replaced by marsh grasses. Shrubs replace the marsh grasses. Eventually, a forest replaces the shrubs. The forest becomes the climax community. This means young maple and beech trees will replace dead maple and beech trees. This process occurs after a long period of time. Follow the steps of pond succession in the drawings below.

Succession in a Pond Ecosystem

1. Layers of soil settle in the pond. The remains of plants and animals add to these layers.

2. As the pond fills in, a marsh develops. Marsh grasses and animals grow and die.

3. In time, the marsh dries up. Grasses and shrubs grow in the new soil.

4. Trees begin to appear. Finally, a forest community lives where a pond once was.

Building Skills: Collecting Data

Does succession happen in a schoolyard?

Steps

1. Look for places in the schoolyard where there is grass. Choose a place where there is also a dandelion plant or other large weed.

2. Place a circle of string on the ground around the dandelion and its leaves. Use the knife to carefully dig up the dandelion.

3. Record the number of grass plants that are growing inside the circle.

4. Lay the same string in a circle on the grass where there are no dandelions. Count and record the number of grass plants inside.

Questions

1. Did the number of grass plants inside the two circles differ? Explain.

2. How does this activity explain what happens during succession?

Materials

string
plastic knife

Step 2

✓ Lesson Checkup

1. What can cause an ecosystem to change?

2. Explain how succession occurs in your lawn.

3. **Think Critically!** In an area that gets very little rain, is the climax plant likely to be a plant with a deep root system or a plant with a shallow root system? Why?

Artificial Reefs

An artificial reef

Natural reefs are ridges of sand, rock, or coral near the water's surface. Reefs provide an environment in which many different plants and animals can grow. Some fish like to hide in the reef's nooks and crannies. Reefs can shelter small fish from strong currents. Reefs also provide a hard surface for some plants and animals to grow on. These plants and animals become the food for other, larger animals.

Scientists are placing carefully chosen objects on the sea floor to create artificial reefs. Some objects are sunken ships. Other are piles of tires. In Palm Beach, Florida, even a Rolls Royce car dumped into the ocean has become an artificial reef. Artificial reefs may increase the number of certain kinds of ocean life. These reefs can be found along the United States coasts.

To be effective, artificial reefs must not pollute the ocean and must be longlasting. In Japan, scientists have designed special tube-shaped reefs made of fiberglass. Fiberglass is stronger than steel. It does not burn, stretch, or rot. These reefs are made on land and floated out to sea where they are sunk. The Japanese hope the reefs will attract ocean life. Then fish can be caught easily in the areas around the reefs.

Think About It

Reefs made of cars and other metal objects will usually rust away in a few years. These structures are not longlasting. A study in Florida, however, showed that the number of fish doubled when an artificial reef was built near a natural reef. Do you think artificial reefs are important to ocean communities? Why or why not?

Making an Aquarium

Problem: What do plants and animals need to survive in an aquarium?

Experimenting

1. Work in a group. Add sand and gravel to the jar. Slowly add water to fill the jar three-quarters full. Leave the jar uncovered for three days.

2. ◇ HANDLE WITH CARE! Add water plants, guppies, and snails to the jar. Make sure your aquarium gets the nonliving factors it needs. Also keep in mind the energy pyramid that will work in your jar.

3. After you have set up your aquarium, feed the guppies. Feed them each day. Label your jar.

4. Observe your aquarium every school day for two weeks. Record your observations.

Materials

4-liter jar
sand and gravel
water
snails
water plants
guppies
guppy food
labels

Recording Data

Day	Condition of plants	Condition of animals	Condition of nonliving factors
1			
2			
10			

Step 4

Drawing Conclusions

1. How did the living things affect the nonliving things in your ecosystem?

2. Did your ecosystem have what it needed to survive? How do you know?

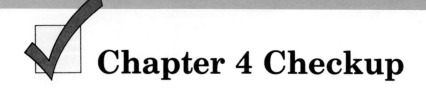

Chapter 4 Checkup

Summary

■ An ecosystem is a community and its nonliving things.

■ As energy passes through an ecosystem, it is used up. This creates an energy pyramid.

■ The oxygen–carbon dioxide cycle and the nitrogen cycle provide materials needed in an ecosystem.

■ Changes occur in an ecosystem through succession.

Science Words

Write a story using each word below. Show that you know what each word means.

climax community
community
ecosystem
energy pyramid
environment
nitrogen cycle
oxygen–carbon dioxide cycle
population
succession

Science Ideas

1. Letter your paper from a to g. Write the cause and effect for each statement.

   a. The amount of food a population can get limits its size.

   b. An ecosystem can be changed by a fire.

   c. Cycles occur when materials are used over and over again.

   d. Survival of all living things depends on where they live.

   e. As you move up an energy pyramid, available energy is lost.

   f. Tiny bacteria change nitrogen gas into nitrogen compounds.

   g. An ecosystem's communities are often determined by the ecosystem's nonliving things.

2. Letter your paper from a to d. Explain how each drawing below could change an ecosystem.

a Volcano

b Fire

c Flood

d Mudslide

3. Look at the picture. What are some of the living and nonliving things a bear needs to survive?

Data Bank

Use the world map on page 382 to answer the following questions.

1. Which continent has more wetlands than any other continent?

2. Which three continents have tundra marshes?

Problem Solving

Ecosystems can change naturally. But humans can cause changes, too. Bombs, air and water pollution, building, and forestry can change ecosystems. Choose one of the examples and go to the library to find out more about it. Write a report on how it would change a particular ecosystem of your choice. What form of succession might occur?

Science Ideas, Question 3

Chapter 5
The Earth's Biomes

In this chapter, you will learn

- what a biome is
- how climate affects living things
- how forest, grassland, desert, and tundra biomes differ
- how freshwater and saltwater ecosystems differ

Keiko is taking her first train trip across the country. She has brought along an outline map to color during the trip. As she leaves her home state of Maine, the trees are turning colors. Keiko colors these forests orange and red on her map. She calls this the "Glowing Forest." It spreads from the east to the Mississippi River.

Gradually, Keiko sees fewer trees outside her window. Flat land stretches as far as she can see. Keiko colors her map golden yellow. This matches the corn and wheat fields she sees. Her name for this area is "Golden Plains."

Then the land changes again. The jagged Rocky Mountains appear. Keiko draws the mountains and forests in her map. She calls it "Purple Mountains."

Soon the land looks very dry. Large patches of tan appear. Keiko draws and colors some scattered plants. She labels this part "Desert Tan." Keiko wonders why the plants change so much from place to place. After this chapter, you can answer Keiko's question.

Lesson 1   Climate and Life

What causes one kind of plant to grow in one place but not another?

Imagine that you could look at all of the earth at once. You would see large land ecosystems in different parts of the world that look alike. For example, some of the ecosystems in California, Arizona, Australia, and Africa are deserts. In a desert ecosystem, the air is dry and hot. Each of these ecosystems may be a part of a very large region. In this lesson you will learn about the desert regions and other regions found on the earth.

Biomes   The earth is divided into a number of large regions. Each region differs from the others. The temperature and rainfall, as well as the kinds of plants and animals, are similar in all parts of the region. Each of these regions is called a **biome.**

There are six major biomes on the earth. These biomes are the tundra, taiga (TY guh), temperate for-

Rain forest, tundra, and temperate forest biomes

ests, rain forests, deserts, and grasslands. One biome differs from another by its rainfall and temperature. These conditions in turn affect the plants that grow in the biome. The most abundant plants in a biome are called climax plants. Climax plants win over other plants for the water and sunlight of the biome. Each biome has its own climax plants.

Look at the grassland pictured below. The grasses found in Africa are different from the grasses found in the United States. But both kinds of grasses need about the same amount of water and sunlight. Therefore, they belong to the same biome, the grasslands.

Notice how the plants in the biomes shown on these two pages differ. Lush, green plants grow in the hot, moist rain forests. The deserts are also hot. But because deserts do not get as much water, desert plants are fewer and different. The tundra is another place where few plants grow. However, the frozen soil and the freezing temperatures are limiting factors in this environment.

Desert, taiga, and grassland biomes

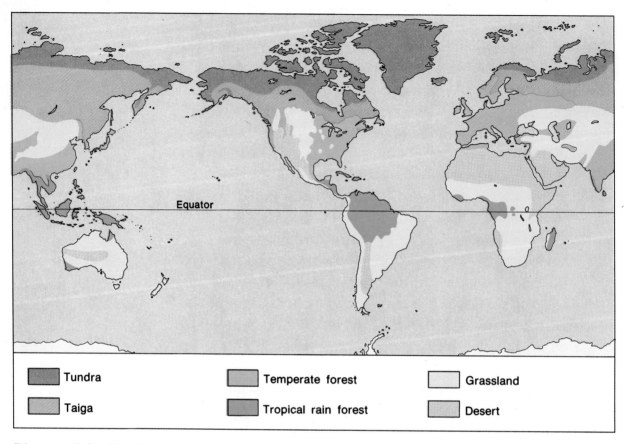

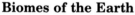 Tundra	Temperate forest	Grassland
Taiga	Tropical rain forest	Desert

Biomes of the Earth

Find the desert biomes on the map above. Notice what other biomes are near the deserts. Biomes do not begin and end abruptly as they seem to on the map. Instead, one biome blends into another at their edges.

Climate   Many plants grow well in one place but not in another. Most living things are adapted for a certain kind of climate. **Climate** is the average weather in one place over a long period of time. Many factors affect the climate in a given place. These include temperature, moisture, sunlight, and wind.

Of all the factors that affect climate, temperature and moisture are most important. The temperature of a biome is determined by the amount of sunlight it

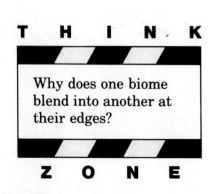

THINK

Why does one biome blend into another at their edges?

ZONE

receives. In general, those land areas near the equator receive the most sunlight. These areas are the warmest. As you move away from the equator, the average amount of sunlight decreases. The temperature also decreases.

You can see on the temperature graph that the temperature range in the tundra is between −27°C and 7°C. These are very cold temperatures. Notice on the map that tundra is located far from the equator.

Moisture falls on the earth in the form of rain, dew, snow, hail, or sleet. This water is called **precipitation.** Much of the water in a biome comes from rain or snow. Look at the precipitation graph. It shows the yearly precipitation for each of the biomes. Which biome has the most precipitation in a year? Which has the least?

Temperatures and Precipitation in the Biomes

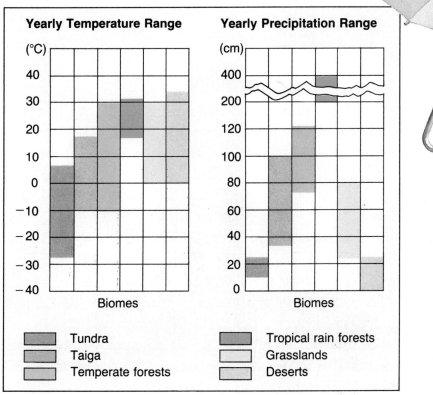

Plant and Animal Life in a Biome The climate affects a plant's growth. A plant can grow only where conditions are right for it. Too little water may stop one kind of plant from growing in a certain area. Too much water may stop another kind of plant from growing there. Some plants grow best when the temperature is very warm. Others grow best when the temperature is cool.

The kinds of plants in a biome determine the kinds of animals found there. Many animals can live only where there are certain plants. For example, animals that eat grass live in a grassland biome. They would not be able to live in a rain forest biome. The koalas in the picture feed only on the leaves of eucalyptus (YOO kuh LIHP tuhs) trees. If these trees disappeared, koalas would soon die.

Eucalyptus leaves

How do koalas depend on their climate for food?

Building Skills: Reading a Graph

Which factors cause biomes to differ?

Step

1. The graphs below show the average temperatures and precipitation of four different cities. Compare these graphs with the graphs on page 107.

Materials

paper

pencil

Question

1. Describe the temperature and precipitation for each city. To which biome does each city belong?

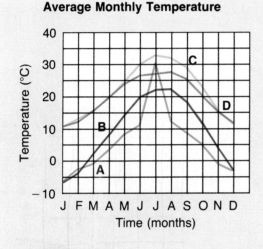

Average Monthly Temperature

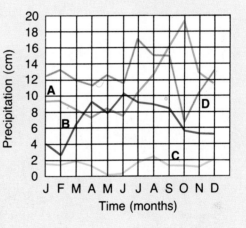

Average Monthly Precipitation

✓ Lesson Checkup

1. What is a biome?

2. What factors cause biomes to differ?

3. **Think Critically!** If there were living things on other planets, do you think they would be like living things on earth? Explain.

Lesson 2   Biomes on Earth

■ What are the climax plants in the six major biomes?

If you could fly over the arctic region in the fall, you might see large caribou (KAR uh boo) herds moving south. As food becomes scarce in the far north, caribou head for a warmer region where there is more food. Caribou move from tundra to a forest biome.

Many animals are able to stay in the same biome all year round. But the temperature and rainfall in a biome may change too much from season to season for other animals. In this lesson, you will read about the climate and organisms of the six major biomes.

Caribou eat grasses.

Caribou move between two biomes to find food.

Tundra   The **tundra** is a treeless biome that circles the northernmost part of the earth. It is a cold, dry region. The layer of soil beneath the tundra surface is always frozen. Only a thin layer of the topsoil thaws each spring. This topsoil stays moist through the summer.

Tundra plants grow rapidly in the three months of spring and summer. Though the seasons are short, the days are very long. The most common climax plants in the tundra are mosses and very low-growing shrubs. Each plant needs similar conditions of soil, temperature, and moisture to grow.

Lichens (LY kuhnz) also grow in the tundra. They are really two different kinds of organisms—algae (AL jee) and fungi. The algae in lichens make food for the fungi. The fungi cannot make food, but they can take in water. The algae and fungi work together to help each other survive.

Caribou, along with ptarmigans (TAHR muh guhns) and lemmings, eat the tundra plants and lichens. Other animals such as arctic foxes, wolves, snowy owls, and falcons feed on the plant-eating animals. Many tundra animals have a white coat in winter and a brown coat in summer.

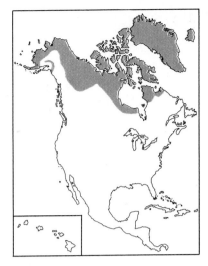

Tundra

Tundra supports lichens, ptarmigans (top right), and lemmings (bottom right).

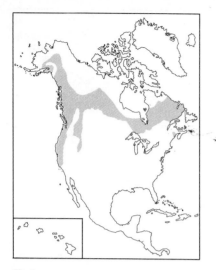

Taiga

Taiga   Next to the tundra is a biome called the **taiga.** Long, cold winters and short, cool summers make the growing season short. The taiga ground is covered with snow during much of the year. Only trees that can survive low temperatures grow there. The taiga's most common plants are trees that make cones. Seeds are made in these cones. The cones below grew on a spruce tree. Lichens, ferns, and mosses may grow on the forest floor. But the trees shade the forest floor so that few plants can grow there.

The trees in the taiga provide shelter for many different animals. The plant-eating animals include deer, moose, beavers, mice, porcupines, and snowshoe hares. The meat-eating animals include woodpeckers, bears, foxes, and wolves. Many animals in the taiga grow a thick winter fur.

Moose, plants with cones, and woodpeckers live in the taiga.

Temperate Forests   Cold winters, warm summers, and plenty of rain produce another kind of forest. It is called the **temperate forest**. The climax plants in temperate forests are trees. These trees have broad leaves and need lots of water. Beech, oak, maple, poplar, and sycamore trees are examples of such trees.

Temperate forests can easily be recognized in winter because most of the trees are bare. Most plants lose water through their leaves. The trees get less water as the ground freezes. In temperate forests, trees shed their leaves. This helps the trees stop water loss. During a long spring and summer growing season, the trees grow new leaves.

Insects, woodmice, deer, and squirrels are common in temperate forests. Gray foxes, owls, hawks, and woodpeckers feed on some of these animals.

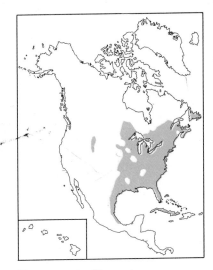

Temperate Forests

Flowering plants, squirrels, and foxes live in temperate forests.

113

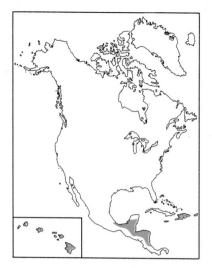

Tropical Rain Forests

Tropical Rain Forests

Heavy rains during the entire year and strong sunlight form a forest rich with plants. This is called a **tropical rain forest.** Because the rainfall in these forests is very heavy, it is always moist. The temperature in a tropical rain forest stays warm. These conditions make it possible for plants to grow year round. Because of this, plants that do not grow anywhere else are found in the rain forest.

A tropical rain forest has about 400 different kinds of trees. These include mahogany, teak, and palm trees. The trees in a rain forest do not lose their leaves in winter.

Many different kinds of animals can live in a rain forest. They include butterflies and other insects, parrots, hummingbirds, monkeys, and deer. Animals that feed on these animals include crocodiles, anteaters, snakes, and eagles.

Many kinds of birds and plants live in tropical rain forests.

The plants in a tropical rain forest are found in several layers. Some trees of the forest are truly giants. These tower above the rest of the trees. The smaller trees form thick layers. The layers keep the sunlight from reaching the forest floor. Without sunlight, few plants can grow on the forest floor. Read about the layers of plants in the drawing below. Notice the different animals that have adapted to live in each layer.

Layers of Plants in a Tropical Rain Forest

Highest layer:
a few giant trees tower above the forest

Forest canopy:
branches of trees, growing close together, form an umbrella over the forest

Medium-size trees:
much smaller trees form a lower layer

Forest floor:
little growth occurs here except in openings where a tree has fallen

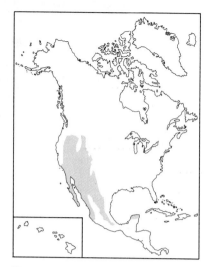

Deserts

Deserts You may think of deserts as places where you can see nothing but sand. Some deserts are like that, but many are not. During a summer day, the temperature in a desert gets very hot. At night, the temperature may drop to half of what it was during the day. Large areas with high daytime temperatures and very little rainfall become **deserts.** You can see two different deserts on these two pages.

The desert climax plant community includes yucca and cactus plants, shrubs, and some grasses. These plants are adapted to the hot, dry conditions of the desert. For example, plants in a desert often have waxy surfaces on their leaves. This keeps the plants from losing water. Some desert plants are "juicy." They survive the heat by storing water. Some desert plants, such as cacti, have spines instead of leaves. Spines lose less water than larger leaves.

Scorpions (top left), snakes, and lizards are common desert animals.

Desert animals are also adapted to the hot, dry conditions. For example, many animals in the desert remain quiet during the heat of the day. They hide in cracks of rocks or burrows. These animals become active at night when it is cooler. Some desert animals have special adaptations that help them survive the heat and lack of water. For example, kangaroo rats can live without drinking water. Their bodies make water from the food they eat. They lose very little water in their wastes. Desert insects and reptiles have waterproof coverings that keep them from drying out.

Some common plant-eating animals in American deserts are kangaroo rats, insects, and jackrabbits. These animals eat the seeds, leaves, and stems of the desert plants. Other animals include snakes, lizards, bats, roadrunners, and vultures. These meat-eating animals get much water from their food.

T H I N K

Most deserts have constant winds. What may be the reason for this?

Z O N E

Roadrunners, yucca plants, and kangaroo rats live in the desert.

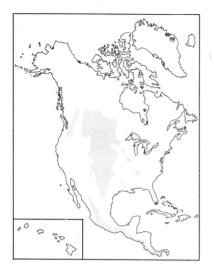

Grasslands

Grasslands   The grassland biome is not as dry as the desert biome. However, it does not get enough water to support trees. **Grasslands** get little rainfall. Grasslands often have great changes in daily temperature, with cold nights and warm days. As you can tell by the name, grasses are the climax plants in the grassland biome. Grain crops such as corn, wheat, and oats are grasses.

Grasses are the primary food in grasslands. Some of the animals that eat grasses are snails, insects, and prairie dogs. Many grassland areas are used to raise cattle and sheep. The large number of insects and seeds in grasslands attract many birds. Prairie chickens, meadowlarks, and longspurs are some examples. Animals that eat other animals include hawks, owls, spiders, weasels, and red foxes.

Meadowlarks, butterflies, bison, and prairie dogs live in grasslands.

Building Skills: Making Models

How can you make a rain forest biome?

Steps

1. ◇ **SHARP!** Cut the top off the bottle as shown.

2. Place a layer of small pebbles in the bottom of the bottle. Cover these with charcoal.

3. Carefully add a layer of potting soil. Cover it with a layer of moss. Wet the soil thoroughly, but do not make it soggy.

4. Plant the small plants. Spread them out so they have space to grow.

5. Tape plastic wrap over the "rain forest." Put it in a place where there is light, but not direct sunlight. Observe the rain forest for two weeks. Record any changes you see.

Questions

1. Why did you not have to water the rain forest?

2. What animals could you add to your rain forest? Could they live without help from you?

Materials

2-liter plastic soda bottle

plastic wrap

small pebbles

charcoal

potting soil

moss

small plants

water

Step 5

✔ Lesson Checkup

1. Compare a tundra biome with a taiga biome.

2. How does a temperate forest differ from a tropical rain forest?

3. **Think Critically!** In Africa, some grasslands are becoming deserts. What may be causing this? What factors are being changed?

Lesson 3   Water Ecosystems

■ Why is most water life found in shallow water or near the water's surface?

Since people live on land, it is easy to forget that almost three fourths of the earth's surface is water. From space, the earth looks like a water planet. It is the only one of its kind in the solar system.

Two kinds of water ecosystems are found on earth: freshwater and saltwater. In this lesson, you will look at these two kinds of water ecosystems.

Freshwater Ecosystems   Only four percent of all the water on earth is fresh water. This means the water is not salty. Much of this water is found underground or is frozen in glaciers and icebergs in the polar

These bears are part of a freshwater ecosystem.

regions. Still, freshwater ecosystems are important. Many different plants and animals live in ponds, lakes, and swamps as well as rivers and streams.

In many ways, it is easier for plants and animals to live in water than on land. For example, water animals do not need complex body systems to save water. Most freshwater fish drink little water. When a fish swallows water, it is actually taking in oxygen. The water passes through gills and then leaves the body.

The temperature in water changes very slowly. Therefore, plants and animals that live in water do not have to adapt to rapid changes in temperature. However, they do have to adapt to changes in light. Water is not always clear. Soil and other matter in water limit the amount of light that reaches water plants.

How have these animals adapted to live around water?

Ducks, dragonflies, and fish often live in pond ecosystems.

A pond is an excellent place to study a freshwater ecosystem. Because a pond is still water, floating and rooted plants do not wash away. These plants grow best in shallow water or near the water's surface where there is sunlight. In deeper water, plants do not get enough sunlight to grow.

Many tiny floating organisms can also live in ponds. They are called **plankton,** which means "drifting." Some plankton are like plants. They are green and can make their own food. Green plankton are producers. Other plankton are like animals. They cannot make their own food. Instead, they feed on the green plankton. Both kinds of plankton are food for animals in the pond. Some animals that feed on plankton are insects, snails, and small fish. These animals then become food for fish, bullfrogs, and ducks.

Saltwater Ecosystems   Most saltwater ecosystems are found in the ocean. One ecosystem is the tide pool. Look at the tide pool in the picture below. A tide pool is left on the shore as the tide goes out. It is a tiny ocean community that people can watch.

Twice a day, rising tides bring ocean plankton to the tide pool. Plankton are the main food of clams, crabs, and tiny fish. But green plankton are not the only food producers in a tide pool. Others include seaweed, green algae, and even grasses. Sea snails and sea urchins eat these producers. Starfish and crabs eat these animals. When the tide is out, much of the animal life is hidden in the rocks or seaweed.

Farther out from shore, two other kinds of ecosystems thrive. One is on the ocean floor. The other is in the water above the ocean floor. In this ecosystem, all living things must float or swim. Of these living things, plankton are very important. Green plankton are the producers of the oceans.

T H I N K

Green plankton are sometimes called the basis of life in the oceans. Explain.

Z O N E

Gulls, starfish, and limpets (bottom right) are part of a tide pool ecosystem.

The organisms floating in water have special adaptations that keep them from sinking to the ocean bottom. Many plankton have needlelike parts on their surfaces. These parts help the plankton float close to the water's surface where there is sunlight. This is important because green plankton need the sun's energy to make food.

Other animals that feed on the producers must be near their food source. Some jellyfish have gas-filled floats that keep them from sinking. Many fish have swim bladders that help them float. These bladders are filled with air or other gases.

Some fish that swim far beneath the surface of the ocean glow. They have a body part containing bacteria that give off light. Fish that live very deep in the ocean do not need light because they cannot see. They feed on food that falls from above, or they feed on one another.

Squid (top left), plankton (right), dolphins, and fish live in saltwater ecosystems.

Building Skills: Controlling Variables

Can brine shrimp live in fresh water?

Steps

1. Label one jar A and the other B. Fill jar A with salt water and jar B with fresh water.
2. Dip two dry cotton swabs into the brine shrimp eggs. Next, dip a swab into each jar.
3. Place the jars in a warm place.
4. The next day, put five drops of water from jar A into a dish. Use the hand lens to count the number of eggs and shrimp you see. Record.
5. Rinse the dropper. Repeat step 4 for jar B.
6. Compare the results of both samples.

Questions

1. In which jar did the brine shrimp grow best?
2. How would you change this activity to test how salty the water can be and still let brine shrimp grow?

Materials

fresh water
salt water
brine shrimp eggs
2 jars
labels
spoon
2 cotton swabs
2 shallow dishes
dropper
hand lens

Step 4

✓ Lesson Checkup

1. Why are plankton important to water ecosystems?
2. Describe one food chain in a pond ecosystem.
3. **Think Critically!** Would you expect to find seaweed in deep ocean water or in shallower water? Explain your answer.

A Rain Forest in the Desert

In 1987, scientists began building a gigantic greenhouse in the middle of the Arizona desert. This greenhouse is called Biosphere II. (Biosphere I is the earth.) When Biosphere II is finished, it will have several "mini-environments" inside. Some of these include a tropical rain forest, lagoons and ocean pools, a desert area, and fields of crops.

After Biosphere II is completed, a group of scientists will enter. The doors will be sealed shut. The people inside will be cut off from the outside world. For two years they will raise their own crops, animals, and fish. Water, air, and waste products will all be recycled. Computers will measure the amount of pollution, water, oxygen, and carbon dioxide in the structure. Scientists hope that this experiment will teach them how to take care of the earth's biomes.

The greenhouse will get its energy from the sun. The air will be cleaned by the natural oxygen–carbon dioxide cycle. People and animals inside Biosphere II will inhale oxygen and exhale carbon dioxide. Plants inside the structure will use the carbon dioxide during photosynthesis. In the process, plants will make fresh oxygen for all the plants and animals.

Think About It

Someday, structures similar to the Biosphere II may be used as colonies on distant planets. On earth, these structures could make useful "labs" for studying problems such as pollution. Can you think of other ways a Biosphere II might be used? Would you like to live in one? Why or why not?

Ladybugs will help control pests in Biosphere II.

Butterfly fish may live in the ocean lagoons.

Exploring Science

Comparing Temperatures

Problem: How do the temperatures on earth change as you get farther away from the equator?

Experimenting

1. Make a data table like the one shown below.

2. Tape a thermometer on a large globe at the equator. This is at 0° latitude.

3. Directly above the first thermometer, at 40° north latitude, tape another thermometer. Your globe should look like the globe in the picture.

4. Shine the lamp's light at the equator, 15 centimeters from the globe. Take temperature readings of the two thermometers every 5 minutes for 15 minutes. Record the data.

Materials

2 thermometers
tape
globe
lamp without shade
metric ruler
clock or watch

Recording Data

Latitude	Temperature			
	Start	After 5 minutes	After 10 minutes	After 15 minutes
0°				
40° N				

Step 4

Drawing Conclusions

1. Which thermometer had light shining more directly on it? Which thermometer recorded the higher temperatures?

2. What caused the differences in temperatures?

3. How does this activity show in part why there are different biomes on the earth?

127

Chapter 5 Checkup

Summary

- Large regions on earth where temperature, precipitation, plants, and animals are similar are called biomes.

- The climate of an area determines the kinds of plants that can grow and the kinds of animals that can live there.

- There are six major biomes. They differ in climate and plant and animal life.

- Freshwater and saltwater ecosystems are different just as land biomes are different.

Science Words

Copy the words below. Define each word in a sentence.

biome
climate
desert
grassland
plankton
precipitation
taiga
temperate forest
tropical rain forest
tundra

Science Ideas

1. Letter your paper from a to g. Write a word(s) that best completes each sentence.

   a. Only four percent of all the water on the earth is ____.

   b. Corn, wheat, and oats are the main grain crops in the ____ biome.

   c. ____ are large areas with high daytime temperatures and very little rainfall.

   d. All water that falls to earth is ____.

   e. ____ is the average weather in one place over a long period of time.

   f. Animals in a water ecosystem feed on drifting organisms called ____.

   g. There are six major ____ on earth.

2. Letter your paper from a to f. Write the correct biome for each drawing below.

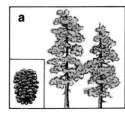

Pine tree

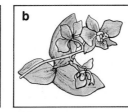

Tropical flower

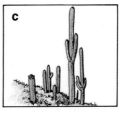

Cactus

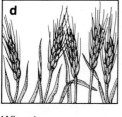

Wheat

Caribou

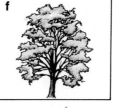

Oak tree

3. Look at the picture. Explain why plants change so much from biome to biome.

Data Bank

Use the table on page 383 to answer the following questions.

1. Which spice listed grows in almost all tropical areas? Which spices grow in Mexico?

2. Where is cinnamon grown? Where is vanilla grown?

Problem Solving

Timothy wanted to do a science fair project to find out in which biome certain vegetables would grow best. Write a brief description of how each of the six biomes could be set up for this experiment. Include information about temperature and water needs.

Science Ideas, Question 3

129

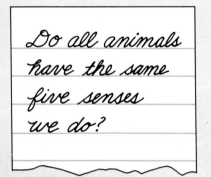

Do all animals have the same five senses we do?

Mrs. Marti Griffin's class at Saigling School in Plano, Texas

Dr. Sheila Stiles

? Ask a Scientist

Dr. Sheila Stiles is a biologist. She works for the United States National Marine Fisheries Service in Milford, Connecticut. In a laboratory, Dr. Stiles does research on heredity in fish. She also studies the effects of pollution on organisms that live in the water.

Dr. Stiles says that the five senses that humans have are sight, hearing, smell, taste, and touch. Many animals have the same five senses that we do. For example, monkeys, horses, dogs, cats, and rabbits have eyes, ears, and noses that work much like ours. However, some of the sense organs of animals are more sensitive than those of humans. For example, dogs can hear very high-pitched sounds that we cannot hear. Dogs also have a better sense of smell than we do. Cats, owls, and raccoons can see things when it is too dark for us to see anything.

Fish have a special sense organ called a lateral line. This organ helps a fish feel the movement of water around it. Then the fish knows if other animals are swimming nearby.

Insects seem to have the same five senses we do, but their sense organs are very different from ours. For example, the eyes of a dragonfly or bee are not like our eyes. Each of their eyes is made up of hundreds of small eyes put together. A grasshopper hears sounds through sense organs on its abdomen. Butterflies can taste food with their legs!

Even very simple organisms, such as paramecia or hydras, can sense things. They do not have eyes or ears or noses. Still, some of these simple animals do respond to touch, flashes of light, and chemicals in their environment.

Careers & Science

Aquarium Guide People visit aquariums to see water animals in their natural environment. Aquarium guides help people make the most of their visits. These guides give information about the organisms in the exhibit and how the organisms interact with one another. The guides also tell visitors about the kinds of environments these organisms require. If you like water animals and like to talk to groups of people, you may enjoy being an aquarium guide. After high school, you can be trained on the job.

Forest Ranger Anyone who has visited a national forest has probably met forest rangers. They protect trees from fires, disease, and insects. Forest rangers make people's camping trips enjoyable. They show films and give lectures about the plants and animals in the forest. They help people appreciate what a wonderful resource a forest is. You may think that working with people and with wildlife would be an exciting life. If so, study forestry or park management in a four-year college.

Agronomist Working with farmers that grow our food are agronomists (uh GRAHN uh mihsts). These soil scientists help farmers grow more and better crops. They experiment with plants to find those that grow best and that have the greatest nutritional value. They work to find ways to improve soil by adding minerals. Some agronomists do research and some teach. Perhaps you like doing experiments with plants and soil. If so, you can study to be an agronomist in a four-year college.

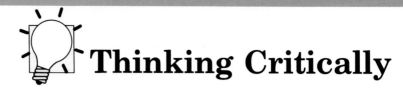

Thinking Critically

Reasoning by Analogy

Sometimes you have to make decisions about things even though you do not have as much information as you would like. When this happens, it helps to think about other things that are similar. This extra information can help you make a better decision.

Suppose it is your job to shovel the driveway each time it snows. It usually takes you two hours. Your neighbor asked if you would be willing to shovel his driveway the next time it snows. He says he will pay you six dollars. Since his driveway is about the same length as yours, you figure it will take you two hours. You want to make at least three dollars an hour, so you tell him six dollars is okay.

You are reasoning by analogy to draw this conclusion. An analogy is a comparison of two things that are similar. In this case, you are comparing the two driveways. To make a good analogy, the things you compare should not be too different. For example, if your neighbor's driveway is uphill, or wider than yours, then it will probably take you more time to shovel it. If the analogy is not good, your reasoning will not lead to a good conclusion. Reasoning by analogy is a thinking skill.

1 Practicing the Skill

Last summer, Joyce planted some zucchini (zoo KEE nee). She followed the directions on the seed packet carefully. She got a large crop. This summer, she planted zucchini, butternut squash, and corn. She decided to use the same procedure to plant the corn and

Zucchini

Butternut squash

Corn

butternut squash that she had used for planting zucchini. The zucchini and butternut squash grew well, but the corn did not.

On what analogies did Joyce based her reasoning? List three differences between zucchini and corn that might explain why her reasoning did not lead to a good decision about the corn. Why was the decision about the butternut squash better?

2 | Thinking About Thinking

How did you figure out why her reasoning by analogy did not lead to a good decision? How did you know if her analogies were good or bad? What can you tell a friend to be careful about when reasoning by analogy?

3 | Using the Skill

Paul does not like peas. When the school cafeteria served corn for lunch, he did not eat it. He said that corn was like peas. On what analogy was Paul's reasoning based? What questions might you ask him in order to decide if his reasoning by analogy led to a good decision?

133

Unit Two
Physical Science

Chapter 6
The Structure of Matter

All things are made of matter. Matter is made of particles. The types of particles and how they are arranged cause matter to differ.

Chapter 7
Sound

Sound is all around you. Sound travels through matter. You make and hear different kinds of sound.

Chapter 8
Motion

Objects move fast, slow, up, down, and around. Different laws can help you to understand and predict motion.

Chapter 9
Energy Resources

Energy is used to heat homes, run cars, and power factories. This energy comes from different sources. Some energy sources are becoming more and more scarce. Saving energy helps these resources last longer.

Chapter 6
The Structure of Matter

In this chapter, you will learn

- how matter is classified as an element, compound, or mixture

- how to describe the parts of an atom

- how atoms combine to form molecules or ions

- how to identify types of mixtures

Philip loved to explore his grandmother's attic. The attic was filled with furniture, clothes, toys, boxes, and suitcases. One day, he found a pocketwatch in an old pair of pants. The pocketwatch did not work.

Philip showed the pocketwatch to his grandmother. Together they took the watch to a watchmaker to have it repaired.

Philip looked on as the watchmaker repaired the pocketwatch. The watchmaker removed the back of the watch. The inside was filled with springs and gears. The watchmaker told Philip that although old watches come in different styles, they have similar parts. These parts are arranged in similar ways. Look closely at the picture of the pocketwatch and its parts. The inside of Philip's watch looked much the same.

The arrangement of the pocketwatch's parts is called its structure. Just as pocketwatches have a basic structure, so does matter. After reading this chapter, you should have a better idea about the basic structure found in all types of matter.

Lesson 1   Matter

■ How are elements and atoms similar?

You live in a world made of matter. Your desk is probably made of wood. The classroom windows are made of glass. Wood and glass are types of matter. All matter has mass and takes up space. Each kind of matter is called a substance.

Substances may differ a great deal from one another. Look at the picture below. The balloons are filled with hot air. Air is matter. It is a gas that you breathe. Iron and hydrogen are two other kinds of matter. Iron is a solid that rusts. Hydrogen is a gas that explodes. While air, iron, and hydrogen are matter, they are very different from each other.

Matter is made of particles. Both the type of particles and the way the particles are arranged cause matter to differ. Because of this structure, matter can be placed into different groups.

Hot air balloons

138

Mercury, Hg

Gold, Au

Bromine gas, Br

Elements   Many substances can be broken down into simpler substances. You can use heat, electricity, or sunlight to change some substances. But all substances reach a point when they cannot be broken down any further. A substance that cannot be changed into a simpler substance is called an **element.**

Gold is an element. It is a yellow solid that can be pounded into different shapes. Like all elements, gold has its own set of properties. Its properties are unlike the properties of any other element. Look at the pictures above. Each picture shows an element. How do mercury and bromine differ from gold?

There are 109 known elements. Scientists use chemical symbols to represent these elements. A chemical symbol is an abbreviation. It often is the first letter in the name of the element. For example, the symbol for hydrogen is H.

Some chemical symbols are two letters. If the names of more than one element begin with the same letter, two letters are needed. For example, the symbol for helium is He. Some chemical symbols come from other languages. The symbol for gold, Au, comes from the Latin word *aurum.*

T H I N K

The symbols for iron and sodium come from Latin names. Which element was named from *natrium?* From *ferrum?*

Z O N E

139

Classifying Elements   Elements are placed into different groups. For example, all elements are classified as either metals or nonmetals. Metals and nonmetals have different properties. Because they have different properties, metals and nonmetals are used in different ways. Some of these different properties are easy to recognize.

Most elements are metals. Most metals are shiny. They also are good conductors. Substances that are good conductors allow heat and electricity to flow through them easily. Examples of metals are copper, silver, and gold.

Nonmetals are found almost everywhere. Many, such as oxygen and helium, are gases at room temperature. Nonmetals are not shiny and are poor conductors. Look at the table below. It gives information on different metals and nonmetals.

Elements					
Name	**Symbol**	**Type**	**State**	**Uses**	
Copper	Cu	Metal	Solid	Coins, electric wire	
Silver	Ag	Metal	Solid	Coins, jewelry, art	
Mercury	Hg	Metal	Liquid	Thermometers	
Helium	He	Nonmetal	Gas	Balloons	
Neon	Ne	Nonmetal	Gas	Signs	

Building Blocks of Elements   Elements are made up of very small particles called **atoms.** Each element has its own type of atom. For example, gold has gold atoms and helium has helium atoms. Atoms are the smallest particle of an element that can exist and still keep the element's chemical properties.

By using a special microscope, scientists have seen shadows of silicon atoms. But atoms are so small that most cannot be seen even with special microscopes. From their studies, scientists make models of what they think an atom looks like.

Look at the models drawn below. As scientists learn new facts about atoms, they change the models. The model on the right is used by scientists today.

Rutherford model

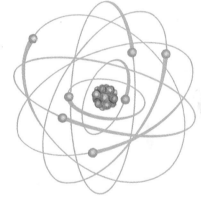

Bohr model

Electron cloud model

Parts of the Atom   According to the electron cloud model, atoms are made of three smaller particles: **protons, neutrons** (NOO trahnz), and **electrons.** Protons and neutrons are located in the center of the atom. This central core is called a **nucleus** (NOO klee uhs). Read about the parts of an atom in the drawing on page 142. As scientists learn more about atoms, this model may also change.

Protons are the only particles in the nucleus with a charge. Therefore, the nucleus has a positive charge. The electrons have a negative charge. Atoms have equal numbers of protons and electrons. So, the number of positive charges equals the number of negative charges. These charges then cancel each other. For this reason, atoms are called neutral.

Even though atoms are very tiny, they are mostly empty space. The protons and neutrons give an atom most of its mass. Yet these particles take up very little space in the atom. Only a tiny part of an atom's mass lies in the electron cloud. Yet the electron cloud makes up almost all of the atom's volume. Imagine the nucleus of a hydrogen atom as big as a marble. The edge of the electron cloud would be more than three football fields away!

Electron Cloud Model of an Atom

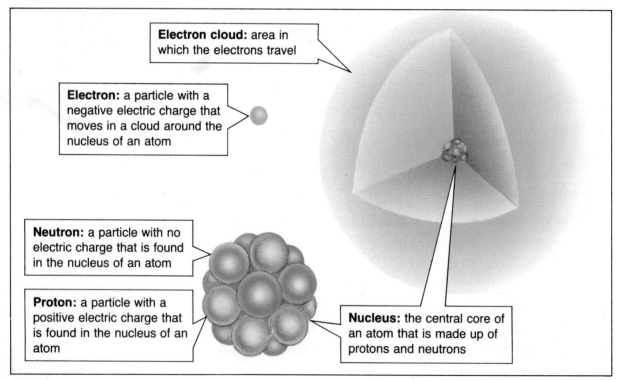

Electron cloud: area in which the electrons travel

Electron: a particle with a negative electric charge that moves in a cloud around the nucleus of an atom

Neutron: a particle with no electric charge that is found in the nucleus of an atom

Proton: a particle with a positive electric charge that is found in the nucleus of an atom

Nucleus: the central core of an atom that is made up of protons and neutrons

Building Skills: Inferring

How can you guess the inside of a box?

Steps

1. With your pencil, carefully punch two holes in each side of the box. Make sure the holes on opposite sides line up.

2. Place four straws through the holes as shown in the picture.

3. Close your eyes. Have someone put the straws through the washers and close the lid.

4. Open your eyes and study the box. Move it but do not open the lid! Draw a diagram of where you think the washers were placed on the straws.

Questions

1. Was your diagram accurate? Why or why not?

2. What clues helped you guess where the washers were?

3. Compare this activity to the way a scientist makes a model of an atom.

Materials

box
pencil
4 straws
3 washers

Step 3

✔ Lesson Checkup

1. Draw an electron cloud model of an atom. Label the parts.

2. If an electron were removed from an atom, what would happen to the atom's charge?

3. **Think Critically!** Explain what makes the substance gold different from silver.

Lesson 2　　Combining Elements

How do elements and compounds differ?

At one time, early chemists believed that it was possible to turn one element into another. For many years, they tried to find a way to change common metals into gold. Although they were never successful, these chemists helped start modern chemistry.

We now know that elements cannot be changed to other elements by simple chemical reactions. But elements can combine with other elements to form new substances. In fact, most substances are a combination of elements. When two or more elements chemically combine, the new substance is called a **compound.** Whenever matter joins chemically, new substances are formed. Although there are only 109 known elements, they combine to form millions of compounds!

Early chemist

Compounds   Chemical compounds have properties that are different from the properties of elements that make them up. Look at the pictures below. Chlorine is a greenish-yellow, poisonous gas. Sodium is a soft, silver-colored metal. When chlorine combines with sodium, the compound sodium chloride is formed. Sodium chloride is common table salt. It is not at all like the elements sodium and chlorine.

Chlorine gas, Cl

Salt, NaCl

Sodium, Na

Sodium and chlorine combine to make salt.

The elements hydrogen and oxygen are colorless and odorless gases. Hydrogen is explosive. Oxygen is needed before anything will burn. When hydrogen and oxygen combine, however, they form water. The properties of water are very different from those of hydrogen and oxygen.

When elements combine, a chemical bond is formed. A chemical bond is a link between atoms. Chemical bonds keep the atoms of compounds joined together. When water is formed, chemical bonds join two atoms of hydrogen to one atom of oxygen. Chemical bonds also join sodium and chlorine atoms to form salt.

Chemical Bonds In nature, most atoms are found joined to atoms of other elements. The chemical bonds that join atoms are caused by the behavior of electrons. An atom may form a chemical bond in either of two ways: (1) atoms can give or receive electrons, or (2) atoms can share electrons.

One way atoms form chemical bonds is by giving or receiving electrons. An atom that has lost or gained at least one electron is called an **ion** (EYE uhn). When an atom gives up an electron, it is left with more protons than electrons. The atom has a positive charge. It is called a positive ion.

The atom that receives an electron will have more electrons than protons. The atom becomes negatively charged. It is called a negative ion.

Particles with unlike charges will attract each other. Particles with the same charge will repel each other. For this reason, ions with different charges attract each other and form a bond.

Table salt is a compound formed from ions. Each sodium atom gives up an electron to a chlorine atom. The sodium atoms become positive sodium ions. The

Salt crystals
and their structure

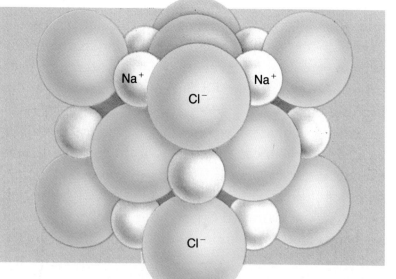

chlorine atoms become negative chloride ions. Since these ions have opposite charges, they attract each other. In this way, the ions form table salt.

The smallest particle of salt that can exist is a combination of one chloride ion and and one sodium ion. Look at the model of sodium chloride on page 146. Why is a sodium ion always surrounded by chloride ions?

Another type of chemical bond is formed when atoms share electrons. An atom can share electrons with one or more neighboring atoms. When this happens, the shared electrons spend part of their time orbiting the nucleus of each atom. In this way, a group of atoms can be linked together in a certain pattern. They form a particle called a **molecule.**

A molecule is made of two or more atoms. Some compounds form as molecules. For these compounds, a molecule is the smallest particle that can exist and still have the properties of the compound. For example, if two atoms of hydrogen share electrons with an atom of oxygen, a water molecule forms. A molecule of water is the smallest particle of water that can exist.

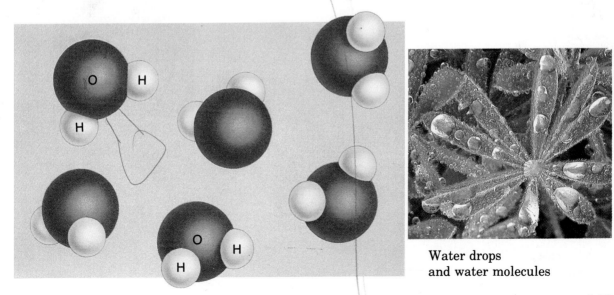

Water drops
and water molecules

T H I N K

The element oxygen may exist as oxygen gas, O_2, or as ozone gas, O_3. Are these gases examples of compounds? Explain.

Z O N E

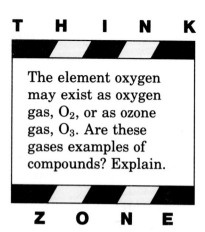

Formulas of Compounds   You have learned that scientists use symbols for the names of elements. Scientists also have abbreviations for the names of compounds. A chemical formula is an abbreviation for a compound. The symbols of elements are used in chemical formulas.

A chemical formula shows the type and number of atoms present in a compound. The formula for salt is NaCl. The symbol for sodium, Na, is combined with the symbol for chlorine, Cl. It tells you that salt has one sodium ion and one chloride ion.

The formula for water, including snowflakes, ice, and steam, is H_2O. Notice the 2 after the H. This tells you that one molecule of water has two atoms of hydrogen. These two hydrogen atoms are joined to one atom of oxygen. Two molecules of water would be written as $2H_2O$.

Compounds are found all around you. Look at the pictures below. Some compounds and their formulas are shown in the different pictures.

Fe_2O_3

H_2O

$C_6H_{12}O_6$

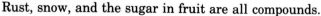

Rust, snow, and the sugar in fruit are all compounds.

148

Building Skills: Making Models

How many combinations of atoms can you make?

Steps

1. Use the following symbols for each nut and bolt.
   Long bolt—Lo   Wing nut—Wg
   Short bolt—Sh   Hex nut—Hx

2. Place a hex nut on a long bolt. Use the symbols to write a formula for this "molecule."

3. Now add another long bolt to the combination you just made. Write a formula for this molecule.

4. Continue making molecules using different nuts and bolts. Write formulas for each molecule.

Questions

1. What was the formula for your nut and bolt combination in step 2? In step 3?

2. How many different combinations did you make?

3. How are your formulas similar to the formulas used by scientists for molecules and compounds?

Materials

2 long bolts
2 short bolts
3 wing nuts
3 hex nuts

Step 2

✓ Lesson Checkup

1. What is a chemical bond?

2. Describe the atoms found in a molecule of hydrogen peroxide. Its formula is H_2O_2.

3. **Think Critically!** A crystal of magnesium chloride contains 2,000 magnesium ions (Mg) and 4,000 chloride ions (Cl). What is this compound's simplest formula?

Lesson 3   Different Mixtures

What is the difference between a solution and a suspension?

Look at the salad bowl in the picture below. If you ate a salad like this, could you taste each individual tomato, pepper, or lettuce leaf? Could you easily remove one type of food?

The salad is a mixture of different foods. A **mixture** contains two or more different substances that are not chemically joined. Though mixed together, each food within the salad remains unchanged. Since the atoms of lettuce and the atoms of tomatoes will not combine, or react, with each other, no change will occur. A tomato will remain red and still taste like a tomato. A lettuce leaf will remain green and still taste like a lettuce leaf. If a reaction had occurred between any of these foods, then a new compound instead of a mixture would have formed.

Salads are mixtures.

Mixtures   The properties of mixtures depend upon the properties of the substances found within them. If orange slices are added to the salad, the salad will look different. It will taste different as well. A mixture changes according to the amount of each substance present. How would the taste of the salad change if more and more oranges were added?

Most mixtures can be easily separated into the substances that make them up. Since no chemical bonds are formed, the substances are not linked together. A fork will easily separate each part of the garden salad. A lettuce leaf can be easily separated from a tomato.

If you add sand to water, you get a mixture. The sand particles do not react with the water. You can separate this mixture using a piece of filter paper. The particles of sand get trapped by the filter paper, while the water molecules pass through the paper. The student below is filtering a sand and water mixture.

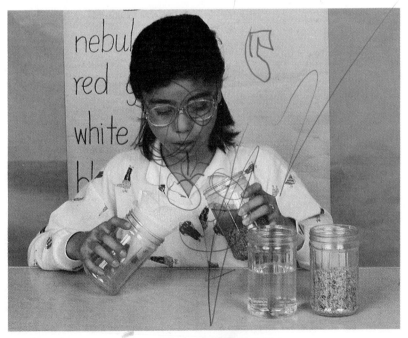

A sand and water mixture can be separated.

Solutions   Some mixtures are called **solutions.** In these mixtures, the different parts mix together evenly. They do not easily separate from each other. Look at the pictures below. They show how a solution forms when you add food coloring to water. At first the food coloring remains in a glob. Then the molecules of food coloring spread out. They begin to mix with the molecules of water. Finally the molecules spread evenly throughout the water. The molecules of food coloring will not settle to the bottom. Such a mixture is called a solution.

What happens when food coloring is added to water?

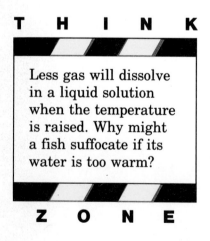

T H I N K

Less gas will dissolve in a liquid solution when the temperature is raised. Why might a fish suffocate if its water is too warm?

Z O N E

Dissolving is when a substance mixes evenly throughout another substance. When a spoonful of sugar is added to a glass of water, sugar molecules mix evenly with the water molecules. Dissolving has occurred. You cannot see the substances in the solution. Dissolved substances will not settle out. Solutions are mixtures that contain dissolved substances.

In order to mix evenly, substances that dissolve must separate into their molecules or ions. When sugar is added to water, the sugar crystals must first separate into sugar molecules. The sugar molecules are small enough to mix evenly among the water molecules. When table salt is added to water, it must first break down into its positive and negative ions. Only then can it mix evenly with the water molecules.

In a solution, the substance in greater quantity is called a **solvent.** If a spoonful of sugar is added to a glass of water, the solvent will be the water. The substance in lesser quantity is called the **solute.** In this case, sugar is the solute.

Solutions are found everywhere. There are gas, liquid, and solid solutions. The air that you breathe is a solution. It contains different gases, such as nitrogen, oxygen, and water vapor. If you were to examine a sample of air, you would find that these gases are evenly mixed throughout.

Look at the table below. It lists some common solutions of liquids, solids, and gases. What is the common solvent for the liquid solutions?

Solutions			
Type	**Example**	**Solute**	**Solvent**
Liquid	Vinegar	Acetic acid	Water
	Soft drink	Carbon dioxide, sugar, and flavorings	Water
	Sea water	Salt	Water
Solid	Brass	Tin	Copper
	Dental filling	Mercury	Silver
Gas	Air	Oxygen and other gases	Nitrogen
	Deep sea diving air	Oxygen	Helium

Oil and vinegar form a suspension.

Suspensions   A suspension is another type of mixture. The substances in a suspension usually remain mixed for only a short time. They do not dissolve. Some of the particles settle slowly when left standing. A suspension must be constantly shaken for its substances to remain mixed.

An oil and vinegar salad dressing is a good example of a suspension. Study the unshaken jar of dressing in the picture. You will see a layer of oil and a layer of vinegar. The contents mix when the jar is shaken. As soon as the jar is put down, however, the dressing will begin to separate. A layer of oil and a layer of vinegar will form again.

Dust in the air is another common suspension. Look at the picture below. Eventually the cloud of dust will settle to the ground.

Suspensions differ from solutions in one important way. The particles in solutions are ions or small molecules. The particles in suspensions are larger. These particles settle out and can usually be separated by filter paper.

Dust in the air is a suspension.

Building Skills: Predicting

How are solutions different from suspensions?

Steps

1. Use the tape to mark a line half way up the jars.
2. Fill each jar with water to the top of the tape.
3. Predict what will happen to the water level if you add three spoonfuls of salt or sand to each jar. Record your predictions.
4. Add three spoonfuls of salt to one jar and three spoonfuls of sand to the other jar.
5. Replace the lids. Shake each jar to make mixtures.
6. Observe the water levels.

Questions

1. How did the water levels change? Explain your observations.
2. Were your predictions correct?
3. Which mixture was a solution? A suspension? Explain your answers.

Materials

2 jars with lids
masking tape
salt
sand
water
spoon

Step 2

✓ Lesson Checkup

1. What are the two parts of a solution?
2. How does a mixture of salad dressing differ from sea water?
3. **Think Critically!** If you got sand in your ice tea at the beach, you would have both a suspension and a solution. Explain.

Seeing Atoms

New technology has allowed scientists to "see" the world of the atom! Scientists have developed a very special microscope. This microscope allows people to see images of single atoms.

This microscope does not use light. Instead, it uses a special beam to "see" an object. A beam of electrons scans a surface by moving back and forth in straight lines. This beam works like the needle on a phonograph. As the electrons pass over high spots in the surface, the beam moves up. As the electrons pass over low spots, the beam moves down.

When the beam finishes a scan, it moves slightly to the side. Then it again moves across the object's surface. This process is repeated until the entire object has been scanned.

The information gathered by the probe is sent to a computer. The computer makes a picture of the object's surface. This picture appears on a television screen. Look at the picture in the drawing on the left. A computer was used to make it. Each bump is the surface of a silicon atom.

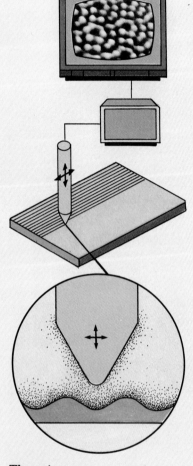

The microscope scans silicon atoms.

Think About It

Silicon is an element used to make important computer parts. The pictures of silicon atoms may help scientists make better computers. Scientists also hope that this microscope will help explain how atoms behave. If you could use the special microscope for one day, what would you look at? Why? What do you think people can learn from using a microscope to look at atoms?

156

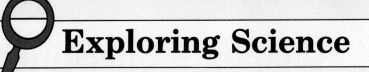

Exploring Science

Separating Mixtures

Problem: How can you separate mixtures?

Experimenting

1. Fill a cup half full with water. Add two spoonfuls of salt to the cup. Then add half a spoonful each of sand and iron filings.

2. Stir the mixture until the salt has dissolved.

3. Fold the paper towel as shown in the drawing.

4. Place the folded towel in the funnel. Put the funnel above the mouth of the other cup. Slowly pour the mixture into the funnel.

5. Place several drops of the remaining solution in a clean dish. Place this dish in direct sunlight. Also set the paper towel aside to dry.

6. After the water evaporates, use a hand lens to look at the dish. Run a magnet under the dried paper towel. Record what you observe.

Materials

2 cups
spoon
salt
sand
iron filings
funnel
paper towels cut in circles
clean dish
dropper
magnet
hand lens

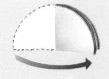

Recording Data

Separation method	Substances separated
Filtering	
Evaporation	
Magnetic attraction	

Drawing Conclusions

1. What were the crystals that formed in step 5?

2. Why was the salt not separated from the water by filtering?

Step 3

157

Chapter 6 Checkup

Summary

- Matter can be classified into elements, compounds, and mixtures.

- Atoms are composed of three kinds of particles: protons, neutrons, and electrons.

- Atoms combine to form ions by giving or receiving electrons, or they combine to form molecules by sharing electrons.

- Solutions and suspensions are two types of mixtures.

Science Words

Copy the list. Find each word in the glossary and write its definition.

atom

compound

electron

element

ion

mixture

molecule

neutron

nucleus

proton

solute

solution

solvent

Science Ideas

1. Group the terms listed into elements, compounds, and mixtures.

oxygen	helium	fruit salad
ocean water	sugar water	table salt
hydrogen	brass	magnesium chloride
mercury	sugar	water
air	soda pop	carbon dioxide
lithium	neon	bromine
dental filling	gold	colored water
sodium	copper	salad dressing

2. Letter your paper from a to d. Write the type and number of atoms in each molecule listed.
   a. $C_6H_{12}O_6$
   b. C_2H_6
   c. C_2H_6O
   d. NO_2

3. Letter your paper from a to d. Write the correct term for each letter in the diagram.

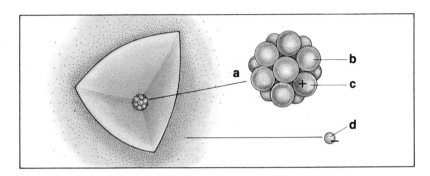

4. Look at the picture. The basic structure of all pocketwatches is similar. How is the structure of all matter similar?

Data Bank

Use the table on page 384 to answer the following questions.

1. Of the elements listed, which has the largest nucleus? The smallest?

2. Of the elements listed, which are solids? Liquids? Gases?

Science Ideas, Question 4

Problem Solving

A student wanted to find out which substances would dissolve in water to form a solution. The substances chosen for the experiment were salt, sugar, corn starch, pepper, and charcoal. All the substances dissolved except the dark-colored ones. The student concluded that white substances dissolve and dark ones do not. What is wrong with this conclusion? How could you improve the conclusion?

159

Chapter 7
Sound

In this chapter, you will learn

- ■ how sounds are made
- ■ how sounds travel through matter
- ■ ways in which sounds are different
- ■ how you make and hear sounds

Standing on tiptoes, with her head tilted slightly, Tiffany suddenly makes an announcement. "The band is coming!" she shouts. "I hear the drums."

Seconds later, the marching band turns the corner. The crowd claps and music fills the air. Trumpets blare, drums thump, cymbals crash, and flutes trill.

As the band marches toward Tiffany, the music grows louder. She notices that the store window behind her is shaking. Soon the band passes down the street. The music begins to fade, but the street is not silent. Impatient people in cars, stopped by the parade, honk their horns. Tiffany puts her hands over her ears to block the loud noise.

Back at home, Tiffany recalls all the sounds she heard. "How can there be so many?" she wonders. "The music was great but not the car horns." And what about the window? "Why did it shake when the parade passed by?" she asks herself.

As you read this chapter, look for answers to Tiffany's questions. You can learn more about sound, and how there can be so many different types of sound.

Lesson 1   How Sound Travels

■ How does sound travel?

You may not even see it, but you know when a bee is nearby. You can hear its telltale buzz. Then the buzzing suddenly stops. The bee has landed on a flower. Why did the sound stop?

While flying, a bee moves its wings back and forth more than 200 times a second. The rapid back and forth movements are called **vibrations**. Vibrations cause a bee's buzzing sound. When a bee lands, it stops moving its wings, so the sound stops. In this lesson, you will read how sound is made and how it travels.

What causes a honeybee to buzz?

How Sound is Made   Vibrations are the source of sound. But without energy, vibrations are not possible. To start something vibrating, an energy source is needed. Energy causes movement. When a bee moves its wings, it uses energy that was stored inside its body.

Sound comes from the energy of movement.

Sound is a type of energy. To make sound, one form of energy is changed to another form of energy. Sound energy comes from changes to the energy of movement. For example, the movement of a bee's wings causes a buzzing sound. This buzzing is sound energy. Sound energy from the marching band caused the window to shake at the parade.

Sound can be produced by hitting, plucking, stroking, and blowing. All of these actions use energy to create vibrations. For example, when a drummer beats a drum, energy from the drummer's moving hands creates vibrations in the drum. The stretched drumhead moves back and forth to produce sound.

There are many kinds of sound. But all sounds are produced in the same way—by vibrations. When the cricket in the picture above rubs its wings together, it makes vibrations. The vibrations cause a chirping sound. When the wind blows through a tree, the leaves vibrate. They make a rustling sound. You are surrounded by sound every day. Close your eyes and listen carefully for a minute. How many sounds can you identify?

163

What causes the confetti to move?

How Sound Travels Through Matter When you speak, sound travels through air. Sound does not stay in one place. Instead, it moves from place to place. If sound did not travel, it would not reach your ears. When you talk, the sound travels from your throat through the air to another person.

Sound can only travel through matter. Molecules of matter pass sound energy from one molecule to another. In the picture, the confetti looks as though it is jumping from the vibrating drumhead. Although you cannot see them, the molecules in air surrounding the drum act much like the confetti. When the drum bulges outward, it pushes the nearby molecules and supplies them with energy.

The moving molecules do not travel far before they hit other molecules. For an instant, the molecules collide, squeeze together, and then spread apart. In the collision, energy is passed between the molecules. As they spread, the molecules hit other molecules. This process goes on from molecule to molecule.

The drawing below shows how sound travels. The dark areas show molecules squeezed together. The light areas show them spread out.

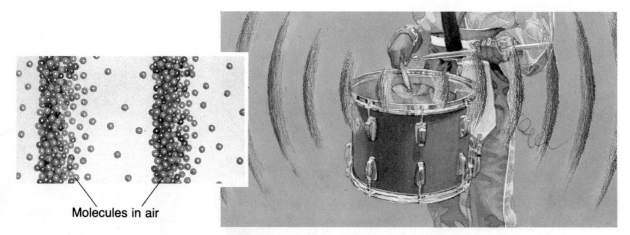

Molecules in air

How Sound Travels Through Matter

If you tap on your desktop with a pencil, sound will travel through air to your ears. If you put your head on one side of your desk and tap the other side, you can hear the sound through the desktop. Even when you swim underwater, you can hear sounds. Sound travels through gases, liquids, and solids.

Speed of sound through air is 330 m/s.

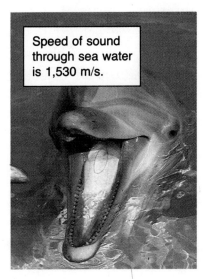
Speed of sound through sea water is 1,530 m/s.

Speed of sound through steel is 5,200 m/s.

Sound travels through all types of matter.

Gases, liquids, and solids are forms of matter. Sound does not travel at the same speed through all these substances. It travels faster in liquids and solids than it does through gases. The molecules of liquids and solids are closer together than the molecules of gases. This makes it easier for molecules to bump into one another. The exact speed of sound depends on the form of matter and its temperature. Look at the pictures above. Compare the speed of sound through air, water, and steel.

Without matter to pass sound energy from one molecule to another, there can only be silence. A space empty of all matter is called a **vacuum.** Sound cannot travel in a vacuum.

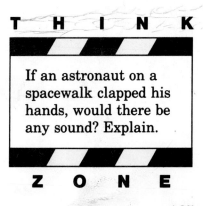

THINK

If an astronaut on a spacewalk clapped his hands, would there be any sound? Explain.

ZONE

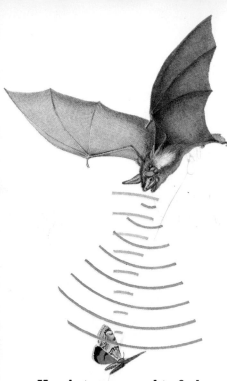

How bats use sound to find food

Sound Reflection and Absorption If sound strikes a hard object, some of the sound reflects or bounces back. The reflected sound you hear is called an **echo.** If you stand in a large empty room and shout "hello," your greeting may be repeated many times. This is because sound vibrations reflect off the walls, ceiling, and floor. These vibrations reach your ears at different times.

Bats use echoes to find food. When flying, a bat makes a series of chirps that you cannot hear. These sounds reflect off objects in front of the bat. The animal's ears pick up the echoes.

The bat's brain interprets the echoes. The bat then knows what is in its path. If the bat is heading for a tree branch, it changes its flight path. If the chirps were reflected off an insect, the bat flies on to catch a meal.

Things that are soft or filled with small air holes absorb sound. You would not hear an echo in a room with drapes, carpeting, and lots of furniture. These things absorb sound.

Which room is more likely to absorb sound?

Building Skills: Observing

How can you build a sound-proof box?

Steps

1. Place the dried beans in the pill bottle and replace the lid. Put the bottle inside the box. Shake the box. Describe the sound.

2. Fill the box with sound-absorbing materials. Put the bottle in the shoe box. Pack the material around the bottle. Place the lid on the shoe box.

3. Shake the box and describe the sound.

4. Repeat the activity. Fill the box with different sound-absorbing materials. Compare the different sounds you hear.

Questions

1. When was the sound of the beans in the box the loudest? Softest?

2. What material was the best sound-absorber? Why do you think it was?

Materials

shoe box

pill bottle

4 dried beans

sound-absorbing materials

Step 3

✓ Lesson Checkup

1. What is sound?

2. Can you hear the sound of a bell ringing inside a jar that has no air? Why or why not?

3. **Think Critically!** Steam, water, and ice are made of the same molecules, but they are different forms of matter. In which form does sound travel fastest? Slowest? Why?

Lesson 2   Why Sounds Are Different

■ Why are some sounds loud and low while others are soft and high?

Scientists estimate that the human ear can tell the difference among 400,000 different kinds of sounds. These sounds can be a dog's bark, a piano's note, or your friends' voices. If you could name these sounds and list one sound each second, it would take you more than four days to finish the list. For each different sound, there are different sound vibrations.

Let's find out how sounds are different and what makes them different.

Sound Waves   Sound vibrations occur in wave-like patterns. The repeating pattern of molecules squeezing together and spreading apart makes up these sound waves. All sound waves have three common features.

First, a wave always has a certain wavelength. The drawing below shows a **sound wavelength.** Each wavelength is the distance between two neighboring bunches of molecules.

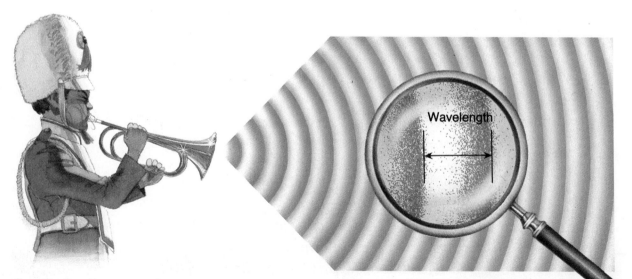

Sound vibrations occur in waves.

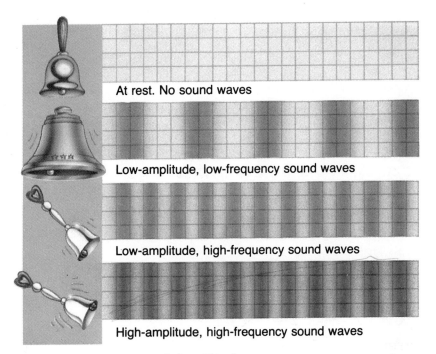

At rest. No sound waves

Low-amplitude, low-frequency sound waves

Low-amplitude, high-frequency sound waves

High-amplitude, high-frequency sound waves

Sound Frequency and Amplitude

Secondly, the source of sound can vibrate at different speeds. **Frequency** is the measure of the number of times a sound source vibrates in one second. The drawings above show sound waves of different frequencies. Notice that as the frequency increases, the wavelength decreases.

A third feature of a sound wave shows how much energy it carries. The amount of energy in a sound wave is called **amplitude.** High amplitude sound is made by objects with great vibrating motion. Look at the drawings above. Find the drawing that shows the greatest amplitude.

The wave drawings do not show the true direction of sound. They show sound moving in only one direction from a source. But if you could see the sound waves produced by a vibrating object, you would discover that the waves move in all directions. Sound waves would surround the object making the sound.

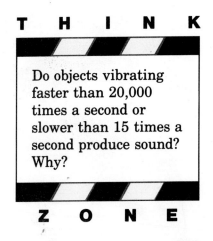

T H I N K

Do objects vibrating faster than 20,000 times a second or slower than 15 times a second produce sound? Why?

Z O N E

How Frequency Determines Pitch

Sounds Differ in Pitch When you hit two different keys on a piano, they make two different sounds. This means they make two different sound waves.

Look at the sound waves for the two different notes shown above. The sound for high C was produced by a piano wire that vibrates 512 times each second. This wire vibrates twice as fast as the wire for middle C. Another way to say this is that the wire for high C vibrates at twice the frequency of the wire for middle C.

Frequency determines the pitch of a sound. **Pitch** is highness or lowness of a sound. As the frequency of vibrating increases, the pitch becomes higher. The opposite is also true. As the number of vibrations decreases, the pitch becomes lower.

Most people can hear sounds made from a wide range of frequencies. A very deep sound may vibrate 15 times per second. It has a low pitch. A very shrill sound may vibrate 20,000 times per second. This sound has a high pitch.

Sounds Differ in Loudness   If you want to get into a locked room, you knock on the door. What do you do if no one answers? You probably pound harder to make the sound of your knocking louder.

The loudness of sound is related to the amount of energy a sound wave has. As you increase the amount of energy you use to knock on a door, the sound of your knocking grows louder. The sound waves have a higher amplitude.

Loudness is measured with units called **decibels.** You can barely hear a sound that measures 0 decibels. When you whisper, the sound of your voice is about 20 decibels. When you speak normally, the loudness of your voice is about 60 decibels. The table lists the decibel values for several sources of sound.

The Loudness of Some Common Sounds	
Sound	**Decibels**
Whisper	20
Telephone ring	70
Police siren	95
Rock concert	110–120
Jet airplane engine	170

Sounds Differ in Quality Even if you were blindfolded, you would not mistake the sound of a trumpet for the sound of a violin. The same notes played on different instruments sound similar, but they are not identical.

A violin's sound is actually a blend of many different vibrations. The strings actually vibrate at several different frequencies and so do other parts of the violin. Each vibration adds its own tone, or sound. The tones are spaced so closely together that you do not hear them as separate sounds. Instead, you hear one note.

The frequencies that combine to produce the violin note are related. Each type of musical instrument produces its own special blend of frequencies. This is why you can tell the difference between a violin and trumpet even when they play the same note. This blend of frequencies is called the quality of sound.

How do instruments make different sounds?

Building Skills: Observing

How can you test the frequency of sounds?

Steps

1. Wrap the five rubber bands around the box and pluck each one. As you pluck, listen to the sound. Describe what you hear.

2. Pluck each rubber band again. Watch the rubber band vibrate. Describe what you see.

3. Use one hand to stretch a rubber band, but only a little. Pluck it with the other hand. Listen. Watch the rubber band vibrate. Describe what happens.

Questions

1. How does the thickness of a rubber band affect the frequency of vibrations? Affect the pitch?

2. Do tight rubber bands vibrate slower or faster than loose rubber bands? Do they make higher-pitched or lower-pitched sounds?

3. If you owned a guitar, how would you change a string's pitch?

Materials

tissue box
5 different rubber bands

Step 1

✔ Lesson Checkup

1. Explain the three ways in which sounds differ.

2. Which sound has the most energy, a bird's soft song or a loud explosion? Why?

3. **Think Critically!** A guitar player strums a low note on his instrument and then strums a very high note. Why do the sounds differ?

Lesson 3   Making and Hearing Sounds

■ What parts of your body help you to speak and hear?

You can both make and hear sounds. With your voice, you make sound waves. You can use your voice to sing, laugh, cheer, cry, and to make many other sounds.

With your ears, you are constantly receiving sound waves. Even when you are asleep, you hear. A strange sound may awaken you from a deep sleep. In a crowd, you can pick out the sound of a friend's voice. The sound of screeching tires or a honking car horn alerts you to danger. You are constantly using sound. In this lesson, you will learn how you make and hear sounds.

How You Make Sounds The human voice, like all sounds, is made by vibrations. Look at the drawing on the next page. It shows the parts of the body you use to make sounds.

How are these people producing sound?

174

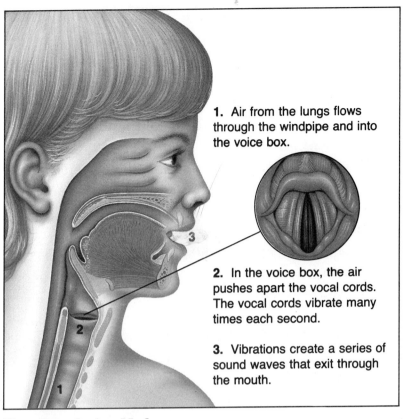

1. Air from the lungs flows through the windpipe and into the voice box.

2. In the voice box, the air pushes apart the vocal cords. The vocal cords vibrate many times each second.

3. Vibrations create a series of sound waves that exit through the mouth.

How Sounds Are Made

With only two vocal cords, you can make a large variety of sounds. **Vocal cords** are thin, elastic bands of tissue that vibrate to produce sound. Small muscles attached to the vocal cords can change the shape of the vocal cords. The muscles can also tighten or loosen them. This controls the pitch of your voice. When you speak in high tones, such as when you are excited, the vocal cords tighten and become shorter. This increases the frequency of vibrations. When you speak in a deep voice, the vocal cords loosen and become longer. Then the vocal cords vibrate more slowly.

Besides your vocal cords, the roof of your mouth, your lips, tongue, head, nose, and chest all vibrate when you speak. These vibrations contribute to the quality of your voice.

How You Hear Sounds When you hear, you use your ears and your brain. An ear has three major parts: an outer ear, a middle ear, and an inner ear. Each part of the ear helps change the messages carried in sound waves into a form that the brain can understand. Study the drawings to find out how sound waves reach your brain.

Only part of your ear is visible. The visible part, the ear canal, and the eardrum form the outer ear. The outer ear gathers sound waves.

Three small bones—the hammer, the anvil, and the stirrup—make up the middle ear. In the middle ear, the air vibrations from the eardrum change to the vibrations of tiny bones.

How Sound Waves Reach Your Brain

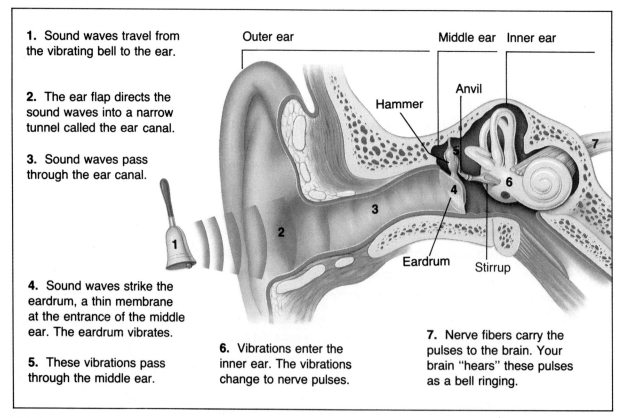

1. Sound waves travel from the vibrating bell to the ear.

2. The ear flap directs the sound waves into a narrow tunnel called the ear canal.

3. Sound waves pass through the ear canal.

4. Sound waves strike the eardrum, a thin membrane at the entrance of the middle ear. The eardrum vibrates.

5. These vibrations pass through the middle ear.

6. Vibrations enter the inner ear. The vibrations change to nerve pulses.

7. Nerve fibers carry the pulses to the brain. Your brain "hears" these pulses as a bell ringing.

Outer ear   Middle ear   Inner ear

Anvil
Hammer
Eardrum   Stirrup

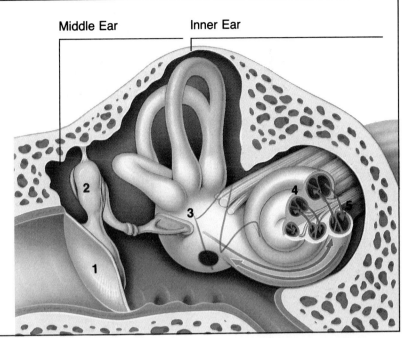

1. The eardrum vibrates differently for each different sound wave.

2. The hammer vibrates, moving the anvil and then the stirrup.

3. The sound energy passes from the stirrup to the inner ear. This causes thick fluid in the snail-shaped cochlea to move up and down like water waves.

4. The fluid causes thousands of fine hairs to shake.

5. Shaking hairs create the nerve pulses carried by nerve fibers to the brain.

How Sounds Are Heard

The **cochlea** (KAHK lee uh) and nerve fibers which connect the ear to the brain form the inner ear. The inner ear changes the vibrations of the middle ear's bones to nerve pulses. Your brain "hears" the pulses as different sounds. You may hear a loud firecracker, a soft whisper, or a ringing bell.

You may wonder why you have two ears, instead of one. Two ears gather sound waves on both sides of your head. Both ears supply the brain with information. This information helps the brain to determine where a sound is coming from.

If you are standing on a street corner and hear a car horn, you probably know where the car is without looking. If the car is on your right, sound waves from the horn will reach your right ear first. A small fraction of a second later, sound waves will arrive at your left ear. Although small, the time difference is enough for the brain to judge the location of the honking horn.

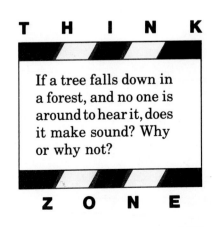

T H I N K

If a tree falls down in a forest, and no one is around to hear it, does it make sound? Why or why not?

Z O N E

Protect Your Hearing Your sense of hearing is very valuable. But sometimes you may take your ears for granted and forget to protect them.

The eardrum punctures easily. It is very delicate and very thin—about as thick as a piece of notebook paper. For this reason, you should never poke objects in your ears. You should be very careful when cleaning your ears.

Loud noises can permanently damage your hearing. At first, you might not notice the hearing loss. Loud noises decrease your ability to hear high-frequency sounds. If you are exposed to loud sounds often, the damage can build over the years. Your range of hearing can be greatly reduced.

At music concerts, the loudness level may reach 120 decibels. Sounds this loud may damage nerves in your ear. These sounds may even cause pain, a sign of injury to parts of the ear. But even sounds at lower decibel levels can cause injury. For this reason, people who work with loud machinery should wear ear plugs.

Why should airport workers wear ear protection?

Building Skills: Observing

How do your lips, cheeks, teeth, and tongue help you to make sound?

Steps

1. Make a variety of letter sounds. Try to determine which mouth parts make the sound. For example, say the letter "s" and stress the hissing sound at the end of the letter. Discover if you use your cheeks, lips, teeth, or tongue to make this sound.

2. Record your observations in a table.

3. Repeat the sounds without moving your cheeks, lips, teeth, or tongue. Check if your first observations were accurate.

Questions

1. How do the parts of the mouth help you speak?

2. What part of the mouth did you use most to make sound?

3. How could the information from your table be used to teach a deaf person to speak?

Materials

paper
pencil

Step 1

✓ Lesson Checkup

1. How is a human voice like a violin? How are the two different?

2. Why should you avoid loud noises?

3. **Think Critically!** In the past, people who had trouble hearing used a funnel-shaped hearing aid. How do you think it helped them to hear?

179

Faster Than the Speed of Sound

This jet flies faster than sound travels.

The jet's sharp nose helps it fly fast.

In 1947, pilot Chuck Yeager flew his air force jet faster than the speed of sound. Yeager was the first pilot to "break the sound barrier."

Today, many airplanes and rockets can travel faster than the speed of sound. But in the United States, only military jets are allowed to travel faster than the speed of sound. One reason is that these jets produce tremendous shock waves. These waves are called sonic booms. You may have heard one. Sonic booms are very loud. By the time you hear a sonic boom, the jet is often out of your sight. All you may see is the jet's vapor trail.

Jets that fly faster than the speed of sound have special features. Look at the pictures on the left. The noses of the jets are sharply pointed. The wings have sharp, thin edges that can knife through the air. These features help the jets fly at such high speeds.

Some scientists want to make a jet that could travel faster than 22,500 kilometers an hour. This is about 20 times the speed of sound. It could travel around the world in only a few hours. Until the jet is tested, no one knows how loud it will be.

Think About It

People who support this idea say the jet could carry passengers. It would travel at such high altitudes that it would not be any noisier than today's jets. Other people believe today's jets are already too loud. They can break windows and cause other damage. In what ways could people use this new jet? How would you feel if you lived near an airport that used this new jet?

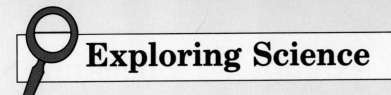

Exploring Science

Waves

Problem: Do sound waves turn corners?

Experimenting

1. Fill the box with about three centimeters of water. Place the box on top of the white paper.

2. Shine the flashlight directly on the box. Dip the ruler in the water. Dip it several times in a row. Record what you see.

3. Place the wood block in the middle of the box, with one edge touching a side. Make waves with the ruler. Draw the wave pattern you see.

4. Move the block around inside the box. Dip the ruler and record the wave patterns you see.

Materials

clear plastic box
flashlight
white paper
metric ruler
wood block
water

Recording Data

Step	Wave pattern
2	
3	
4	

Drawing Conclusions

1. What happens to the water waves when they meet an obstacle?

2. Think about Tiffany, who was at the parade described at the beginning of this chapter. She could hear the sound of music before she could see the band. Can you use your observations from this activity to explain why?

Step 4

Chapter 7 Checkup

Summary

■ Sound is made by vibrations which move from one molecule to another.

■ Sound can travel through solids, liquids, and gases.

■ Sounds are different in terms of waves, pitch, loudness, and quality.

■ We make sounds with our vocal cords, mouth, lips, tongue, head, nose, and chest.

■ We hear sounds because of how sound vibrations affect our ears and brain.

Science Words

Write a story using each word below. Show that you know what each word means.

amplitude
cochlea
decibel
echo
frequency
pitch
sound wavelength
vacuum
vibration
vocal cords

Science Ideas

1. Letter your paper from a to i. Write the word that matches each definition.

   a. The amount of energy in a sound wave

   b. The highness or lowness of a sound

   c. A space where there is no matter

   d. Thin, elastic bands of tissue that vibrate to produce sound

   e. The measure of the loudness of sound

   f. Rapid back and forth movements

   g. Made of the hammer, the anvil, and the stirrup

   h. The vibration of matter

   i. The number of times a sound source vibrates in one second

2. Letter your paper from a to d. Write whether each thing pictured below would tend to reflect or absorb sound.

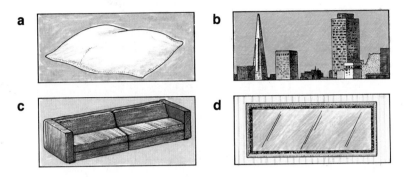

a   b

c   d

3. Look at the picture. While Tiffany watched the parade, a window began to shake. What do you think caused the shaking? Explain your answer.

Data Bank

Use the table on page 385 to answer the following questions.

Science Ideas, Question 3

1. Which animal listed has a range of 7,900 cycles per second?

2. Which animal listed has the largest range of hearing? The smallest?

Problem Solving

Have you ever noticed a "quiet zone" sign near a hospital? People who are sick need lots of rest. However, loud noises can disturb their rest. This noise is a form of pollution. Cars, airplanes, factories, and other things contribute to noise pollution. What could be done to limit noise pollution around your home or school? Write a few paragraphs describing your ideas.

Chapter 8
Motion

In this chapter, you will learn

- how to find the speed of an object
- what the three laws of motion are
- how gravity and friction affect motion

Craig and his family were on their way to the amusement park for Craig's birthday. They were making up "What if" stories. It was his sister Sandy's turn.

"All right. Ready? What if there were no motion?" Sandy said.

"That's easy," said Craig. "Everything would be very still. Nothing would be moving. That's all."

"Clouds wouldn't move across the sky. We'd never have rain or snow," Sandy said. She was watching a huge cloud float north.

"Your heart wouldn't beat, so you wouldn't even be alive," said Craig.

"Amusement parks would be very dull places," said their father. "There would be no rides, no shows, no games. And popcorn for us to eat would not be popping in the machines."

Sandy said, "I'm glad my story was just pretend. The park would be no fun at all without motion!"

What kinds of motion would you experience at an amusement park? Do you know what makes things move? You will learn about motion by reading this chapter.

Lesson 1   Speed of Motion

■ How do speed and acceleration differ?

Have you ever watched a movie in slow motion? It seems to take forever for things to change position. The picture below shows motion that appears to have slowed down or stopped. When you watch a film in fast motion, everything changes position quickly. Either kind of motion looks funny!

Motion is a change of position. You know something has moved when it is not in the same position.

Clues to motion are found by looking at other objects. When you are on a bus, you might see a tree move by the window. Yet, you know it is the bus that is moving. You expect the bus to be moving and the tree outside to be still. You have used the tree as a **reference object.** Motion can sometimes confuse you when reference objects are moving too.

By using reference objects, you follow changes in the motion of things. In this lesson, you will learn about changes in motion.

Gymnast in motion

186

Speed   Look at the picture below. On Memorial Day weekend, drivers race cars at the famous Indianapolis 500 Speedway. All the drivers start at the same time. Those that finish the race will travel the same distance—805 kilometers. But one driver will reach the finish line before the others. The people watching the race will know that the winning driver had the fastest speed.

When figuring speed, you need to know two things. First, you need to know the distance traveled from one place to another. Also, you need to know the time it takes to go that distance. **Speed** is the distance an object moves in a certain amount of time. By measuring the distance traveled and the time it takes an object to go that distance, you can figure the object's speed.

Suppose your family goes to a lake that is 225 kilometers from your home. It takes you three hours to travel there. What is your speed? You can find the speed by dividing the distance traveled by the time.

speed = distance ÷ time
speed = 805 km/3h
speed = 268 km/h

On the Indianapolis 500 Speedway

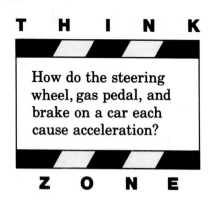
Acceleration

Objects in motion change speed and direction many times. When the drivers race in the Indy 500, they drive very fast. They also change direction and speed during the race.

As the drivers go around the track, they turn left at the corners. As they turn corners, the drivers slow down and then speed up. When the cars get low on fuel, the drivers slow down and stop for a pit stop. After they leave the pit, the drivers once again speed up their cars. Any change in speed or direction is called **acceleration** (ak SEHL uh RAY shuhn).

The change in speed during acceleration can be a speeding up or a slowing down. Speeding up is called positive acceleration. Slowing down is negative acceleration or deceleration (dee SEHL uh RAY shuhn).

Many moving objects accelerate. Notice the baseball players below. After a player hits the ball, he starts running to first base. He accelerates. When the player rounds second base, he also accelerates. In the last picture, the player slides to a stop. What kind of acceleration is that?

Running, turning, and stopping are accelerations.

Building Skills: Measuring

Can you find the speed of moving objects?

Steps

1. Make a data table like the one shown.

2. Work with a partner. Place one end of the tube on three books. Let the other end touch a wall.

3. Prepare to time. Your partner will let go of the marble at the top of the tube. When you are ready to start timing, say "Go," and watch the clock. When you hear the marble hit the wall, note the time. Record the time in the data table. Make ten trial runs.

4. Calculate the speed for each trial. The distance is the length of the tube.

Questions

1. Which was the fastest trial? The slowest?

2. Why were all the speeds not the same?

3. Find the average speed for all ten trials.

Materials

plastic tube

marble

3 books

clock or watch to measure seconds

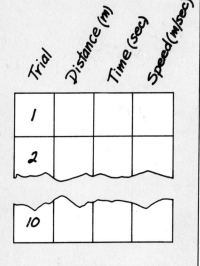

✓ Lesson Checkup

1. How can you figure the speed of an object?

2. Describe the accelerations of a baseball being tossed straight up and down.

3. **Think Critically!** Suppose you are going to a camp, which is 240 kilometers away. If the bus travels at a speed of 80 kilometers per hour, how long will the trip take?

Lesson 2   Laws of Motion

What are the three laws of motion?

Have you ever watched someone who was riding the rapids in a river? If you have, you saw many kinds of motion! The person had to pull and swerve to keep from tumbling over the rocks. These movements followed certain laws of motion. These laws were not made up by people. They are laws of nature that explain why things behave as they do.

During the 1660s, the English scientist Isaac Newton studied what happens when something moves. He developed the three laws of motion to explain how all things move.

First Law of Motion   Suppose you saw some leaves blowing across the schoolyard. You were certain that the leaves did not move by themselves. Someone or something had to move the leaves to their new position in the schoolyard.

A kayak tumbles in whitewater.

Perhaps the football in the picture at the right can provide a clue to what happened to the leaves. The football is resting at the 40-yard line. It will stay there until a player kicks it. Newton would explain the change in motion this way.

If something is at rest, it will stay at rest unless a force acts on it to move it.

A force is any kind of push or pull. The wind can be a force that pushes leaves across a schoolyard. What kind of force moves a football? A football can move quickly or slowly and change direction many times. These changes do not happen by chance. A force makes each change happen. Newton explained how things move in this way.

An object in motion stays in motion in a straight line at constant speed, unless a force changes the motion.

When both parts of what Newton said are put together, the statement becomes Newton's **first law of motion.**

Objects at rest stay at rest and objects in motion stay in motion in a straight line at constant speed, unless a force acts on them to move them or change their motion.

Second Law of Motion   Notice the boy in the center drawing below. He is not pushing or pulling, so the wagon is not moving. Its speed is zero. Any change in the speed or direction of the wagon will be an acceleration. Follow the drawings below to learn how force and mass affect the acceleration of an object.

The Second Law of Motion

As force increases, acceleration increases.

When two forces act in the same direction, acceleration increases.

As mass increases, acceleration decreases.

When two forces act in opposite directions, acceleration decreases.

The drawings show how acceleration is related to force and mass. When the boy applies enough force, the wagon moves. The harder he pulls, the more it moves. With someone's help, the wagon will go faster. In all the examples, the wagon accelerates.

What happens when another dog jumps into the wagon? The extra dog adds extra mass. The wagon will not change its motion unless more force is used. What happens if someone pulls the wagon in the opposite direction that the boy is pulling? The wagon stands still if the two forces are equal. Or it moves toward the person pulling with the most force. When this happens, the wagon accelerates.

Newton observed situations like those in the drawings on page 192. He put all these ideas together into the **second law of motion.**

> An object's acceleration depends on the mass of the object and the size and direction of the force acting on it.

Third Law of Motion   Suppose you are trying to lift weights. The weights are heavy. You can feel them pulling on your hands. At the same time, your hands are pulling on the weights. Two forces are at work—the force of the weights and the force of your hands. Each force acts on a different object. The force of the weights acts on your hands. The force of your hands acts on the weights.

The two forces are equal. The weights pull down on you with the same amount of force as you pull up on them. However, the directions of the two forces are opposite. The weights pull down as your hands pull up.

T H I N K

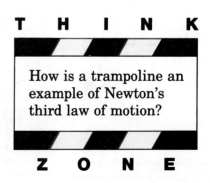

How is a trampoline an example of Newton's third law of motion?

Z O N E

Newton's third law of motion explains how forces work in pairs but on two different objects. Newton showed that if you press on a stone with your finger, the stone presses back on your finger. That is like saying whatever you touch touches you back. You could also say whatever you pull pulls you back, or whatever you push pushes you back.

Newton described this in his **third law of motion.**

For every force, there is an equal and opposite force.

The rocket takeoff is a good example of Newton's third law of motion. When the gases burn inside the rocket engine, they push in all directions with equal force. But some of the gases are allowed to escape through a narrow opening at the back. This makes the force inside the rocket engine less in the back than it is in the front. This force pushes the rocket upward.

Forces of man and weights are equal.

Building Skills: Defining Operationally

How can you show the first law of motion?

Steps

1. ◇ **SHARP!** Cut off the top of the milk carton. Use the bottom. Cut away one side. You should now have a three-sided box.

2. Put the rubber ball inside the box.

3. Slide the box quickly on the top of your desk. Make the open side of the box face forward. When the box gets to the edge of the desk, stop it suddenly.

4. Observe what happens to the rubber ball.

Questions

1. What was the force in this activity? On what two objects was the force acting?

2. What happened to the rubber ball when you stopped moving the box?

3. Explain this activity, using the first law of motion.

Materials

milk carton
scissors
rubber ball

Step 3

✓ Lesson Checkup

1. Describe the three laws of motion.

2. How do mass and force affect the acceleration of an object?

3. **Think Critically!** If you were a bicycle racer, would you want a lightweight bicycle or a heavy bicycle? Explain.

Lesson 3 Gravity and Friction

How do the forces of gravity and friction affect moving objects?

Imagine a great baseball player hitting a home run. The ball takes off with a loud whack and sails through the air. The eyes of the crowd search the sky. The ball looks as if it will never land. But of course it does, and someone in the stands goes home with a special prize!

What causes the ball to slow down and finally drop? Two forces cause this change in motion—gravity and friction. Gravity is a force that pulls on giant planets and on tiny pebbles. It is an important part in the lives of everyone on the earth. Friction is another force that also acts on objects. Let's take a look at how both of these forces affect motion.

Gravity and friction will soon act on the ball.

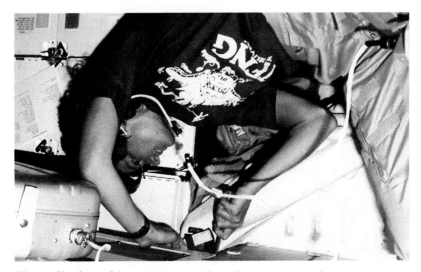

The pull of earth's gravity is reduced in space.

Gravity Do you think it would be fun to float around your room like an astronaut? But no such luck! You are pulled to the earth by a force called gravity. The earth's gravity pulls all objects toward its center. Everything on earth stays on the ground because of gravity. No matter where you are on earth, you are pulled by gravity.

But the earth is not the only thing with gravitational pull. All objects exert this force. **Gravity** is a force that pulls all things toward each other. You probably never thought that you pull on the earth while the earth pulls on you.

Two factors affect the pull of gravity between two objects: their masses and the distance between them. The greater the mass of the objects, the greater the pull of gravity between them. The pull is very small unless the mass of at least one object is large. For example, the pull of gravity between you and a friend is too small to be measured. Your two masses are too small. But the earth has a great mass. The force of gravity between you and the earth can be measured.

The pull of gravity keeps you on earth.

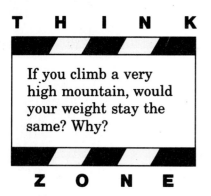

If you climb a very high mountain, would your weight stay the same? Why?

Distance also affects gravity. When two objects are far apart, gravity is less. The distance to the center of the earth is greater for an astronaut in space than it is for a person on earth. This makes the pull of earth's gravity less on the astronaut than on the person.

Comparing Weight and Mass The measure of the pull of gravity on an object is called **weight.** Weight is a force. An astronaut weighs more on earth than in space. Weight depends on where an object is in the universe and what is pulling on the object.

Some people confuse weight and mass. Mass is the amount of matter in an object. An astronaut's mass is the same in space as it is on earth. She still has the same amount of matter in either place. In fact, she would have the same mass anywhere in the universe.

Scientists use kilograms as units to measure mass. They use a different unit to measure weight—the **newton.** An object that has a mass of 1 kilogram weighs about 10 newtons on earth. So if your mass is 40 kilograms, you weigh 400 newtons on earth.

Weight varies in the universe but not mass.

Friction   Where would it be easier to slide the heavy box in the picture—on the ground or on a polished floor? You probably picked the polished floor. The rough surface of the ground would rub against the bottom of the box. The box would be harder to move. Whenever two objects touch each other, there is friction between them. **Friction** is a force that resists motion between two objects in contact. Friction either stops things from moving or it slows things down.

Friction resists motion.

The force of friction exists between all objects that touch one another. Your chair stays in place because of friction between the legs of the chair and the floor. Your bike slows down when you press on the brakes. The brakes create friction with the turning wheel. This causes the wheel to slow down or stop. Friction between your feet and the ground lets you run or walk.

Notice in the picture how useful friction can be. Rubber boots with treads increase the friction between the boots and snow. This keeps people from slipping and falling in snow. A world without friction would make motion very difficult to control.

Boots increase friction and act as brakes.

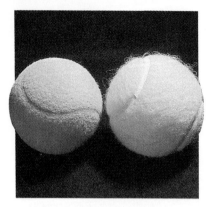

Friction made the tennis ball on the left wear out.

Reducing Friction Friction can work against you. It makes things hard to move. Friction makes things wear out. In the picture, you can see what happens when a tennis ball is hit many times. Bouncing and hitting cause friction.

Friction can cause machines to heat up. Rub your hands together quickly. The same kind of heat is produced when machine parts rub together. Most work is harder to do because of friction.

What happens when you put soap and water on your hands? You probably notice that it is easier to rub them back and forth and they do not get as hot. The soap and water reduce the friction between your hands.

Grease and oil reduce friction in machines the same way that soap and water reduce friction between your hands. Grease makes the parts in a machine slide over each other smoothly. The biker in the picture adds a little oil when a wheel squeaks. The oil reduces friction and keeps the wheel part from wearing out.

Using oil to reduce friction

Building Skills: Reading a Table

How does a rock's weight change in the solar system?

Steps

1. Find a rock in the schoolyard. Wrap the rock with the rubber band. Weigh your rock with the scale.

2. Use the table to predict where in the solar system the rock will weigh the most and the least.

3. Find out how much the rock would weigh on each object listed in the table. To do this, multiply the rock's weight in newtons by the object's pull of gravity.

Questions

1. Where would the rock weigh the most in the solar system? The least?

2. Were your predictions correct? How does the table help you predict weight?

3. Would you weigh more on Jupiter than on Mars? Why or why not?

Materials

newton spring scale

rock

rubber band

Object	Pull of gravity compared to earth
Earth	1.00
Sun	27.90
Venus	0.88
Moon	0.17
Mars	0.38
Jupiter	2.34
Saturn	0.92

✔ Lesson Checkup

1. What is friction?

2. What is the difference between mass and weight?

3. **Think Critically!** The earth has more mass than the moon. Yet if two astronauts were on the moon, the moon's pull of gravity on them would be much stronger than the earth's pull. Why?

Technology Today

Experimenting in Microgravity

Microgravity experiment in space

Some people think that the earth's pull of gravity is absent in space. It is not. Objects in space still have forces acting on them. The very small forces that still remain are known as microgravity.

Astronauts perform many experiments to test the effects of microgravity on different things. For example, materials combine differently in microgravity. On earth, oil and water do not mix. Gravity pulls the water down, while the oil floats on top. In microgravity, oil and water stay mixed together.

Astronauts study themselves in space. Microgravity causes some changes in the astronauts' bodies. If astronauts are in space for a long time, their bones lose small amounts of calcium and other minerals. Their faces may become puffy, too. These changes, however, do not seem to last. Tests suggest that people are able to adapt to life in space.

Bees in microgravity have produced honeycombs similar in size and shape to honeycombs made by bees on earth. Plants in space can grow in water and chemicals instead of soil just as on earth. This information may one day help feed people living in space and on earth.

Think About It

An experiment performed in space will often have different results from the same experiment performed on earth. Consider the experiments you have done in your own classroom. How might microgravity change their results? Plan an experiment you would do in microgravity and predict its outcome.

Growing plants in space

Exploring Science

Reducing Friction

Problem: Which factors cause a greater amount of friction?

Experimenting

1. Make a data table like the one shown below.

2. Glue sandpaper to the bottom of box 1. Leave the bottom of box 2 as it is.

3. Put a rubber band around each box.

4. Attach a spring scale to the rubber band on box 1. With the spring scale, pull the box across the board.

5. Record how much force is needed to overcome the friction between the two surfaces.

6. Repeat steps 4–5 with box 2.

7. Add rocks to the boxes. Repeat steps 4–5 with both boxes.

Materials

2 empty boxes
coarse sandpaper
glue
board
rocks
newton spring scale
2 rubber bands

Recording Data

Box	Without rocks	With rocks
1		
2		

Drawing Conclusions

1. Which box bottom caused the most friction? Why?

2. Which box bottom caused the least friction? Why?

3. What effect did extra mass have? Why?

4. How else could you decrease or increase friction? Why might you want to?

Step 7

203

Chapter 8 Checkup

Summary

- Speed is the distance an object moves in a certain amount of time.

- Objects at rest stay at rest and objects in motion stay in motion in a straight line at constant speed, unless a force acts on them to move them or change their motion.

- An object's acceleration depends on its mass and the size and direction of the force acting on it.

- For every force, there is an equal and opposite force.

- Friction resists motion.

Science Words

Copy the words below. Write a paragraph using all the words.

acceleration
first law of motion
friction
gravity
motion
newton
reference object
second law of motion
speed
third law of motion
weight

Science Ideas

1. Letter your paper from a to e. Write the word that best completes each sentence.

   a. Any change in speed or direction is called (motion, acceleration, mass, gravity).

   b. The force that resists motion between objects in contact is (friction, newton, mass, gravity).

   c. A change in position is (friction, speed, motion, acceleration).

   d. The force that pulls things toward each other is (weight, friction, gravity, motion).

   e. To find speed, you (multiply distance and time, divide time by distance, divide distance by time).

2. Letter your paper from a to d. Identify the force acting on the object in each picture.

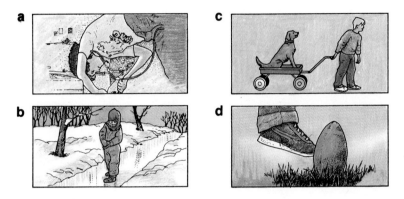

3. Look at the picture. Does the fun from amusement park rides come from their speed or their acceleration? Why?

Science Ideas, Question 3

Data Bank

Use the bar graph on page 384 to answer the following questions.

1. What was the average speed of the winning car in 1985? In 1982?

2. In which year was the average winning speed the fastest? The slowest?

Problem Solving

You may have read in science fiction about antigravity machines, or machines that let you float free from gravity. Scientists do not have the knowledge or technology to make these machines, but maybe someday they might! Think of some ways to use an antigravity machine. How could it be beneficial to our society? How could it be harmful?

Chapter 9
Energy Resources

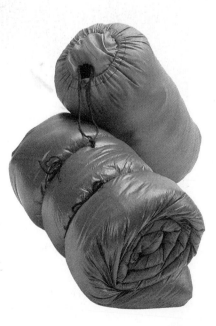

In this chapter, you will learn

- about different sources of useful energy
- what renewable and nonrenewable energy resources are
- ways to conserve energy in your home and community

The Turner family was camping in the mountains. Jenna and Len had just finished inspecting the campsite the family had picked. Len said he was glad he had brought his energy pack.

"What in the world is an energy pack?" asked Jenna. Instead of answering, Len started to unroll his sleeping bag. A flashlight tumbled out. Len tossed it to Jenna. "There you are—stored electric energy!"

"Big deal," said Jenna. But she kept watching as Len unrolled the sleeping bag some more. They both grabbed for the granola bars that appeared. Len said, "These are pure energy. You can use this energy to do work—like carrying the firewood!"

"This is the best thing yet," he said as he shook out the sleeping bag. "My body gives off lots of heat. When I'm in my sleeping bag, my body heat will stay in and keep me warm."

Is there energy in flashlights and granola bars? What are the different sources of energy? What kind of energy source is firewood? The answers to these and other questions can be found in this chapter.

Lesson 1   Today's Energy Resources

■ What major energy resources are used today to meet our energy needs?

Energy is very important in your life. You use energy to run a race or play baseball. Your family uses energy for cooking and for heating your home.

The world's energy needs grow each year. Scientists are always looking for new sources of energy to take care of these needs. We also need to make wise use of our current sources of energy. In this lesson, you will learn the major sources of today's energy.

The sun—our most important energy source

The Sun and Energy   Something has energy when it is able to do work. In fact, **energy** is the ability to do work. Without energy, nothing moves or changes. A school bus has stored energy when it has gasoline in its tank. The bus needs this energy in order to move. A runner has stored energy after eating a meal. A light bulb gets energy when the electric switch is turned on.

Almost all the energy used on earth can be traced back to the sun. The sun is the source of most of the energy you use. Look at the drawing below. It shows how energy from the sun flows from one thing to another. The sun's energy flows to the school bus, the runner, and the light bulb.

Even the wind energy that drives windmills can be traced to the sun. The earth receives light energy from the sun. Sunlight changes to heat when it strikes the earth. But the earth is not heated evenly over its entire surface. Some of the air around the earth becomes warmer in some places than in others. This causes winds to form. Since wind is able to move things, it has energy to move the blades of a windmill.

Energy Pathways

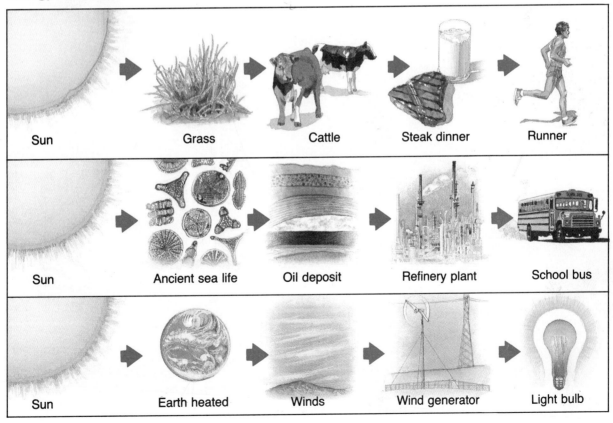

| Sun | Grass | Cattle | Steak dinner | Runner |

| Sun | Ancient sea life | Oil deposit | Refinery plant | School bus |

| Sun | Earth heated | Winds | Wind generator | Light bulb |

Replacing Energy Sources   The sun sends us a continuous supply of energy. This energy is replaced as it is used. Sources of energy that are easily replaced are called **renewable resources.** Like the sun, the wind is a renewable resource. The wind that turns a windmill is always being produced by the uneven heating of the earth.

Some energy sources cannot be quickly replaced. For example, the gasoline used to run a school bus cannot be easily replaced. It takes millions and millions of years to form the oil that is used to make gasoline. Oil is a **nonrenewable resource.** This means it is used up faster than it can be replaced in a person's lifetime.

Renewable and nonrenewable energy sources

Drilling for Oil

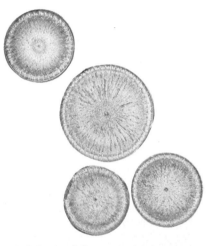

Oil formed from ancient sea life that looked much like these organisms.

Energy from Oil, Coal, and Gas

The energy in oil, coal, and gas can be traced back to the sun. Millions of years ago, many plants lived on the land and millions of tiny organisms lived in the sea. These living things used the sun's energy to make food, just as plants today make food. The sun's energy was stored in the plants and tiny organisms.

After these plants and small organisms died, they were buried under sand and mud. They decayed beneath the sand and mud. For millions of years, more sand and mud piled up. This caused heat and pressure on the decaying organisms. The combination of time, heat, pressure, and decay changed the organisms into oil, coal, and gas. These energy sources that formed from dead organisms are called **fossil fuels.**

The type of fossil fuel that formed depended on the organisms that died. It also depended on where they were buried. Small sea organisms that died and were buried beneath ancient seas formed deposits of oil and gas. Ancient plants that died and were buried on land formed deposits of coal.

Today, people use fossil fuels to heat homes, drive cars, and power factories. But supplies of fossil fuels will not last forever. These supplies are limited. Because fossil fuels take millions of years to form, they are nonrenewable resources.

Fossil fuels are used to make fuels and plastics.

Energy from Flowing Water The motion of water can be used to make electricity. Moving water has energy and is able to do work. Like fossil fuels and the wind, this source of energy can be traced back to the sun.

When the sun shines on the earth, it heats the oceans as well as the land. Water evaporates from the oceans and rises into the air. In time, water vapor in the air cools and changes back to water. Most of it then falls back to the earth as rain. This water runs off land into streams or rivers that flow back to the ocean.

Special dams are built to capture the energy of water flowing back to the oceans. In dams, water passes into tubes that lead to large fan-shaped turbines (TER buhnz). The rushing water turns the blades of these turbines. The movement of the turbine is used to run a generator. The generator then makes electricity. Electricity produced this way is called **hydroelectric power.**

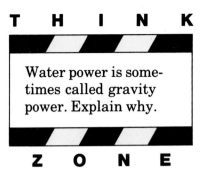

T H I N K

Water power is sometimes called gravity power. Explain why.

Z O N E

Using Hydroelectric Energy to Make Electricity

213

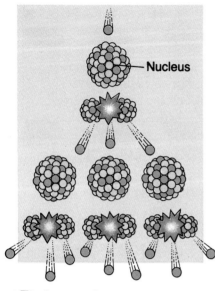

Fission—a chain reaction

Energy from Atoms You might be surprised to know that there is a lot of energy locked inside a tiny atom. This energy is stored in the center, or nucleus, of the atom. The energy locked up in the nucleus of an atom is called **nuclear energy.**

An element called uranium (yu RAY nee uhm) is a common source of nuclear energy. When the nucleus of a uranium atom splits, large amounts of energy are released.

The splitting of an atom's nucleus is called **fission** (FIHSH uhn). During fission, many smaller particles shoot out from a splitting nucleus. These particles smash into other atoms, causing them to split. More particles are released. These particles then smash into still more atoms. In a short time, many atoms split and give off energy. This process is called a chain reaction.

Nuclear reactors, like the one shown, have been built to produce electric energy from fission. The energy from fission heats water and makes steam. The steam drives turbines that run electric generators.

Using Nuclear Energy to Make Electricity

214

How does a turbine work?

Steps

1. ◇ SHARP! Using the compass and pencil, mark your piece of foil as shown in the drawing.

2. ◇ SHARP! Cut along the outside circle with your scissors. Then cut along the dotted lines.

3. Fold the four marked corners toward the center of the pinwheel until they overlap.

4. ◇ SHARP! Stick a pin through the center of the pinwheel. Attach it to the pencil's eraser.

5. Blow against the blades of the pinwheel.

6. Hold your pinwheel over a pan. Slowly pour water on the blades of the pinwheel.

Questions

1. What powered the pinwheel in step 5? In step 6?

2. How is a windmill similar to a turbine in a hydroelectric power plant?

Materials

heavy duty foil
compass
pencil
scissors
straight pin
cup of water
pan

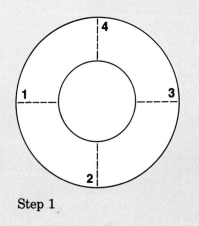

Step 1

✔ Lesson Checkup

1. How is energy from fossil fuels different from nuclear energy?

2. Why might depending on nonrenewable resources cause future energy problems?

3. **Think Critically!** Explain how energy from Niagara Falls could have started from the sun.

Lesson 2　　Future Energy Resources

■ What energy resources can be used to increase our energy supplies?

Suppose you are lost in the woods. All you have to eat are three crackers with peanut butter. As the day goes on, you know you will be very hungry unless you find another food source. You will be very careful not to waste the food you have.

Like the food in the story above, there are limited supplies of some energy resources. You know that fossil fuels are a nonrenewable resource. Once these supplies are gone, other energy sources must be found.

The graph below shows the energy resources that are used most. Notice that 90 percent of our energy resources are nonrenewable. Scientists are looking for new sources of energy. We must be ready for the day when we run out of nonrenewable resources.

Energy Use in the United States

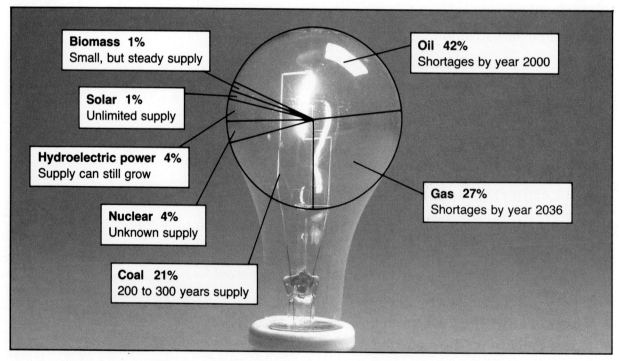

Biomass 1%
Small, but steady supply

Solar 1%
Unlimited supply

Hydroelectric power 4%
Supply can still grow

Nuclear 4%
Unknown supply

Coal 21%
200 to 300 years supply

Oil 42%
Shortages by year 2000

Gas 27%
Shortages by year 2036

Energy from the Sun   You have learned that the sun is the main source of energy on earth. Scientists are finding ways to use energy directly from the sun to make electricity and to heat homes. Energy from the sun is called **solar energy.**

A solar panel is a device that uses solar energy directly. Solar panels collect sunlight. The house in the drawing uses solar panels to collect sunlight and change it to heat.

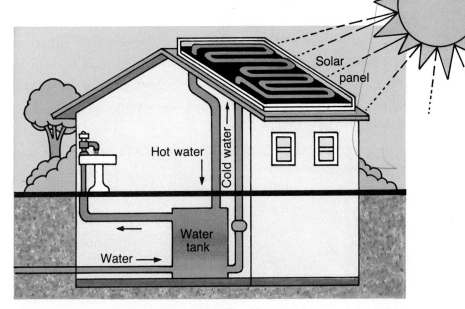

Using Solar Energy to Heat Water

Water is pumped through the panels. In the panels, water is heated by the sun. The heated water is carried to a storage tank. This water supplies hot water for people living in the house. The hot water can also be pumped through the house as a source of heat.

Solar energy is renewable. But not all places receive enough sunlight to make solar energy useful. And the equipment used to collect the sunlight is costly. Scientists are finding other uses for solar energy. They are also finding cheaper ways to collect it.

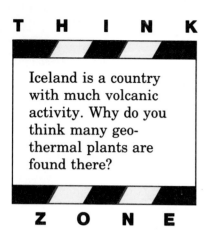

T H I N K

Iceland is a country with much volcanic activity. Why do you think many geothermal plants are found there?

Z O N E

Energy from Inside the Earth   Deep beneath the earth's surface, the temperature is very hot. In some places where this heat comes near the surface, it serves as a valuable source of energy. Energy that comes from the heat trapped inside the earth is called **geothermal energy.** Look at the drawing below. The drawing shows how geothermal energy can be used to make electricity.

Using geothermal energy has some advantages over other energy sources. It does not add smoke and harmful wastes to the air. Also, geothermal energy is renewable. As long as heat from the earth's interior can reach the surface, this kind of energy will be available. However, there are only a few places on earth where the earth's heat reaches the surface.

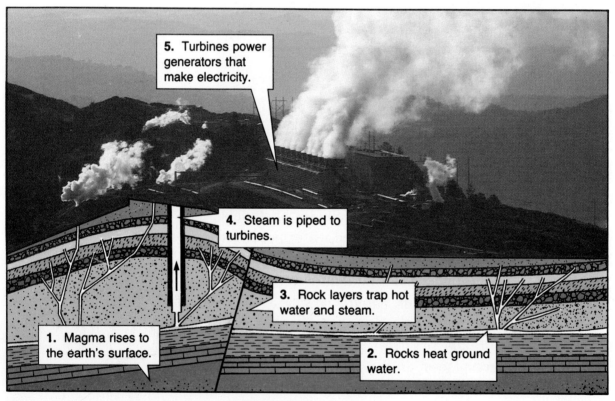

5. Turbines power generators that make electricity.

4. Steam is piped to turbines.

3. Rock layers trap hot water and steam.

1. Magma rises to the earth's surface.

2. Rocks heat ground water.

Using Geothermal Energy to Make Electricity

218

Wind turbines

Energy from the Wind   The windmills in the picture above make electricity. These windmills are called wind turbines. The wind turns the blades of the turbines. These turbines are hooked up to generators that produce electricity for nearby cities.

There are both good and bad things about wind energy. Two good things are that it causes no air pollution and it is a renewable resource. But winds blow strong and steady in few places. Wind turbines are also expensive to build.

Energy from Tides   Every day, the gravity of the moon and sun creates tides. Tides are the rising and falling of the water level along a shoreline. The energy from rising and falling sea water is called **tidal energy.** This energy is renewable.

Tidal energy can be used to produce electricity. This can be done when a dam is built to trap sea water. When the tide falls, the trapped water is slowly released back into the sea through openings in the dam. Turbines are placed at these openings. As the water moves back to the sea, it turns the turbines. The turbines power generators to make electricity.

Energy from Living Things   Another source of energy comes from remains or wastes of plants and animals. This source of energy is known as **biomass.** Unlike fossil fuels, energy from biomass is renewable.

Wood is one example of biomass. When people burn wood, they use the wood's stored energy. Burning wood changes the stored energy to light and heat energy.

Plants like corn and sugar cane are also biomass. The sugar in corn and sugar cane can be used to make a type of alcohol. This alcohol is mixed with gasoline to make a fuel called gasohol. Replacing some of the gasoline with alcohol helps save gasoline.

Even garbage is a type of biomass. Certain power plants burn garbage to produce energy. Some dumps even make energy from rotting garbage. The picture below shows land that was once a garbage dump site. Beneath the layers of soil is rotting garbage. When garbage rots, it produces a natural gas called methane. Methane gas can be collected for fuel. Methane can be used to power cars and heat homes.

How can garbage produce energy?

220

Building Skills: Making Models

How can you make a solar collector?

Steps

1. Line the inside of a shoe box with black paper. Label this box 1. Line the other box with white paper. Label this box 2.

2. Set the boxes in sunlight. Put one jar of water in each box. Measure and record the water temperature in each jar.

3. Carefully cover the boxes and jars with plastic wrap. Tape the wrap to the boxes.

4. After two hours, measure and record the temperature of the water in each jar. Cover the jars with plastic wrap again.

5. Next, move the boxes into shade. After one hour, measure and record the water temperatures.

Questions

1. Which heated faster, the water in box 1 or box 2? Which cooled faster?

2. Why do you think solar panels are painted black?

Materials

2 shoe boxes
black paper
white paper
2 small jars
water
thermometer
plastic food wrap
tape

Step 4

Lesson Checkup

1. In what way can solar energy be used directly?

2. How do biomass and fossil fuels differ?

3. **Think Critically!** Which of the energy resources in this lesson do you think has the most promise for the future? Why?

Lesson 3   Energy Conservation

■ How can you and your community save energy?

Factories in the United States make millions of products every day. In order to keep making products, these factories need a lot of energy. In fact, the United States uses one fourth of all the energy produced in the world. In 1975, Congress passed a law requiring factories to use less energy. And the law is helping! Now some factories are using almost one fourth less energy than they did in 1975. Yet they are producing more goods.

The government has also asked builders and home-owners to make homes that use energy better. Houses are built to prevent heat loss. Heating and cooling systems that use less energy have been developed. Even with these efforts, we will someday run out of nonrenewable resources. By not wasting the fossil fuels we use, we can make supplies last longer. In this lesson, you will learn ways to conserve energy.

Making a home more energy efficient

Saving Energy at Home

Saving Energy at Home   One fifth of all the energy used in the United States is used in homes. Notice in the graph below that heating and cooling a house uses half of a home's energy needs. By heating and cooling only part of your home, you can save energy. Look at the drawing below. You will find other energy-saving ideas.

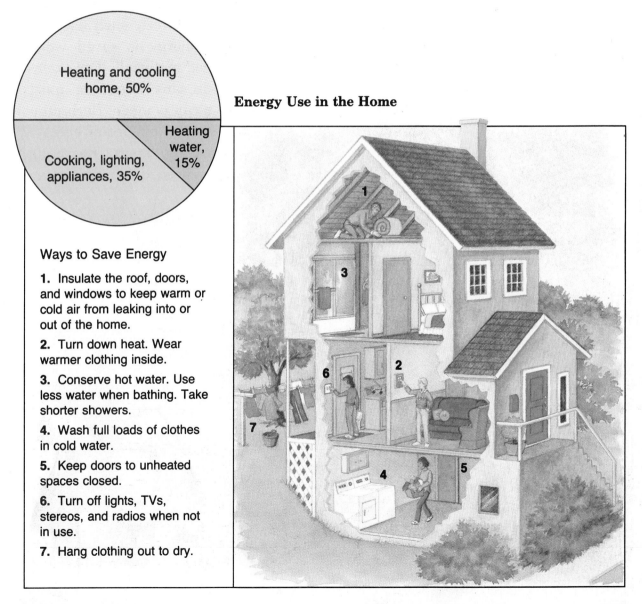

Heating and cooling home, 50%

Cooking, lighting, appliances, 35%

Heating water, 15%

Energy Use in the Home

Ways to Save Energy

1. Insulate the roof, doors, and windows to keep warm or cold air from leaking into or out of the home.

2. Turn down heat. Wear warmer clothing inside.

3. Conserve hot water. Use less water when bathing. Take shorter showers.

4. Wash full loads of clothes in cold water.

5. Keep doors to unheated spaces closed.

6. Turn off lights, TVs, stereos, and radios when not in use.

7. Hang clothing out to dry.

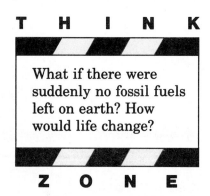

T H I N K

What if there were suddenly no fossil fuels left on earth? How would life change?

Z O N E

Saving Energy in the Community Many communities try to help people save energy. Public transportation such as buses and trains is used to move people in cities. A bus carrying 25 people uses much less fuel than 25 cars carrying one person each.

Centers like the one in the picture are set up where people can take their used aluminum cans, glass bottles, and paper. These materials are then **recycled,** or used again.

Recycling saves valuable resources, such as trees and aluminum. In addition, energy is saved when products are made from recycled materials. For example, aluminum metal is used in cans. The metal must be mined and cleaned before a can is made. Each mining and cleaning step uses a great amount of energy. Recycling aluminum avoids these steps. Recycling saves 95 percent of the energy needed to make a can from raw metal!

People can make a difference when it comes to the future of energy. They can help make fossil fuels last longer by not wasting them. They can also support the search for more renewable energy sources.

What kinds of energy sources does recycling save?

224

Building Skills: Reading a Table

How much energy does your family use?

Step

1. Copy the table shown below. Estimate the number of hours per week your family uses each appliance listed below. Complete the table to find the energy costs of your family during a summer month.

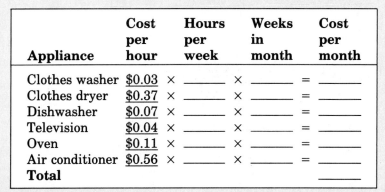

Appliance	Cost per hour		Hours per week		Weeks in month		Cost per month
Clothes washer	$0.03	×	_____	×	_____	=	_____
Clothes dryer	$0.37	×	_____	×	_____	=	_____
Dishwasher	$0.07	×	_____	×	_____	=	_____
Television	$0.04	×	_____	×	_____	=	_____
Oven	$0.11	×	_____	×	_____	=	_____
Air conditioner	$0.56	×	_____	×	_____	=	_____
Total							_____

Materials

paper
pencil

Questions

1. How does the cost per month of each appliance relate to its use of energy?

2. Where could your family best cut down on its use of energy?

Step 1

 **Lesson Checkup**

1. Name three ways to save energy at home.

2. How does recycling save energy?

3. Think Critically! Even if new fossil fuel sources are found, why is it still necessary to save energy?

Energy from Sea Water

Scientists in Princeton, New Jersey, are testing a new source of energy. This source is sea water, a substance that covers more than three fourths of the earth. How can you get energy out of sea water?

The process used to get energy from sea water is the same process that the sun uses to make its energy. This process is called fusion. In fusion, the centers of two atoms are fused, or joined, to make one large particle. When the centers of the two atoms join, a tremendous amount of energy is released. The atoms used in fusion are hydrogen atoms. The form of hydrogen that scientists need is found in sea water.

Fusion, however, only happens at very high temperatures. These temperatures can be hard to produce in a laboratory. In Princeton, a special reactor called a tokamak (TOH kuh mak) has created these high temperatures. The tokamak reactor has heated a cloud of hydrogen gas to a temperature ten times hotter than the center of the sun!

However, too much energy is used to create the very high temperatures needed for fusion. For fusion to work as an energy source, more energy must be made than is used to keep the reaction going. If scientists can do this, an endless supply of energy can be used to make electricity.

Think About It

You have just read how sea water can be used to supply the hydrogen needed in fusion. Do you think fusion is a useable future source of energy? Give your reasons for your conclusion.

The sun—a fusion machine

Tokamak

Exploring Science

Designing a Heat Saver

Problem: How can you make a container that saves heat?

Experimenting

1. Make a data table like the one shown.
2. Choose the material you think will best keep the water hot. Wrap one can in that material. Leave the other can bare.
3. Pour equal amounts of hot water in both cans. Cover the opening of each can with cardboard.
4. Measure and record the temperature of the water in each can after 5, 10, and 15 minutes.
5. Repeat steps 2–4, using other materials.
6. Make a graph using the data.

Materials

2 metal cans
hot water
thermometer
2 pieces of cardboard
insulating materials
tape

Step 2

Recording Data

	Temperature		
Can	**At 5 minutes**	**At 10 minutes**	**At 15 minutes**
Bare			
With wrapping 1			
With wrapping 2			

Drawing Conclusions

1. What material kept the water warmest?
2. If you did this experiment again using cold water instead of hot water, what material would keep the water coldest?

Step 4

227

Chapter 9 Checkup

Summary

- Almost all the energy used on earth can be traced back to the sun.

- The major sources of useful energy include fossil fuels, fission, and flowing water.

- A renewable energy source is one that can be replaced as it is used.

- Nonrenewable energy sources, such as fossil fuels, are used up faster than they can be formed in a person's lifetime.

- To save resources, energy should be conserved at home and in the community.

Science Words

Copy the words below. Define each word in a sentence.

biomass
energy
fission
fossil fuel
geothermal energy
hydroelectric power
nonrenewable resource
nuclear energy
recycle
renewable resource
solar energy
tidal energy

Science Ideas

1. Letter your paper from a to f. Tell whether each statement is fact or opinion.

   a. Solar energy is a better type of energy than nuclear energy.

   b. Electricity produced by rushing water and turbines is called hydroelectric power.

   c. Nuclear energy is locked up in the nucleus of an atom.

   d. The energy from rising and falling sea water is called tidal energy.

   e. Biomass, in the form of gasohol, is the best type of fuel for automobiles.

   f. Recycling saves valuable resources, such as trees.

2. Letter your paper from a to d. Write the type of energy produced by each source in the pictures.

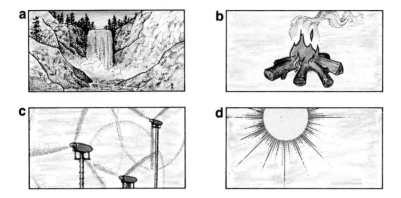

3. Look at the picture. What energy resources are used while camping?

Data Bank

Use the table on page 382 to answer the following questions.

1. Which city listed would be the best in which to place a solar energy collector?

2. Which cities average about six hours of sunshine out of a possible ten hours?

3. Which city has less than one half of its possible ten hours of sunshine?

Science Ideas, Question 3

Problem Solving

Two students want to do a science fair project to discover which kind of batteries have the most stored energy. Their hypothesis is that alkaline batteries are the best. Design an experiment to test their hypothesis. What materials would you need?

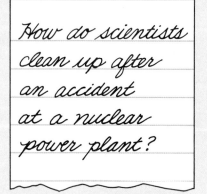

How do scientists clean up after an accident at a nuclear power plant?

Mrs. Maxine Ishiyama's class at Iliahi Elementary School in Wahiawa, Hawaii

Dr. Fred Begay

Dr. Fred Begay is a physicist who works for Los Alamos National Laboratories in New Mexico. He does research on peaceful uses of atomic energy. Dr. Begay is an American Indian. In his spare time, he enjoys Navaho dances and ceremonies.

If an accident occurs at a nuclear power plant, says Dr. Begay, the first thing to do is quickly find out how serious it is. Determining if any radioactivity has been released is also important. If people, either inside the plant or in the surrounding area, may be in danger, a warning is issued.

If radioactivity has escaped from the plant into the surrounding air or water, people who live nearby may be told to stay inside for a few days. Sometimes the people may have to leave and go where there is less radioactivity. Farm animals are tested for radioactivity in their bodies. Milk and food supplies are also checked.

Cleaning up after an accident can be very difficult and take a long time. If there is lots of radioactivity, workers must wear radiation-proof suits. Rooms and equipment are washed with special cleaning chemicals. Some things in the plant are taken apart and placed in big containers that do not let radioactivity escape. These containers are stored in a safe place. Often, the containers are buried deep in the ground.

Some kinds of radioactivity do not last very long. Other kinds, however, can last thousands of years. Therefore, it is important to do a good cleanup job. It is also important to keep records of exactly what happened. Then, similar accidents may be prevented in the future or cleaned up better if they do happen.

Careers & Science

Drafter When an automobile, a building, or an appliance is designed, a drafter makes very exact drawings of it. The drafter uses special tools so that the drawings are exact. The drawings show the dimensions and every possible view of the object. The drawings are then used by people who actually make the object. To be a drafter, you must be good in math. You will also have to study mechanical drawing in high school or at a technical school.

Telephone-Line Installer What happens when you talk to a friend on the telephone? Wires connect your home to a central telephone office. Wires from your friend's home do the same. A switching system at the central office connects the two phones. Telephone-line installers put up the wires needed for you to talk to your friend. They often work from trucks that lift them to the tops of telephone poles. If you enjoy working outside and doing physical work, you might like to be a telephone-line installer. You can learn on the job during four years as an apprentice.

Chemical Engineer Imagine an engineer making peanut butter! Chemical engineers design ways to process large amounts of all kinds of foods, cosmetics, and even explosives. They do experiments in a laboratory to find the most efficient way to process products. They understand the laws governing heat and evaporation. They know what happens when certain chemicals are combined. They make it all happen smoothly. To be a chemical engineer, you must study chemical engineering in college.

Thinking Critically

Evaluating Sources

Have you ever bought something you saw advertised and found out it was not as great as the advertisement made it sound? If so, the ad was not a very reliable source of information about the product.

Before you buy a product you have to decide whether the product can really do what the ad claims it can do. An ad is just one source of information about a product. Before making a decision based on this information, you have to evaluate the source of the information. A reliable source can be trusted. If the source is not reliable, the information is probably not accurate. Evaluating sources is a thinking skill.

1 Practicing the Skill

Laura saw an ad for a new shampoo. The ad claimed the shampoo would make hair curly but not frizzy. Included in the ad was a telephone number. Anyone could call the number and talk to someone about the product.

You'll look great after just one shampoo!

New

Sheen Shampoo

Get curly, not frizzy, hair!

Recommended by users— just call 555-1234 and talk to someone about *Sheen Shampoo!*

232

Laura decided to call the number. She made a list of questions to ask the person who answered the telephone. She wanted to make sure that the person on the telephone could give reliable information about the shampoo.

1. Have you used the shampoo?

2. Did it make your hair curly? Frizzy?

If you were Laura, what other questions would you ask? Are there any other, more reliable sources you could go to? Why might they be more reliable?

2 Thinking About Thinking

Answer your list of questions the way a person who is a reliable source of information would. Answer the same questions the way a person who is not a reliable source of information might.

List at least three things that you should look for to evaluate whether someone is or is not a reliable source of information.

3 Using the Skill

Pretend you are a salesperson. Think of a product that you would like to sell—a kind of food or clothing, a game, or something else. You want people to buy your product. How would you convince people that you are a reliable source of information about this product? To what other reliable sources of information could these people go? Why would these sources be reliable?

Unit Three
Earth Science

Chapter 10
The Earth's History

Fossils are records of ancient plants and animals. These records are usually preserved in sedimentary rock. Scientists study fossils to understand the earth's history.

Chapter 11
Oceans of the Earth

Most of the earth's surface is covered with water. Ocean water moves in waves, currents, or tides. Features of the ocean floor look like land features.

Chapter 12
The Changing Weather

A thick layer of air surrounds the earth. Conditions in this layer of air cause weather. When conditions change, the weather changes.

Chapter 13
Motion in Space

The sun, moon, and earth are always in motion. The spinning earth causes day and night. Other motions in space affect the earth in different ways.

Chapter 10
The Earth's History

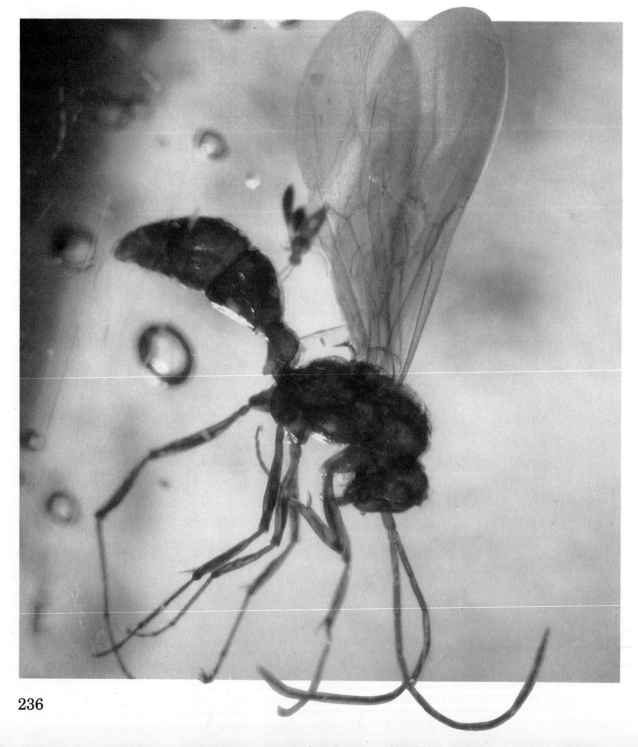

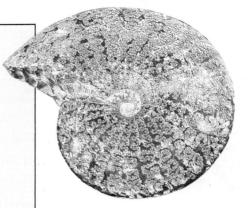

In this chapter, you will learn

- how the order of rock layers is a clue to the rocks' age
- how fossils form
- how fossils show that the earth and life on earth have changed
- the four time periods into which the earth's history is divided

"This piece of amber is millions and millions of years old," said Beth. "I'm taking it to science class today." Beth was holding a piece of amber that looked like the picture on the left.

"It looks like a piece of yellow plastic with an insect inside," said her friend Rashan.

"My aunt gave it to me," said Beth. "She said this insect lived when dinosaurs were alive. My aunt is smart. She's a geologist."

"But the insect looks just like a bug I saw yesterday! Wouldn't it have rotted away by now?"

"Don't you remember the fossils we saw at the museum?" asked Beth. "They looked real, too. And they were old. This is just another kind of fossil."

Just then, their school bus came. Both students stopped talking and got on the bus. Do you know what fossils are? In this chapter, you will learn about fossils and other interesting things about the earth's past.

Lesson 1   Reading the Rock Record

■ Why are fossils found in sedimentary rock?

Rivers often make deep cuts through the earth's crust. These cuts uncover layers of rock that formed millions of years ago. The Colorado River has cut into the earth more than 1.5 kilometers deep. This action formed the Grand Canyon. You can see the Grand Canyon's rock layers in the picture below.

Rock layers contain clues about the earth's past. For example, people have found the remains of some plants and animals in the walls of the Grand Canyon. These plants and animals lived millions of years ago when the layers of rock formed. In this lesson, you will learn about rock layers and the remains of organisms found in them.

Fossilized sea lily

Remains of organisms can be found in the walls of the Grand Canyon.

Rock Layers   Some layers of rock form from sediment. Sediment is tiny bits of matter that settle, or come to rest, in water. The rock that forms from the deposit of sediment is called sedimentary rock. Sedimentary rock is usually made of layers. There are many types of sedimentary rock. They differ depending on the kind of sediment from which they are made.

Some layers form from sand particles. These particles are cemented together to make sandstone. If the layers are made of very fine mud, then shale is formed. Layers of tiny shells from tiny sea organisms harden into limestone. Sandstone, shale, and limestone are examples of sedimentary rock.

No matter what kind of sedimentary rock forms, the process is the same. The drawings below show the three main steps in forming sedimentary rock.

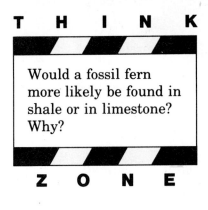

T H I N K

Would a fossil fern more likely be found in shale or in limestone? Why?

Z O N E

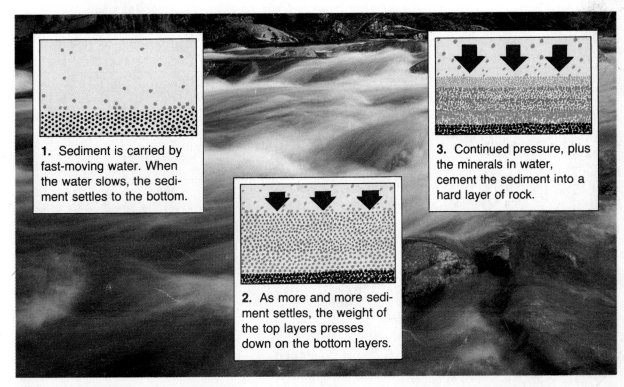

1. Sediment is carried by fast-moving water. When the water slows, the sediment settles to the bottom.

2. As more and more sediment settles, the weight of the top layers presses down on the bottom layers.

3. Continued pressure, plus the minerals in water, cement the sediment into a hard layer of rock.

How Sedimentary Rock Forms

You can decide the age of a rock layer by finding its position in a series of layers. Younger rock will form near the top. Older rock will be in the layers near the bottom. When you look at the exposed layers of rock near the bottom of the Grand Canyon, you are looking millions of years into the past. By looking at layers of rock, scientists are able to study the history of the earth.

Forces within the earth can change the rock layers' position. These forces can push up to bend or tilt layers of rock. The drawings below show how the position of rock layers can change.

Sometimes it is hard to tell the original order of the rock layers. Bent or tilted rock may have older rock on top of younger rock. Or, younger and older rock may be side by side. However, by comparing the rock layers, scientists can often learn their proper order. They can also learn about past earth movements.

Two Ways Rock Layers Can Change Position

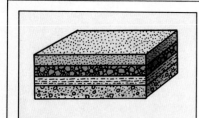

1a. Original position of rock layers

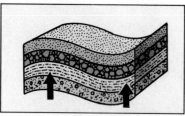

b. Forces within the earth push up and fold the rock layers.

c. Erosion of the rock's surface uncovers the folded rock.

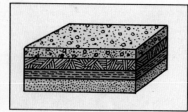

2a. Original position of rock layers

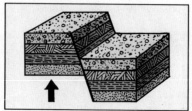

b. Forces within the earth push up and tilt the rock layers.

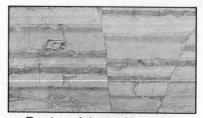

c. Erosion of the rock's surface uncovers the tilted rock layers.

Fossils   When layers of sediment are deposited, the bodies, skeletons, or shells of dead organisms become buried. Over the years, the remains of these organisms become saved in the layers of rock. These remains or prints of organisms are called **fossils.** Fossils are most often found in sedimentary rock.

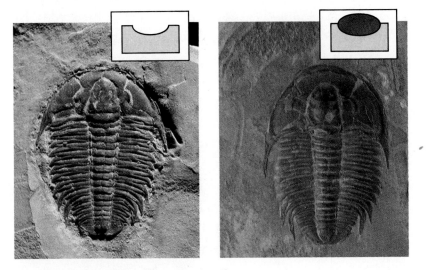

A mold fossil (left) and a cast fossil

Organisms buried in sediment become fossils in several ways. One of the simplest ways is for rock to harden around a dead plant or animal. When the dead organism rots, a hollow space in the shape of the organism is left in the rock. This kind of fossil is called a **mold.**

If minerals are deposited in a mold by water, another kind of fossil forms. The minerals form the shape of the mold. This kind of fossil is called a **cast.** The actual remains of an organism can form casts, too. A cast of a shell looks like the shell itself. Notice the mold and cast fossils in the pictures above.

Some fossils show an animal's activity. You probably have walked in mud and left footprints. Many dinosaurs walked in mud and left footprints which later hardened into rock. These footprints are fossils, too. Fossils that show an animal's activity are called **trace fossils.** Animal footprints, trails, and burrows in rock are examples of trace fossils.

Some fossils form when minerals replace the remains of dead organisms. The petrified wood in the picture was made this way. Over many years, each tree cell was slowly replaced by hard minerals. In time, a rocklike fossil was left behind. This fossil looks very much like the real wood.

Sometimes fossils are the unchanged remains of organisms or the parts of organisms. Hard animal parts like teeth, bones, and shells may become fossils in this way. They are called **true form fossils.**

Some insects become true form fossils. For example, insects may get trapped in tree sap. The sap then hardens over many years. The insect is saved inside a clear, golden case called amber. The wasp on page 236 was trapped in sap more than 25 million years ago.

  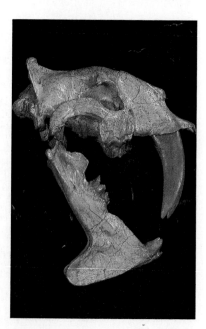

What kinds of fossils are these?

Fossils Tell a Story   Sediment that settled one billion years ago contains the fossils of animals or plants that died one billion years ago. Sometimes these fossils help scientists date the rock. Fossils that help scientists date rocks are called **index fossils.**

To be an index fossil, a fossil must meet two conditions. First, the fossils must form from plants or animals that lived for only a certain time in earth's past. For example, crablike animals called trilobites (TRY luh byts) lived for a short time 500 million years ago. Therefore, rock layers with these fossils probably formed 500 million years ago when trilobites lived.

Second, index fossils must also be found in many places around the world. Trilobites have been found on many different continents. If an index fossil is found in rock layers at two different places, it means that the layers are probably the same age. The drawing shows how index fossils are used to match rock layers of the same age that are found in different places.

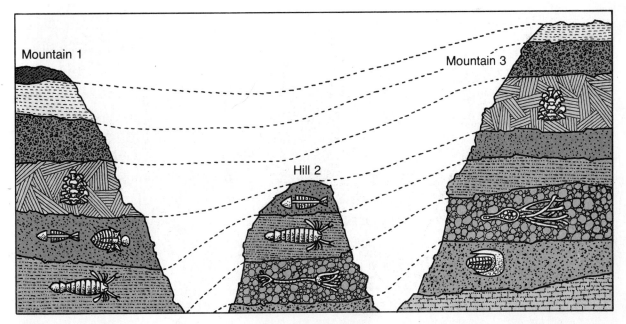

Using Index Fossils to Match Rock Layers

How a landscape today (inset) may have looked when dinosaurs lived there

Fossils often give clues to changes in the earth's climate. Many plants and animals need just the right temperature to grow. Changes in temperature can change the number and types of living things found in an area. For example, palm trees grow in a tropical climate. A rock layer containing palm leaf fossils can sometimes be found between layers of rock containing fossils of plants that grew only in cooler climates. Scientists learn from these fossils that the climate in that area probably changed from cool to warm and back to cool again.

Fossils are also clues of changes in the earth's surface. For example, seashell fossils can be found on land far from the ocean. Fossils of seashells found on land show that the land was once under water.

Building Skills: Defining Operationally

How do fossils form?

Steps

1. Pour a layer of mud on the cookie sheet.

2. Put the sheet outdoors. Sprinkle birdseed, fruit, or meat on the mud.

3. The next day, check the mud for prints. Set the milk carton over a print.

4. Prepare a mixture of plaster of Paris and water. Follow the directions on the package.

5. Pour the mixture slowly into the milk carton until you have a layer about a centimeter thick.

6. When it is dry, carefully remove the plaster.

Questions

1. What kind of "fossil" formed in the mud? In the plaster?

2. Based on this activity, explain two ways in which fossils can form.

Materials

mud
cookie sheet
birdseed, fruit, or meat
empty milk carton, with top and bottom cut off
plaster of Paris
metric ruler

Step 5

Lesson Checkup

1. Describe three ways fossils can form.

2. How do fossil molds and casts differ?

3. **Think Critically!** A scientist found two fossils. One was 300 million years old and the other 150 million years old. Which was probably found in a deeper rock layer? Explain.

Lesson 2　Millions of Years Ago

What are the divisions of the earth's past?

Most scientists believe that the earth is 4.6 billion years old. They have divided the earth's past into four large units of time called **eras.** The oldest era is called the Precambrian. Next is the Paleozoic Era, followed by the Mesozoic Era. The most recent era is the Cenozoic. You live in the Cenozoic Era.

The history of the earth can be shown as a clock. Look at the graph below. The 4.6 billion years are squeezed into a twelve-hour time scale. How many hours does each era represent?

Since people did not live during the early eras, scientists are not certain what happened then. Scientists make good guesses about how the ancient animals and plants looked by studying fossils. In this lesson, you will learn what some scientists think plant and animal life was like during the four eras.

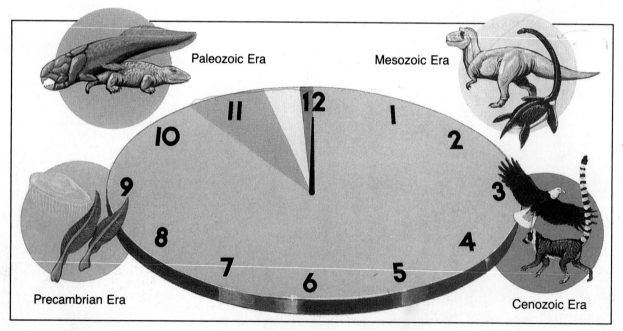

Paleozoic Era

Mesozoic Era

Precambrian Era

Cenozoic Era

The Earth's Eras

Precambrian Era In the early Precambrian Era, the earth's crust was still forming. Volcanoes helped form an atmosphere of many gases, including carbon dioxide, nitrogen, ammonia, and methane. Water was also present, but the early atmosphere had no oxygen in it. Oxygen was later released into the air by early forms of life. The climate varied from warm and moist to cold and dry. At the end of the era, large sheets of ice covered much of the land.

Scientists believe that the earliest forms of life were bacteria and blue-green algae (AL jee). Most organisms were single-celled. No organisms had hard skeletons or shells. Therefore, fossils from the Precambrian Era are hard to find. A variety of life forms began late in the era. Jellyfish, sponges, worms, and other tiny organisms shared the earth with the bacteria and algae. Notice the drawing below. The sponges, jellyfish, and other organisms are like organisms found today in warm, shallow sea water.

Organisms of the Precambrian Era

Paleozoic Era   In the Paleozoic Era, the land changed greatly. Sedimentary layers began sinking. This caused many inland seas to spread over great areas of land. Later, mountains began to form. Bodies of fresh water collected between these mountains.

Thoughout the beginning of this era the climate was mild. As inland seas formed, the climate became warm and humid. As mountains rose, the climate varied even more. Many areas were still warm, but conditions ranged from dry to moist.

Many fossils of organisms that lived during the Paleozoic Era have been found. For this reason, the era is called "The Age of Ancient Life." Early in the era, trilobites lived in great numbers. Seaweeds and land plants appeared. The first air-breathing animals appeared. They were scorpions and millipedes. Fish became numerous. Amphibians and wingless insects lived in swamplike forests. Late in this era, reptiles appeared. By the end of the era, trilobites had died out.

Organisms of the Paleozoic Era

Ocean Organisms of the Mesozoic Era

Mesozoic Era   The Mesozoic Era is known as "The Age of the Dinosaurs." Dinosaurs were the dominant animals of this time.

At the beginning of this era, broad areas of land were deserts. Mountains continued to build up. As they did, wind and water caused them to erode. Later, large areas of the continents became lowlands with inland seas. At the end of this era, the oceans flooded much of the low regions in the continents.

The climate of the early Mesozoic Era varied from moist to very dry. When the land had many lowlands and inland seas, the climate was mild. Later, the climate became warm and moist. At the end of the Mesozoic Era, the climate became cool.

Large reptiles lived in the seas during the Mesozoic Era. The plesiosaur (PLEE see uh sawr) measured 15 meters, most of which was its neck. Notice other organisms in the drawing above.

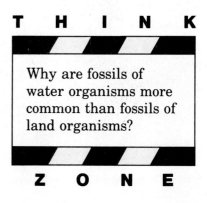

THINK

Why are fossils of water organisms more common than fossils of land organisms?

ZONE

Dinosaurs, the most familiar of all prehistoric animals, first appeared in the early Mesozoic Era. These dinosaurs were the size of present-day chickens and dogs. But by the middle of the era, many very large dinosaurs appeared. The longest dinosaur was longer than three school buses lined end to end. These giants are the largest land animals that have ever lived.

Very small mammals also appeared during the Mesozoic Era. Insects and the first birds also appeared. The most common trees were cone-bearing and palm-like trees. The drawing below shows some of the more common land animals and plants.

Near the end of this era, flowering plants covered the land. For reasons not well understood, dinosaurs became extinct. Mammals then began to take the place of the dinosaurs.

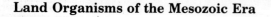

Land Organisms of the Mesozoic Era

Cenozoic Era   The Cenozoic Era is called "The Age of Mammals." Mammals became common and grew larger in size.

The high mountains that formed in the Mesozoic Era remained. Swamps formed, covering large areas of land. By the middle of the Cenozoic Era, mountain building started again. Volcanic eruptions were common. Late in the Cenozoic Era, large sheets of ice, or glaciers, covered large areas of land. These glaciers melted and then returned to cover the land again. Each period of time when glaciers covered the land became known as an "Ice Age."

The early Cenozoic climate was hot and moist. Many areas had heavy rainfall. Later, the climate was generally mild. It became drier and cooler with each approaching Ice Age.

Organisms of the Cenozoic Era

Organisms of the Different Eras

Flowering plants thrived in the hot moist climate of the early Cenozoic Era. Forests covered many large areas, but grasslands also developed. The ancient mammals looked very different from the mammals of today. The first horses and whales appeared. By the middle of this era, all the modern groups of mammals were present. The first signs of humans on earth appeared at this time. Late in the Cenozoic Era, mammoths were abundant. You can see a mammoth in the drawing on page 251. Like dinosaurs, the mammoths also disappeared.

Fossils found in rocks give scientists a record of life on earth. This record is shown in the table below. There are few traces of life before 600 million years ago. However, 3.4 billion-year-old fossils of bacteria have been found. The time table shows the order of life forms from the past to the present.

The Eras of Geologic Time		
Era	**Event**	**Years Ago**
Cenozoic	First humans	3 million
	Mammals spread out	70 million
Mesozoic	Dinosaurs die out	70 million
	First flowering plants	75 million
	First birds	150 million
	First mammals	175 million
	First dinosaurs	225 million
Paleozoic	Trilobites die out	225 million
	First reptiles	300 million
	First amphibians	400 million
	First land plants	450 million
	First fish	500 million
	First trilobites	550 million
Precambrian	Soft-bodied invertebrates	650 million
	First fossils	3.4 billion
	First earth rock	3.9 billion
	Formation of earth	4.6 billion

Building Skills: Making a Graph

How do the lengths of the eras compare?

Steps

1. Use the table on page 252 to figure the number of years for each era. Letting one centimeter equal ten million years, figure the number of centimeters for each era.

2. Make a mark with chalk at one end of the playground. Label it "Formation of Earth."

3. From the mark, draw a chalk line that measures the length of the Precambrian Era. Make a mark at the end of the line. Label it "Precambrian Era ends."

4. Continue the chalk line. Measure, mark, and label all the eras.

Question

1. Which era was longer than all the other eras combined? What was its length?

Materials

metric ruler
chalk

Step 2

✓ Lesson Checkup

1. What are the four eras in earth's history?

2. What are the main differences between the Mesozoic and Cenozoic Eras?

3. **Think Critically!** A scientist found five bird fossils and ten reptile fossils. Does this mean that more reptiles than birds lived in the past? Explain.

Accelerator used in carbon dating

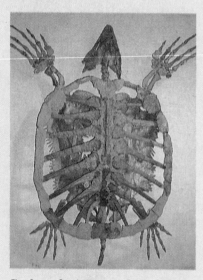

Carbon dating can find the age of a turtle fossil.

Finding the Age of Fossils

A substance called carbon 14 is found in all living things. When plants and animals die, the carbon 14 slowly changes into nitrogen gas. By measuring the carbon 14 left in a fossil, its age can be found.

To find the age of a shell, for example, part of it is ground up and burned. A special machine measures the amount of carbon 14. This amount is compared to an amount of ordinary carbon. The older the shell is, the less carbon 14 there will be compared to ordinary carbon.

Carbon dating often requires the grinding and burning of whole fossil skeletons. Using this method, the scientist learns how old the object is. Unfortunately, the scientist no longer has the fossil to study. A new method of carbon dating solves this problem. This method is called accelerator dating. It uses three very small samples of the fossil being dated. First, the small samples are broken down into carbon atoms. Then a special machine accelerates the atoms to speeds of thousands of kilometers per second. Magnets in the machine and the fast speeds separate the carbon 14 atoms from other carbon atoms. By comparing the carbon atoms, scientists can then date the fossil.

Think About It

Some people do not believe carbon dating is accurate. Scientists who use carbon dating assume that carbon 14 changes to nitrogen at a constant rate. They also assume that this rate has been constant throughout all history. Why do you think scientists make assumptions like these?

Exploring Science

Making Fossil Molds

Problem: Where are fossils most likely to form?

Experimenting

1. Fill each cup halfway: one with clay, one with sand, one with pebbles, and one with a mixture of clay, sand, and pebbles.

2. Add enough water to moisten the clay. Add a similar amount of water to the other cups. Make a smooth surface in each cup.

3. Press the screw into each cup. Carefully remove and rinse it with water each time.

4. Describe the impressions left by the screw.

5. Let the materials in the cups dry. Look at the impressions. Describe what you see.

Recording Data

Cup	Description of impressions	
	While wet	**While dry**
Clay		
Mixture		

Materials

4 cups

clay

sand

pebbles

spoon

water

screw

Step 3

Drawing Conclusions

1. In what cup was the impression most like the screw? Why do you think it worked best?

2. Did the impressions change as the materials dried? If so, how?

3. In what types of environments are fossils likely to be preserved best?

Chapter 10 Checkup

Summary

■ In rock layers, younger rock is found near the top and older rock near the bottom.

■ Fossils form when bodies of dead organisms are buried in sediment.

■ There are five fossil types: molds, casts, trace fossils, petrified fossils, and true form fossils.

■ Fossils can help scientists date rocks and give clues about changes in the earth's climate and crust.

■ The earth's history is divided into four eras: the Precambrian, the Paleozoic, the Mesozoic, and the Cenozoic.

Science Words

Copy the words below. Write a story using all the words.

cast
era
fossil
index fossil
mold
trace fossil
true form fossil

Science Ideas

1. Letter your paper from a to f. Write the word or phrase that does not belong.

   a. Precambrian Era: volcanoes, jellyfish, mammals, blue-green algae

   b. True form fossil: insects, teeth, bones, tracks

   c. Mesozoic Era: dinosaurs, mammals, flowering plants, humans

   d. Fossils: mold, organic, trace, cast

   e. Paleozoic Era: first dinosaurs, first fish, first reptiles, trilobites

   f. Cenozoic Era: swamps, grasslands, first mammals, Ice Ages

2. Letter your paper from a to d. Place the following organisms in the order of their appearance on earth.

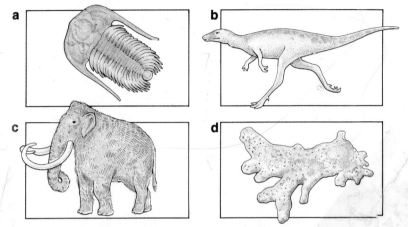

3. Rashan and Beth were looking at an insect in amber. What kind of fossil was it? How did it form?

Data Bank

Use the graph on page 383 to answer the following questions.

1. How long has it been since the first reptiles appeared on the earth?

2. How long were fishes on the earth before amphibians appeared?

Science Ideas, Question 3

Problem Solving

The dinosaurs, which existed millions of years ago, died out. Scientists have many theories about what caused this. Visit your library and read what you can about dinosaurs. Pick the theory that you think best describes why the dinosaurs died. Write an essay that describes why you think the theory is best. Be sure to include the reasons for your conclusion.

Chapter 11
Oceans of the Earth

Dan liked to spend his summer afternoons at the beach. One day, he built a huge sand castle near the water's edge. It was a fine castle with towers, gates, and many walls. He even dug a moat around these castle walls. When Dan had completed the castle, he decided to go swimming.

Dan enjoyed playing in the ocean waves. His favorite sport was body surfing. In order to body surf, Dan had to choose the tallest waves. As these waves approached the shore, Dan would swim onto their cresting tops. If he found the correct spot, the wave's energy would carry Dan on a fast and exciting ride.

When Dan finished body surfing, he returned to where he had played in the sand. Something was different. His castle had disappeared! The same waves that had carried Dan through the surf had destroyed his sand castle.

As you read this chapter, you will learn more about the oceans. You will even discover what causes an ocean wave to crash against the shore.

259

Lesson 1   The Ocean Water

■ How does ocean water move?

Imagine looking at the earth from outer space. What do you think you might see? Beneath a cotton-like layer of clouds, most of the earth's surface is covered by water. All of the earth's water is called the **hydrosphere.** The hydrosphere contains the water found in lakes, rivers, ice, ground water, and oceans. Water that exists in air as water vapor and clouds is also part of the hydrosphere. In this lesson, you will learn about ocean water and the ways it moves.

Sea Water   The water found in the earth's oceans is called sea water. Sea water contains salts, other minerals, and many different chemicals.

Water covers most of the earth.

Most of the minerals found in sea water come from the earth's crust. Rivers flow from the mountains to the oceans. As the rivers flow over the land, they pick up minerals and carry them to the oceans.

Minerals also enter sea water from deep in the ocean floor. This happens when cracks form in the ocean bottom. Lava flows and gases bubble from these cracks. Sea water seeps into the cracks and becomes very hot. It then dissolves minerals from the surrounding rock.

Look at the pictures below. One picture shows river water pouring into the ocean. The water is muddy because it contains sediments. The other picture shows sea vents. They are chimneylike holes in the ocean floor. Sea vents spout hot water and minerals into the surrounding water.

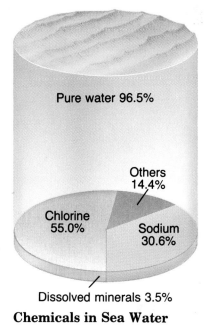

Chemicals in Sea Water

Runoff water and sea vents add minerals to ocean water.

261

Waves   If you blow on a dish of water, tiny ripples form over the surface. Wind blowing over an ocean's surface creates waves in a similar way. The strength of the wind determines the size of the wave. When wind blows hard over the water, large waves form and crash onto the shore.

All waves have four parts. They are the **crest, trough** (TRAWF), **wave height,** and **wavelength.** Look at the drawing below. Locate each wave part. The tallest ocean wave ever measured had a wave height taller than a ten-story building!

You probably think that waves push water over the ocean's surface. But have you ever watched an object

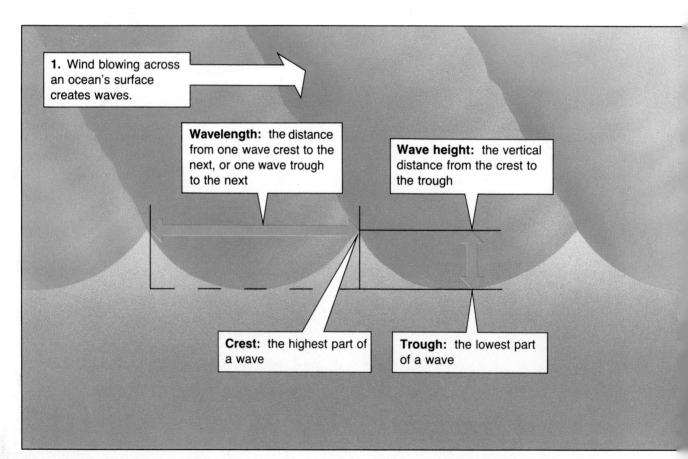

1. Wind blowing across an ocean's surface creates waves.

Wavelength: the distance from one wave crest to the next, or one wave trough to the next

Wave height: the vertical distance from the crest to the trough

Crest: the highest part of a wave

Trough: the lowest part of a wave

Wave Parts and Wave Action

as it bobbed up and down on the ocean? Look at the drawings of the bird floating on the ocean's surface. The bird does not move across the water with the waves. It just moves up and forward, and then down and backward with each passing wave. Water particles within a wave act the same way. Like the bird, the water moves in circles as the waves move through the water.

As a wave approaches shore, its shape changes. Shallow water causes a wave to get higher. Waves may build so high that they become unsteady. The crests of unsteady waves tumble and fall, or break. Waves that break along the shore are called **breakers.**

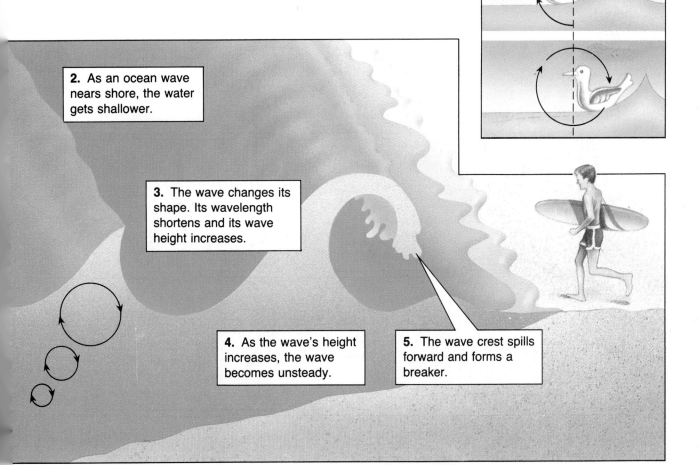

Direction of wave

2. As an ocean wave nears shore, the water gets shallower.

3. The wave changes its shape. Its wavelength shortens and its wave height increases.

4. As the wave's height increases, the wave becomes unsteady.

5. The wave crest spills forward and forms a breaker.

T H I N K

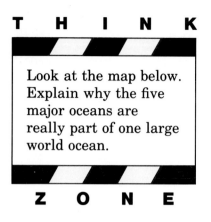

Look at the map below. Explain why the five major oceans are really part of one large world ocean.

Z O N E

Currents   Within every ocean, there are huge rivers of moving water. These large riverlike movements of water are known as ocean currents. There are two major kinds of ocean currents: surface currents and deep water currents.

Surface currents are caused by winds blowing over the ocean. The spinning of the earth and the position of the continents determine the paths of these surface currents.

The spinning earth causes surface currents in the Northern Hemisphere to turn to the right. In the Southern Hemisphere, these currents turn to the left. You can see these movements in the map below.

Locate the West Wind Drift on the map. This current completely circles the earth. If it were not for the

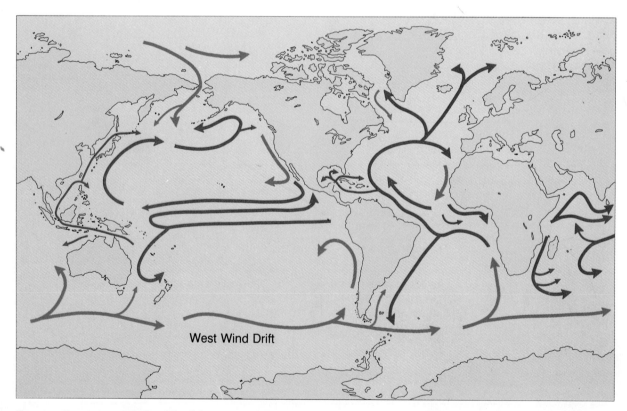

West Wind Drift

Ocean Currents of the World

continents, the other surface currents would completely circle the earth, too. However, when the moving water meets land, the current is forced to flow in a new direction.

Some currents do not flow along the surface. Instead, they move deep below the surface. Differences in water temperature cause these deep water currents.

As cold water spreads along the ocean bottom, it pushes up warmer water. The warmer water moves toward the poles.

Cold, salty water at the poles sinks and slowly moves toward the equator.

Cause of Deep Water Currents

Cold ocean water is denser than warm ocean water. When mixed with warmer water, cold water sinks. The cold water then pushes up warmer water. Deep ocean currents form near the North and South Poles. As the icy waters sink and spread across the ocean floor, currents form.

Deep currents move toward the equator. There they will push up warmer water. The deep currents move very slowly. Deep water that comes to the surface today may have begun its journey millions of years ago.

Tides

Tides   The two pictures show the same place at different times of the day. Notice how the water level has changed. This change takes about six hours. The slow change in water level is called a **tide.**

When the water level is highest, it is called a high tide. Later the level of water drops. When the water level is at its lowest point, it is called low tide. Most places on the coast have two high tides and two low tides every day.

How the Moon Causes Tides

High tide and low tide at a beach

Tides are caused mostly by the moon's gravitational pull on the earth. The moon's gravity creates two large bulges of ocean water. One bulge is on the side of the earth closest to the moon. The other bulge is on the side farthest from the moon. As the earth spins, these large bulges move over the oceans. When the bulges reach the shore, we notice changes in the height of the water. This change in water level is a tide.

Building Skills: Making Models

How can you make a model of a current?

Steps

1. Fill a small cup with cold water.

2. Add ice and ten drops of food coloring to this cup. Use the soda straw to stir in the mixture. The color in the water should be easily seen. If not, add a few more drops of food coloring.

3. Fill the jar with warm water.

4. Use the dropper. Carefully add ten drops of the colored cold water to the jar.

5. Observe what happens inside the jar.

Questions

1. What happened to the colored water as it mixed with the warmer water? How do you know?

2. How does this activity show what happens to water in the oceans?

3. How would you change this activity to see the movement of warm water?

Materials

small cup
jar
food coloring
warm water
cold water
ice
dropper
soda straw

Step 4

✓ Lesson Checkup

1. Draw an ocean wave. Label its crest, trough, wave height, and wavelength.

2. Compare how waves, currents, and tides are formed.

3. **Think Critically!** How can both evaporation and rainfall affect an ocean's saltiness?

Lesson 2   The Ocean Bottom

■ What are the features of the ocean bottom?

Years ago, people thought that the entire ocean bottom was smooth and flat. As scientists learned more about the ocean, their opinions changed. We now know that the ocean floor has many different features. It has a variety of landscapes such as mountain ranges, plains, slopes, canyons, and deep trenches.

The ocean covers more of the earth's surface than the continents do. What would the ocean bottom look like if all of the sea water disappeared? Look at the drawing below. Which features can you identify? In this lesson, you will learn about these features of the ocean floor.

The Ocean Floor

Exploring the Oceans Scientists who study the oceans are called oceanographers. Oceanographers use many different types of instruments to learn about oceans.

One instrument uses sound waves to gather information about the sea bottom. Sound waves from a ship are aimed at the ocean floor. These sound waves strike the floor and reflect, or echo, back to the ship. The bottom's depth is measured by timing how long it takes for the sound waves to return. This method of studying the ocean floor is called echo sounding.

Oceanographers use special cameras to photograph the ocean bottom. They use special submarines to look at the ocean bottom, too. These cameras and submarines help people learn more about the oceans.

A rocky shoreline

The Continental Shelf The land that borders the ocean is called the shoreline. There are different types of shorelines. Some shorelines are rocky. Others are made of sandy beaches. The two pictures show how these shorelines differ.

The ocean bottom closest to the shoreline is called the **continental shelf.** The continental shelf is flat and shallow. It is made up of the same rocks that form the land. Look at the map below. As you can see, the width of the continental shelf changes from place to place. Along some coasts the shelf is wide. Off other coasts it is very narrow.

The waters above the shelves contain many nutrients. These nutrients support large plant and fish populations. Some of the best fishing areas in the world are found in these waters.

A sandy shoreline

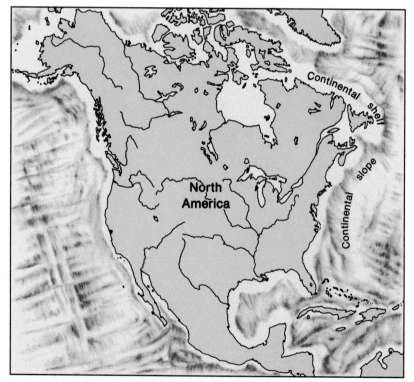

The Continental Shelf of North America

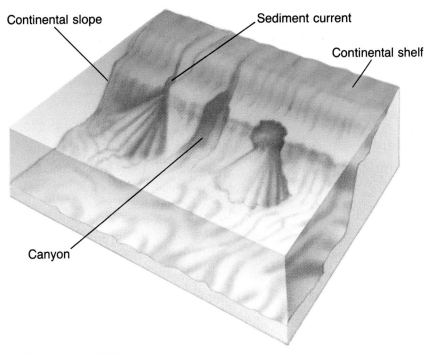

Continental slope

Sediment current

Continental shelf

Canyon

A Continental Slope

Slopes and Canyons Beyond the continental shelf, the ocean bottom drops more steeply to the deep ocean floor. This steep region is called the **continental slope.** If you imagine that the ocean is like a giant tub, the continental slopes form the sides of the tub.

Some of the continental slopes are smooth. Others have large valleys and canyons. Many of these canyons are formed by sediment currents. These currents slide down the continental slope and move great masses of mud, sand, and gravel. This movement cuts deep valleys and canyons into the slope.

As the walls of the slope get closer to the deep ocean floor, they gently level off. The bottom of the slope blends into the rolling hills of the deep ocean floor. Sand and rocks that have been carried by the underwater currents can be found along the bottom of the slope.

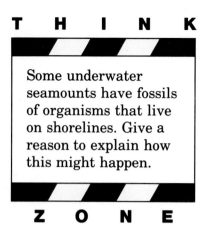

T H I N K

Some underwater seamounts have fossils of organisms that live on shorelines. Give a reason to explain how this might happen.

Z O N E

The Deep Ocean Floor The deep ocean floor begins where the continental slopes end. This region of the ocean bottom has many kinds of features, including plains, gentle hills, volcanoes, and even giant mountain ranges!

Just beyond the edge of the slope, the ocean bottom becomes a landscape of gentle hills. Sand and mud, brought to the floor by currents, cover much of these hills. The sand and mud can also form large flat areas known as **plains.** The plains are the flattest regions of the ocean bottom.

Sometimes, large mountains arise from the sea floor. These large underwater mountains are called **seamounts.** Some of these mountains are so tall that they poke above the ocean's surface. We call them islands. All seamounts are volcano cones. Some seamounts have flat tops. Their tops were made flat by crashing waves.

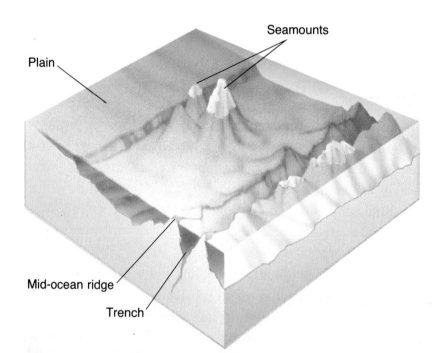

Features of the Deep Ocean Floor

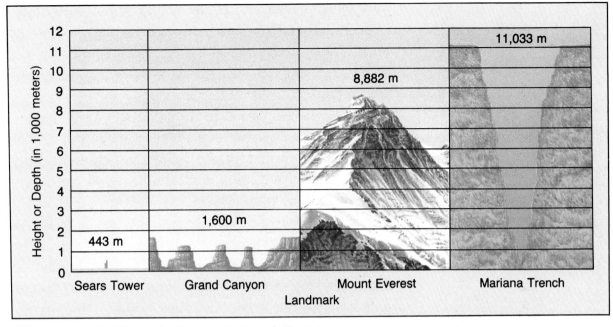

Comparing the Mariana Trench to Land Features

In some parts of the world, the continental slopes do not gently blend with the ocean floor. Instead, the slopes drop sharply downward. Deep ocean valleys called **trenches** form. These trenches are narrow cracks in the ocean floor.

Trenches are the deepest parts of oceans. Their bottoms are often more than twice as deep as the normal ocean floor. Some of the trenches are deeper than the height of the world's tallest mountains. The Mariana Trench is the deepest trench in the world. Notice the graph above. Compare the depth of the trench to some common land features.

Most oceans contain large underwater mountain ranges. These ranges are called **mid-ocean ridges.** The tall, rugged mountains that belong to these ranges divide the ocean into large sections. The mid-ocean ridge of the Atlantic Ocean extends the entire length of this huge ocean. It separates the ocean into eastern and western halves.

In some places, the peaks of the mid-ocean ridges are so tall that they poke through the surface of the water. These above water peaks form islands in the middle of oceans. Iceland is really the top of an under-water mountain in a mid-ocean ridge.

A valley can be found in the middle of many ridges. The valley may run the entire length of the ridge. This underwater valley is called a **rift valley.** The mid-ocean ridges often have earthquakes and volcanoes near rift valleys.

The picture below looks like a colorful map of the ocean bottom. However, it is really a picture of the ocean water. The water's surface is not flat. Instead, it rises over mid-ocean ridges and dips into ocean trenches. The red areas are places where the surface rises. The blue areas are places where the surface dips.

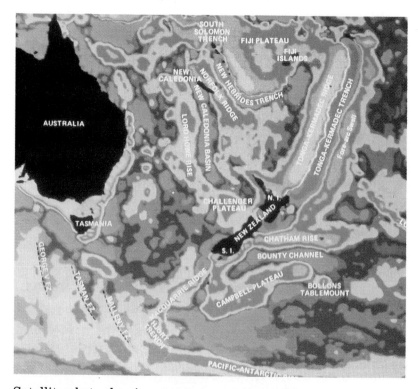

Satellite photo showing an uneven ocean surface

Building Skills: Communicating

How do sand deposits change the ocean floor?

Steps

1. Place a layer of modeling clay (about two centimeters thick) on the bottom of the pan.

2. Work the modeling clay into a landscape of small hills and valleys.

3. Fill the pan with water.

4. Slowly sprinkle five spoonfuls of sand over the water. Observe what happens to the landscape.

Questions

1. What happened to the sand? How did the landscape of clay change? Explain.

2. Explain how this is similar to what happens in the ocean.

Materials

metric ruler
foil pie pan
modeling clay
large spoon
water
sand

Step 1

Lesson Checkup

1. How does echo sounding work? What information does it give scientists?

2. Draw an ocean bottom. Include as many features of the bottom as you can.

3. **Think Critically!** Sound travels at 330 meters per second. How deep is the ocean bottom if it takes a total of four seconds for sound waves to leave a ship, reflect off the bottom, and return to the ship?

Lesson 3 Ocean Resources

What are some resources of the ocean?

Since earliest times, boats have sailed the ocean waters. Currents and winds moved these boats to carry many people across the ocean. Even today, boats transport people and materials around the world.

People have always used the resources of the oceans. They have removed chemicals from sea water and taken fish from oceans for food. In this lesson, you will learn more about ocean resources.

Minerals When sea water evaporates, it leaves behind a mixture of many substances. Most of this mixture is common salt. Near the ocean, people obtain table salt by evaporating large amounts of sea water. But sea water also contains more than 50 elements, including gold!

Transporting coal

How do people get oil and gas from the ocean?

Many minerals found on land are also found on the ocean floor. Ocean rocks contain metals such as manganese, iron, copper, and nickel. These minerals can be used to make pots, pans, cars, and cans.

Many areas of the continental shelf contain deposits of oil and gas. Tiny plants and animals live in the surface waters of the oceans. As they die, they sink to the sea bottom and are buried by sand and mud. Slowly, these dead plants and animals are changed into oil and gas.

Large oil deposits have been found in the continental shelves off Alaska. By drilling into the ocean bottom, crude oil and gas deposits can be reached. The crude oil and gas are pumped to the surface. They are then carried by oil tankers and large pipelines to refineries. At the refineries, they are changed to the kind of oil and gas people can use.

T H I N K

Could an echo sounder be used to locate schools of fish? Explain.

Z O N E

Food   The oceans have always been a source of food. For thousands of years, people have gone to sea and returned with boatloads of fish. Over the years, the fish populations have declined. Some people think that pollution is the reason. Others feel that we have taken too many fish from the oceans. These fish are taken from the oceans faster than they can reproduce.

On land, people grow crops or raise cattle to get the food they need. Scientists are trying to "farm" the oceans, too. Some people now farm kelp. Kelp are large seaweeds that grow in shallow ocean water. Some types of seaweeds are used as vegetables. Others are made into a tasteless, colorless material called agar (AH gar). Agar helps thicken foods such as ice cream and gelatin.

People also raise sea animals. For example, wooden racks with baby shellfish are placed in the oceans. When the shellfish grow large enough, they are removed. Even fish are grown in ocean fish farms.

Fish are one of many food sources in the ocean.

How can you compare the amount of salt dissolved in water?

Steps

1. Label the dishes 1, 2, 3, and 4. Add a spoonful of water to dish 4.

2. Place a spoonful of salt solution 1 in dish 1, solution 2 in dish 2, and solution 3 in dish 3.

3. Move all four dishes into direct sunlight where they will not be disturbed.

4. When the water in each dish has evaporated, use a hand lens to examine the remaining contents.

Materials

4 dishes
3 salt solutions
spoon
water
hand lens
labels

Step 2

Questions

1. What is the identity of the substance that was left on the dishes?

2. Which solution had the largest amount of this substance? Why?

✔ Lesson Checkup

1. What are two of the ocean's resources? How are they used by people?

2. How can ocean farming help provide more food for people?

3. **Think Critically!** If crude oil and gas deposits come from sea life, why is so much oil and gas found in the middle of continents?

Robot Submarines

Angus

There is a new kind of ocean explorer. It is called a remotely operated vehicle, or ROV for short. ROVs are robot submarines that explore the deep ocean floor.

Angus is a ROV that is towed behind a ship. As Angus glides above the ocean bottom, instruments collect data and photograph the ocean bottom. The first pictures of the sunken luxury liner Titanic were taken by Angus.

Another robot submarine is Jason Jr. It, too, was used to photograph the Titanic. Unlike Angus, however, Jason Jr. moves without being connected to a ship. A small video camera on Jason Jr. tells an operator where it is. The operator uses these pictures to move Jason Jr. from place to place. By watching pictures of Jason Jr.'s position, an operator was able to guide the robot deep into the hull of the Titanic. There it took remarkable pictures of the interior of this once great ship.

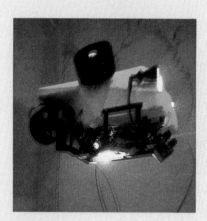

Jason Jr.

Jason is another ROV that can move on its own. This robot submarine rides on top of Angus. If a close-up picture is needed, Jason can leave Angus and move in for a closer look.

Think About It

Few people have seen the ocean bottom. To make maps of the ocean floor, people need to know how deep the water is. How can ROVs be used to map the ocean floor? What other ways can ROVs be used? Use your imagination. List advantages of ROVs for each use. How can ROVs be best used by scientists? Explain your answer.

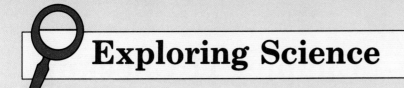

Exploring Science

Exploring an Ocean Landscape

Problem: How can you map the ocean floor?

Experimenting

1. Stand the box up lengthwise. Using the clay, make seamounts and valleys in the box as shown.

2. ◇ **SHARP!** Cut off the top side of the box. Tape on the lid. Trade boxes with a neighbor.

3. Use the tape to make a line across the top of the box. Put a mark on the tape every three centimeters. Number each mark.

4. Tie the sinker to a string. Hold the string next to a mark and lower the string into the box. Measure and record how far the sinker drops.

5. Repeat step 4 at each tape mark.

6. Using the data you have collected, draw what you think the bottom of the box looks like. Then compare your drawing with the box's "landscape."

Materials

shoe box
modeling clay
masking tape
lead sinker
string
metric ruler
scissors
tape
marker

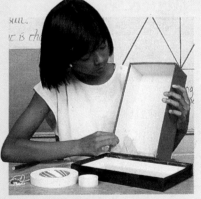

Step 1

Recording Data

	Tape mark number				
	1	2	3	4	5
String length					

Drawing Conclusions

1. How can this method be used to determine the depth of the ocean bottom?

2. How would you change this activity to get a better drawing of the bottom of the box?

Step 4

✓ Chapter 11 Checkup

Summary

- Ocean water contains salt, other minerals, and many different chemical compounds.

- Waves, currents, and tides cause the ocean waters to move.

- The ocean bottom has features such as mountain ranges, plains, slopes, deep trenches, and canyons.

- Some important ocean resources are minerals and food.

Science Words

Copy the words below. Find each word in the glossary and write its definition.

breaker
continental shelf
continental slope
crest
hydrosphere
mid-ocean ridge
plain
rift valley
seamount
tide
trench
trough
wave height
wavelength

Science Ideas

1. Letter your paper from a to g: Write the word in each list that does not belong.

   a. Wave: crest, current, wavelength, trough

   b. Deep ocean floor: plains, volcanoes, mudslides, waves

   c. Hydrosphere: oceans, lakes, mountains, ice

   d. Ocean water: fresh water, salt, minerals, chemical compounds

   e. Exploring oceans: echo sounding, submarines, photographs, hydrospheres

   f. Continental shelf: mountains, shallow, nutrients, fishing grounds

   g. Mid-ocean ridges: rift valley, mountains, islands, plains

2. Letter your paper from a to d. Write the correct term for each letter in the drawing.

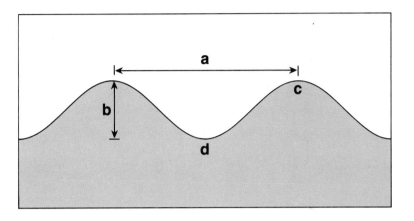

3. Look at the picture. What causes ocean waves to crash against the shoreline?

Data Bank

Use the bar graph on page 382 to answer the following questions.

1. How many millions of metric tons of shrimp are caught each year?

2. What kinds of fish make up the greatest catch each year?

Science Ideas, Question 3

Problem Solving

Gas and oil deposits are found in the continental shelf off the United States. Oil companies drill to collect these valuable resources. Some people believe that off-shore drilling is a bad idea because oil spills can, and have, polluted the oceans. Others say we need this oil to become less dependent on foreign oil. What do you think? Explain why.

Chapter 12
The Changing Weather

In this chapter, you will learn

- what causes changes in weather
- the three main cloud types
- what air masses are and where they form
- three different types of weather fronts
- four kinds of storms and the weather they cause

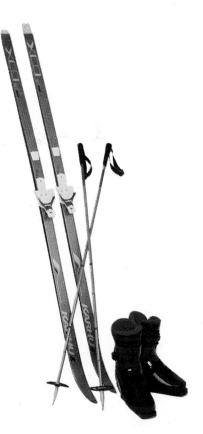

Marcos and Becky Rivera carried their skis to the car. They were careful not to step in puddles. A rainstorm had passed over their house during the night. The morning, however, looked sunny and bright. It was a perfect day to start their ski trip. Their father was in the house calling the weather bureau for the weather conditions where they planned to ski. When he appeared in the doorway, he looked sad.

"I'm sorry, kids. We'll have to postpone the trip until next week. Last night's storm is heading for the mountains. They are expecting a snowstorm today."

"Can't we go anyway?" begged Marcos.

"No, Marcos. It's very dangerous to be in the mountains during a heavy snowstorm. The new snow will be perfect for skiing next weekend."

What made the weather change? How did the weather bureau know that the weather was changing? In this chapter, you will learn the answers to weather questions.

Lesson 1   The Causes of Weather

■ What four conditions determine weather?

When you wake up in the morning, you look to see what kind of day it is. If the sun is shining brightly, you might think it is warm outside. But frost on the windows tells you the air is cold. The condition of the air at a given time and place is called **weather.**

To understand the weather, scientists study four things:

1. Temperature of the air (Is it hot or cold?)

2. Wind (Is it windy or calm?)

3. Moisture in the air (Is it cloudy or clear?)

4. Air pressure (Is the pressure changing?)

These four conditions produce weather changes.

You know that sunny days are caused by the sun. But did you know that rainy days and windy days are caused by the sun, too? In fact, the sun affects all the conditions that make weather. In this lesson, you will learn how.

Ice storms and clear skies are caused by the sun.

Air Temperature and Wind   The sun provides the energy that heats the earth's surface. The heated surface of the earth warms the air above it. But the sun does not heat all of the earth's surfaces evenly. Some places become warmer than others. The differences in air temperature cause wind.

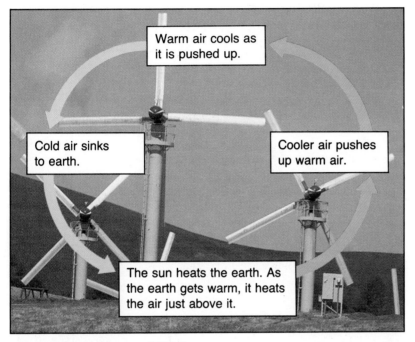

Warm air cools as it is pushed up.

Cold air sinks to earth.

Cooler air pushes up warm air.

The sun heats the earth. As the earth gets warm, it heats the air just above it.

How the Sun Causes Wind

To understand how temperature differences cause wind, you first have to know how warm air and cool air differ. When air warms, the molecules in air spread apart. When air cools, these molecules move closer together. Because of this, warm air weighs less than colder air.

These differences in the weight cause air to move. Because the cool air is heavier than warmer air, it sinks. As the cool air sinks, it pushes up warm air. This movement is wind. The drawing above shows how winds form.

T H I N K

Sometimes people say, "It's too cold to snow!" Why might they say this?

Z O N E

Water in Air   A small puddle of water does not last long on a sunny day. The sun heats the water and causes it to evaporate, or turn into a gas. The gas, called water vapor, escapes into the air. There is always some water vapor in the air. Most water vapor comes from the ocean. The amount of water vapor in the air is known as **humidity.**

Warm air has more space between its molecules than cold air. With this added space, warm air can hold more water vapor than cold air. For this reason, warm air is usually more humid than cooler air.

Suppose warm, moist air over a certain place has all the water vapor it can hold. When cold air moves

Types of Clouds

Cirrus clouds are thin, wispy, and made almost entirely of ice crystals. They form where the temperature is below freezing.

Cumulus clouds are separate, puffy clouds. They form at almost any altitude.

Dark stratus clouds are called nimbostratus clouds. They are rain clouds. In Latin, the word *nimbus* means "rainstorm."

Fog is really a stratus cloud that has formed near the earth's surface.

in, the warm air will be pushed up into the atmosphere. As the warm air rises, it cools and the molecules in the air move closer together. This causes the water molecules to be "squeezed out" of the air.

The cooling of warm, humid air also causes clouds to form. As warm air cools, water vapor gathers on bits of dust in the air and changes to liquid. The bits of dust and water form tiny water droplets. Millions of these water droplets join to form clouds.

The drawing below tells about three main types of clouds: **cumulus, cirrus,** and **stratus.** Combinations of the three cloud types also occur. These clouds differ in their shapes and the altitudes at which they form.

Dark cumulus clouds are called cumulonimbus clouds. They cause thunderstorms.

Stratus clouds form in wide sheets across the sky. The base of the clouds is near the earth's surface. A fine drizzle may fall from stratus clouds.

Air Pressure　You might be surprised to know that air has weight. A beach ball with air weighs more than one without air. You do not notice it, but air is always pressing against you in all directions. The push of air is called air pressure.

Temperature can affect air pressure. Since cold air is heavier than warm air, cold air presses against you more than warm air does. Heavy, cold air forms areas of high pressure called highs. High-pressure areas usually have clear skies. Warm air forms pressure areas called lows. Low-pressure areas usually have cloudy skies.

Wind always moves from areas of high pressure to areas of low pressure. The greater the difference in pressure between two areas, the greater the wind speed.

A sudden change in air pressure usually means the weather also will change. A drop in air pressure usually means that warm, moist high-pressure air is moving in. What does a rise in air pressure mean?

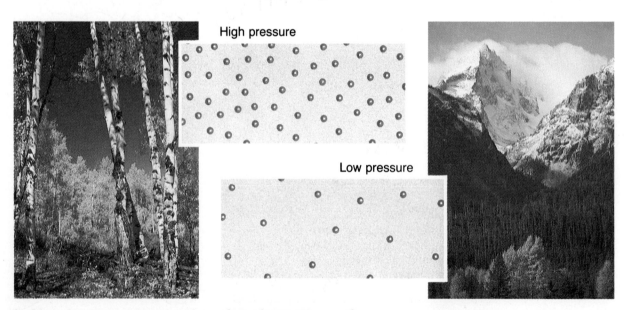

High pressure

Low pressure

Sudden changes in air pressure produce changes in weather.

How can you make a cloud?

Steps

1. Heat the bottle by immersing it in hot water for a few minutes. Do not let water enter the bottle.

2. Place the ice in a self-lock bag. Seal the bag.

3. ◇ **HOT!** Place a piece of incense in the pie pan. Ask your teacher to light it.

4. Turn the bottle upside down. Let some smoke from the incense rise into the bottle.

5. Turn the bottle right side up and quickly place the bag of ice cubes over the mouth of the bottle. Observe what happens in the bottle.

Questions

1. What caused the cloud to form?

2. How does your model compare with how clouds form in the air?

Materials

clear plastic bottle
hot water
2 ice cubes
self-lock bag
cone incense
foil pie pan

Step 4

✓ Lesson Checkup

1. Name four conditions that affect weather.

2. Why do you see your breath outside in the winter, but not in the summer?

3. **Think Critically!** Land warms up faster than water. Where would you expect to find more winds, over the deep ocean or near the shore? Explain your answer.

Lesson 2   Storms

■ What weather conditions are caused by air masses?

Wind brings weather to different places. But the type of weather depends on the air itself. In the picture below, clouds cover part of the United States. This area has a great deal of warm, moist air. Other areas of the map have very few clouds. These areas have drier air. Any large body of air with the same temperature and amount of moisture is called an **air mass.**

Air masses constantly form and move across the earth. In this lesson, you will learn how the movement of air masses can cause weather to change.

Air masses can cause changes in weather.

Oceans of Air   Four terms are used to describe most air masses: warm, cold, moist, and dry. Which term is used depends on where the air mass forms.

In general, air masses come from the tropics or from a polar region. Air masses that form in tropical regions bring warm air. Those that form over polar regions bring cold air.

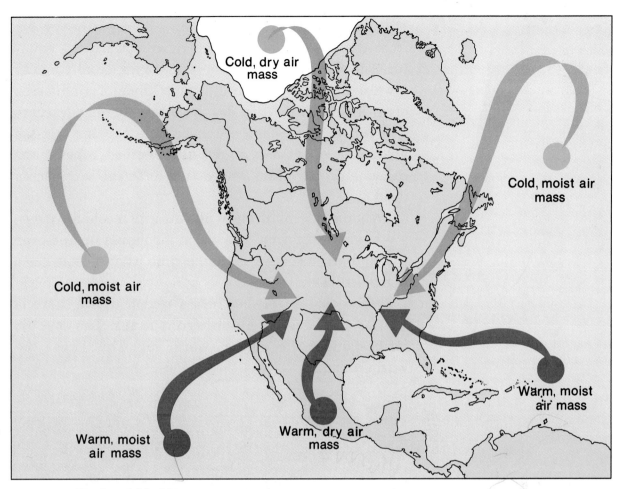

Different Kinds of Air Masses

The surface over which they form may be either land or water. When an air mass forms over land, the air is dry. If an air mass forms over water, the air will be moist.

Look at the map above. A cold, dry air mass from northern Canada is a polar air mass that begins over land. Another polar air mass begins over water. It is cold and moist.

Now look at the air masses coming from tropical regions. Those forming over water carry warm, moist air. What kind of air is carried by the air masses forming over land?

When Air Masses Meet   The cold, heavy air from the poles usually moves down toward the equator. The warm, light air from the tropics usually moves toward the poles. These different kinds of air masses often meet. When they do, the different temperatures and amounts of moisture keep the two air masses apart. The air masses do not mix. Instead, a boundary called a **front** forms where two different air masses meet.

When a warm air mass pushes into a cold air mass, a **warm front** forms. The warm air moves up and over the cold air mass. At the same time, the cold air mass is pushed back.

When cold air pushes into a region where there is a mass of warm air, a **cold front** forms. The cold air pushes under the lighter, warm air. This forces the warm air up.

What forms where air masses meet?

Sometimes the boundary between two air masses does not move. This front is called a **stationary front.** Either a warm front or a cold front can become a stationary front. This condition can last for a few hours or several days. Usually, however, a front moves.

Weather Fronts   The boundary or front between two different air masses usually brings a change in weather. The greater the difference in temperature between the air masses, the greater the weather change will be along the front.

Warm fronts usually bring milder and more gradual changes in weather. This is because the warmer air slides slowly over the colder air. The slow rise of warm air forms a gentle slope, as shown in the drawing below. Layers of clouds form as the air slowly rises along the sloping front.

How a Warm Front Forms

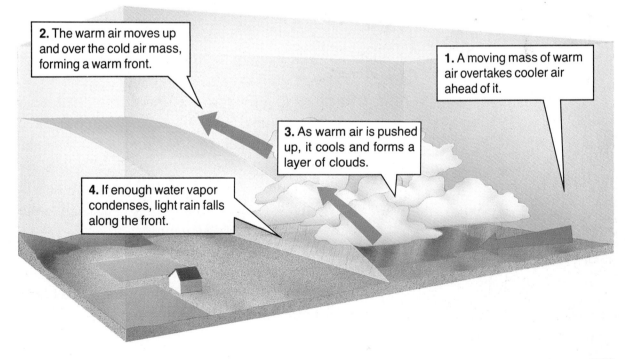

2. The warm air moves up and over the cold air mass, forming a warm front.

1. A moving mass of warm air overtakes cooler air ahead of it.

3. As warm air is pushed up, it cools and forms a layer of clouds.

4. If enough water vapor condenses, light rain falls along the front.

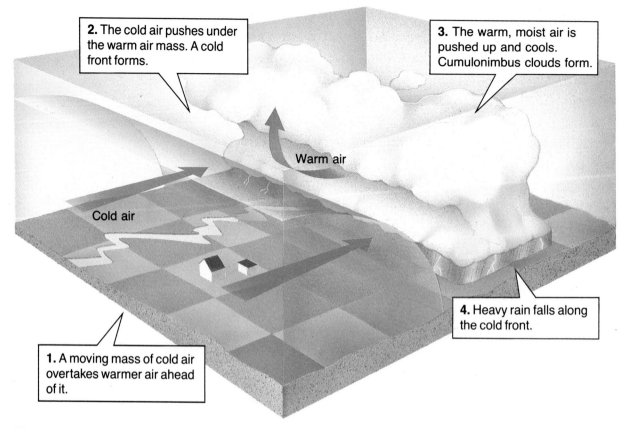

2. The cold air pushes under the warm air mass. A cold front forms.

3. The warm, moist air is pushed up and cools. Cumulonimbus clouds form.

Warm air

Cold air

4. Heavy rain falls along the cold front.

1. A moving mass of cold air overtakes warmer air ahead of it.

How a Cold Front Forms

Light rainfall usually occurs along a warm front. A steady drizzle of rain may last several hours or longer. After a warm front passes, the temperature in the area often rises as the warm air replaces the cooler air.

Along a cold front, the cold air forces the warmer air mass upward. The upward movement of warm air produces a steep slope. Thick storm clouds form as the warm air is pushed up. The more moisture in the warm air mass, the larger the clouds get.

Because the air moves quickly and rises rapidly, a cold front brings violent weather such as thunderstorms. Rain is usually heavy, but does not last as long as it does along a warm front. For example, a thunderstorm may last only a few minutes.

Thunderstorms   From time to time, weather conditions will create violent storms. These can be thunderstorms, blizzards, tornadoes, or hurricanes.

Storms form when the air masses that meet have great differences in temperature and humidity. These differences can be measured as changes in air pressure. The pressure is low over warm areas. It is high over cooler areas.

A change in the air pressure usually is a sign that the weather may change. When the air pressure is high, the weather is fair. When the air pressure is low, the weather is cloudy or stormy. If the air pressure drops suddenly where you live, you can usually expect a storm.

One common type of storm is a thunderstorm. A thunderstorm begins when warm, humid air rises rapidly and cools. This rapid rising and cooling usually occurs along a cold front. The water vapor in the

How a Thunderstorm Forms

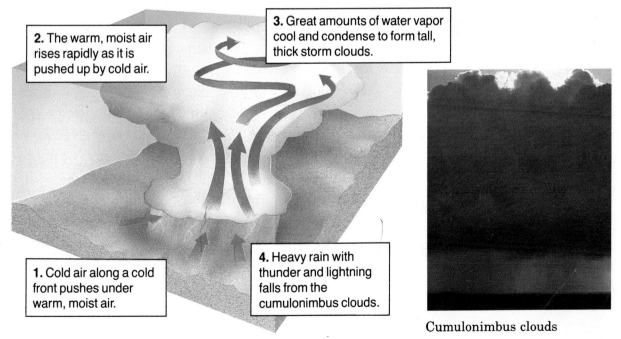

2. The warm, moist air rises rapidly as it is pushed up by cold air.

3. Great amounts of water vapor cool and condense to form tall, thick storm clouds.

1. Cold air along a cold front pushes under warm, moist air.

4. Heavy rain with thunder and lightning falls from the cumulonimbus clouds.

Cumulonimbus clouds

Cumulonimbus clouds and lightning

T H I N K

Why do you think
thunderstorms often
occur during the
summer months?

Z O N E

warm, humid air cools and condenses to form large clouds called thunderheads. Thunderheads are cumulonimbus clouds. These clouds become taller as more and more water vapor in the air condenses.

Thunderheads create lightning and huge downpours of rain. Lightning heats the air, causing the air to expand quickly in all directions. When the warm air crashes into the cool air around it, you hear thunder.

Tornadoes　When air masses have great differences in temperature, the warm air is pushed upward very rapidly by the colder air. This may cause a small, but violent, windstorm called a **tornado.** A tornado is a rotating column of air that looks like a funnel-shaped cloud. It may extend down to the ground from a cumulonimbus cloud.

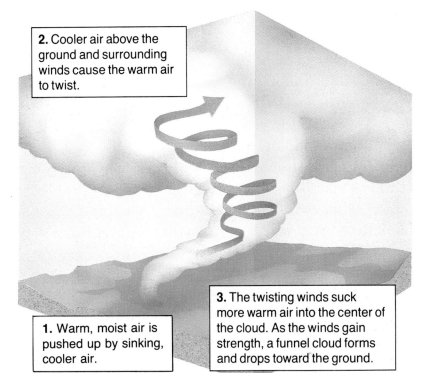

2. Cooler air above the ground and surrounding winds cause the warm air to twist.

3. The twisting winds suck more warm air into the center of the cloud. As the winds gain strength, a funnel cloud forms and drops toward the ground.

1. Warm, moist air is pushed up by sinking, cooler air.

How a Tornado Forms

A tornado touching the ground

The winds in a tornado are the strongest winds at the earth's surface. The winds in a tornado travel at speeds of up to 800 kilometers per hour. These winds usually last only a few minutes. A tornado may be as wide as a car or wider than ten football fields.

Blizzards A blinding snowstorm with strong winds from 56 to 72 kilometers per hour is called a **blizzard.** When the air temperature is below freezing, conditions similar to a thunderstorm cause a blizzard. It happens when cold air forces warm, humid air to rise along a cold front. Since the warm air has so much moisture, the amount of snowfall can be heavy. So much snow blows during a blizzard that it is often hard to see. Houses, cars, and animals can be quickly covered with snow.

A blizzard

Hurricanes   Another kind of powerful storm is called a **hurricane.** It is a low pressure area that forms over the ocean. Hurricanes bring high winds and very heavy rains. The average hurricane is 600 kilometers across. This is large enough to cover an area the size of Wyoming. The wind speeds may be more than 115 kilometers per hour.

Hurricanes form in large masses of warm, moist air. The cool air surrounding the storm has a higher pressure than the warm air within the storm. This difference in air pressure starts winds flowing rapidly inward. The spinning of the earth causes the winds to whirl in a spiral motion. You can see this spiral pattern below in the picture below.

If the hurricane remains over warm water, it may last for a long time. Most last less than a week. Some hurricanes last up to 20 days. Hurricanes weaken when they travel over colder water or over land.

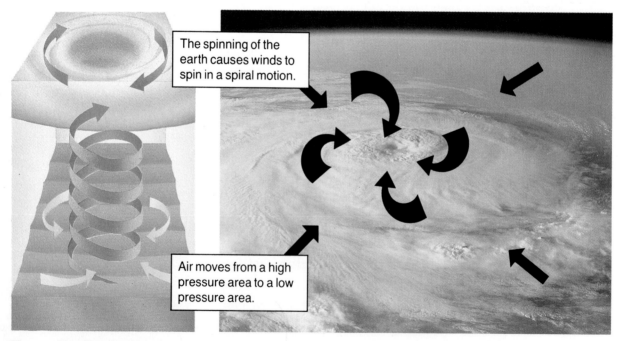

The spinning of the earth causes winds to spin in a spiral motion.

Air moves from a high pressure area to a low pressure area.

How a Hurricane Forms

Building Skills: Defining Operationally

What happens when cold water mixes with warm water?

Steps

1. Add fifteen drops of red food coloring to the water. Stir until the food coloring dissolves. Make sure the water is a deep red. Add more food coloring if you need to.

2. Fill an ice cube tray with this colored water. Put the tray in a freezer.

3. When the cubes are frozen, fill a large jar halfway with warm water.

4. Gently drop an ice cube into the warm water.

5. Watch what happens in the water for the next five minutes.

Questions

1. After step 4, what happened to the ice cube? To the warm water?

2. Although you are observing water and not air, describe how this helps explain what happens when a cold air mass meets a warm air mass.

Materials

red food coloring
dropper
jar of water
ice cube tray
large, clear jar
warm water

Step 4

✓ Lesson Checkup

1. Name the four types of violent storms.

2. How do warm fronts differ from cold fronts?

3. **Think Critically!** Would you expect a tornado to form on a clear, sunny day? Explain your answer.

Predicting Weather Changes

Have you ever planned to go on a picnic, but changed your plans because of rain? Predicting weather is very difficult to do. Weather usually changes because the wind shifts. For this reason, most new weather tools measure wind speed and direction.

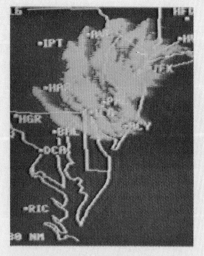

Doppler radar image of a hurricane

Doppler (DAHP luhr) radar is one such weather tool. It helps weather forecasters predict wind changes. Doppler radar sends microwave beams into storm clouds. The beams bounce off the dust and water carried in the air. Computers measure the frequency of the microwaves reflected back to the radar. If the objects are moving towards the beam, the frequency increases. If the objects are moving away from the beam, the frequency decreases.

Airports use Doppler radar to help prevent flight delays. Unpredicted wind changes can cause planes to wait before takeoff or landing. This wastes time and money. Doppler radar tells air traffic controllers in advance that the wind direction will change. The controllers can then keep the airplanes moving.

Besides saving time and money, Doppler radar also saves lives. It spots very sudden changes in wind speed and direction called wind shears. Wind shears can cause a plane to crash when taking off or landing.

Think About It

Farmers, power companies, and home builders all need to know when the weather will change. Think about how weather can affect these people or businesses. How can Doppler radar help save time, money, and perhaps lives?

Making and Using a Wind Vane

Problem: How does a wind vane help you to know the direction of the wind?

Experimenting

1. Tape a piece of poster board to your desk. Put the large eraser on the poster board. Draw a circle around it. Use a compass to find north, east, west, and south on the circle. Label these points.

2. Push the pencil into the eraser, as shown.

3. ◇ SHARP! Use the scissors to cut a slit three centimeters long at one end of the straw. Fold the index card in half lengthwise. Place it in the slit.

4. ◇ SHARP! Use a push pin to make a hole through the middle of the straw. Stick the straight pin through this hole and into the pencil end. Make sure the straw can spin.

5. Move around the wind vane and blow on it. Observe the direction it points. Record your results.

Materials

poster board
tape
large eraser
compass
pencil with eraser
scissors
soda straw
metric ruler
index card
push pin
straight pin

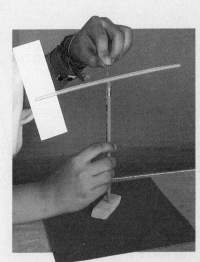

Step 4

Recording Data

Trial	Direction from which wind blows	Direction wind vane points
1		
2		

Drawing Conclusions

1. What does a wind vane tell you about the wind?

2. How can a wind vane help you predict a change in the weather?

Summary

- Four conditions determine weather: 1) the temperature of the air, 2) wind, 3) the moisture in the air, and 4) air pressure.
- The three main cloud types are cirrus, stratus, and cumulus clouds.
- Cold fronts usually cause violent weather while warm fronts usually bring light rain and warmer temperatures.
- The four kinds of storms are thunderstorms, blizzards, tornadoes, and hurricanes.

Science Words

Copy the words below. Draw a picture that shows what each word means.

air mass
blizzard
cirrus cloud
cold front
cumulus cloud
front
humidity
hurricane
stationary front
stratus cloud
tornado
warm front
weather

Science Ideas

1. Letter your paper from a to e. Write the word that best completes each sentence.

    a. A large storm that forms over the ocean is a (tornado, hurricane, front, blizzard).

    b. The amount of water vapor in the air is called (air pressure, rain, clouds, humidity).

    c. The clouds that cause thunderstorms are called (cirrus, stratus, nimbostratus, cumulonimbus) clouds.

    d. Cold air is heavier than (warm air, rain, snow, water droplets).

    e. When a cold front forms, warm air (moves up and down, moves down, moves up, does not move).

2. Letter your paper from a to d. Tell whether each of the weather conditions listed below happens along warm or cold fronts.

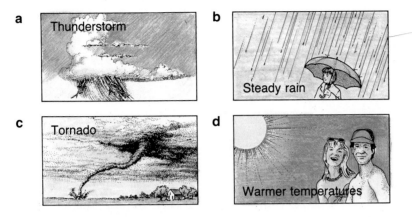

a Thunderstorm

b Steady rain

c Tornado

d Warmer temperatures

3. Marcos and Becky had to postpone their ski trip because the weather changed. What possible conditions could have caused the weather to change?

Data Bank

Use the chart on page 384 to answer the following questions.

1. List the items in order from largest to smallest.

2. How many times larger than a dust devil is an average tornado?

Problem Solving

Lightning is common during stormy weather. Go to the library and read what you can about lightning safety. Use the information to write a list called "Lightning Safety Rules" for your home and school. Make a poster to display the rules and warn others of the possible dangers of lightning.

Science Ideas, Question 3

Chapter 13
Motion in Space

In this chapter, you will learn

- what causes night and day
- what causes the changing seasons
- why the moon seems to change shape
- what happens when the moon or earth blocks the sun's light

On February 26, 1979, the sky grew dark in the middle of the day. The air got colder. It seemed as if a storm was coming.

Scientists around the world had prepared for this day. They aimed special cameras at the sun. The scientists had to be careful not to look directly at the sun. A special satellite in space was ready to take pictures, too.

Slowly, the moon appeared to move across the sun. For a few minutes the sun's light was completely blocked by the moon. Only the glowing gases that surround the sun could be seen. These gases are only seen when the moon blocks the sun. Stars were seen in the sky. Daytime was like nighttime. Scientists recorded the event with their special cameras. The picture on the left was taken from the space satellite.

What was this strange event? As you read this chapter, you will learn about movements of the earth, moon, and sun. And you will learn how these movements cause special events like the one just described.

Lesson 1   Movements of the Earth

What movements of the earth cause day and night and the seasons?

Pretend that you are riding a horse on a merry-go-round. If you look straight ahead, the objects around you seem to move. As the merry-go-round spins, trees and people pass by. Of course, the trees do not really move. They just seem to move.

Motions in the solar system are a lot like the motions at an amusement park. Many of the things we think are moving are not moving in the way we see them. Motion can be real or apparent. Real motion is when something actually moves. Apparent motion is when something is not moving but seems to move. In this lesson, you will learn about the real and apparent motions of the earth, sun, and moon.

If you were riding on a merry-go-round, which of the top pictures shows what you would see?

Day and Night   You have seen the sun rise, move across the sky, and then sink below the horizon. What is moving—the earth or the sun? To explain night and day, you need to understand the motions of the earth.

The earth spins or rotates on an imaginary line called an **axis.** The axis passes through the earth at the North and South Poles. The globe in your classroom probably has a rod that goes through its center. This rod is an axis that you can see. However, the earth's axis is imaginary. You cannot see it.

The earth makes one turn, or **rotation,** on its axis every 24 hours. One rotation is called a day. Even though you are sitting on the earth, you do not feel it rotate. You do not feel the motion, yet you are spinning at 1,670 kilometers per hour.

Day and Night

As the earth spins, sunlight shines on only half of the earth at any one time.

The time spent in the lighted side is called day.

The time spent in the dark side is called night.

The spinning of the earth causes most places on the earth to move in and out of sunlight.

309

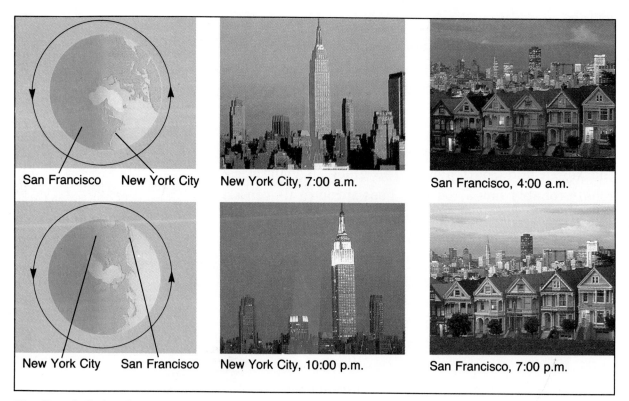

San Francisco New York City	New York City, 7:00 a.m.	San Francisco, 4:00 a.m.
New York City San Francisco	New York City, 10:00 p.m.	San Francisco, 7:00 p.m.

The Earth Spins from West to East

The earth spins from west to east on its axis. You can see in the top left picture that it is sunrise in New York City. This means that the East Coast of the United States is just entering sunlight. Three hours later the East Coast is well into daylight. At that time, the West Coast is just entering daylight. It is sunrise on the West Coast. While someone in New York is eating lunch, someone in California is having breakfast. Which coast will be the first to see the sun set?

The drawing on page 309 shows that the earth is tilted on its axis. This means that as the earth spins, some areas are tilted away from the sun while other areas are tilted toward the sun. At each of the poles, during a certain time of the year, the sun never sets. During another part of the year, at each pole, the sun never rises.

The Earth Revolves   As the earth spins on its axis, it also moves around the sun. The motion around the sun is called **revolution.** One revolution around the sun is called a year. It takes $365\frac{1}{4}$ days for each revolution around the sun. Therefore, a year is $365\frac{1}{4}$ days long.

The path the earth takes around the sun is called an **orbit.** The shape of the earth's orbit is not a perfect circle. Instead, it is a flattened circle called an **ellipse** (ih LIHPS). As the earth moves in an ellipse, it is closer to the sun during some parts of its trip than it is during others. In fact, you may be surprised to know the earth is closer to the sun during winter than it is during summer.

Because the earth orbits the sun, different stars are seen in the night sky during different times of the year. Look at the drawing of the earth's orbit below. Notice that the stars seen in the summer sky are different from the stars seen in the winter sky.

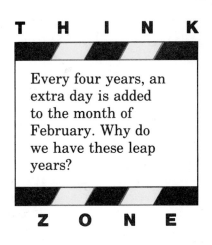

T H I N K

Every four years, an extra day is added to the month of February. Why do we have these leap years?

Z O N E

The Earth's Orbit

Summer Triangle

North Star

Big Dipper

The summer night sky

Big Dipper

North Star

Gemini

Taurus

Orion

The winter night sky

Seasons   During the earth's yearly trip around the sun, we experience different seasons. The seasons are not caused by the distance the earth is from the sun. Instead, seasons are caused by the tilt of the earth's axis.

Look at the drawing below. It shows that as the earth orbits the sun, its axis always points in the same direction. This causes the northern and southern halves of earth to tilt toward and away from the sun at different times of the year. Notice which half is tilted toward the sun in each season. Then read about the seasons in the drawing.

The angle at which sunlight strikes the earth is affected by earth's tilt. The half of the earth that points toward the sun receives rays of sunlight more directly.

Seasons in the Northern Half of Earth

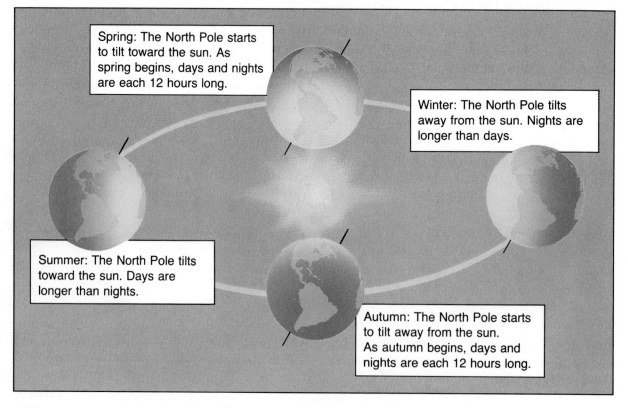

Spring: The North Pole starts to tilt toward the sun. As spring begins, days and nights are each 12 hours long.

Winter: The North Pole tilts away from the sun. Nights are longer than days.

Summer: The North Pole tilts toward the sun. Days are longer than nights.

Autumn: The North Pole starts to tilt away from the sun. As autumn begins, days and nights are each 12 hours long.

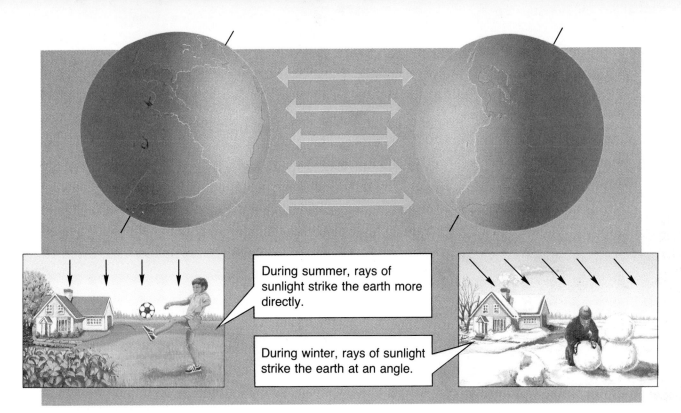

During summer, rays of sunlight strike the earth more directly.

During winter, rays of sunlight strike the earth at an angle.

Summer and Winter

The half that tilts away from the sun has rays of light striking at more of a slant or angle. You can see this in the drawing above. Sunlight that strikes more directly is absorbed in greater amounts by the surface of the earth. When sunlight strikes at an angle, less is absorbed. The more light that is absorbed, the warmer the earth's surface gets.

This makes it easy to understand that summer occurs on the half of the earth that is tilted toward the sun. Direct sunlight and longer days allow that half of the earth to get more energy from the sun. Therefore, places tilted toward the sun will be warmer than places tilted away from the sun.

The half of earth that tilts away from the sun gets less direct sunlight and has shorter days. Therefore, when the northern half of the earth is having summer, the southern half is having winter.

Movement Through Space   As the earth spins on its axis and revolves around the sun, it also moves through space. This movement is tied to the movement of the sun.

Like the earth, the sun revolves. Scientists believe that the sun is on the outer edge of a huge system of stars known as the Milky Way galaxy. They believe the sun and all the other stars are spinning around the center of the galaxy. As the sun travels through the outer edge of the Milky Way galaxy, the earth and all the other planets travel with it.

Two Views of the Milky Way Galaxy

Side view

Top view

Building Skills: Making Models

Can you tell time with a sundial?

Steps

1. Place a pencil upright in a lump of clay.
2. Find a window that gets sunlight all day. Tape a piece of paper on the window sill. Set the pencil and clay on the paper near the window pane.
3. Draw a half circle around the pencil.
4. Draw a line on the paper where the pencil's shadow falls. Draw the line from the clay to the circle. Label this line with the time of day.
5. Every hour mark the shadow's position. Label each mark with the time of day. Do this for one full day.
6. Use this sundial to tell time the next day and one week later. Compare the sundial's time with a watch.

Question

1. Was the sundial time the same as the watch each time you compared the two? Explain.

Materials

pencil
clay
tape
paper
ruler

Step 4

✓ Lesson Checkup

1. How long does it take earth to complete one rotation? One revolution?
2. Explain why it can be dáytime in one city and night in another.
3. **Think Critically!** Where on earth would you notice the least change in seasons? The most? Explain.

315

Lesson 2   Movements of the Moon

What three events can happen because of the earth's movement?

The earth is not alone in its yearly journey around the sun. All the planets in the solar system are also revolving around the sun. These planets are satellites of the sun. A **satellite** is an object that revolves around a larger object.

Many of the planets have satellites called moons. For example, Jupiter has 16 of these satellites. Our moon is also a satellite. All moons revolve around planets. In this lesson, you learn about our moon and its movements around the planet earth.

Why is the moon called a satellite?

How the Moon Moves   Like the sun, the moon appears to move across the sky. This motion is not caused by the actual movement of the moon. Instead, as with the rising and setting sun, the moon's motion is caused by the earth's rotation. Therefore, the movement of the moon we see is apparent motion.

But the moon really does move. In fact, it has two real motions. It rotates and revolves, just like the earth does.

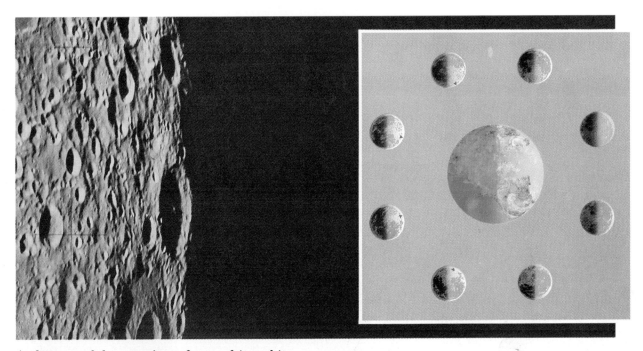

A close-up of the moon's surface and its orbit

The moon orbits the earth once every month. Look at the drawing above. It shows the moon orbiting earth. Notice that as the moon goes around earth, the moon slowly rotates. In fact, it takes the moon as long to make one rotation as it takes it to make one revolution. For this reason, the same side of the moon always faces the earth. As long as you stay on the earth, you will see only one side of the moon!

The Moon's Phases   The moon is shaped like a ball. But if you look at the moon every night, you would notice that its shape seems to change. One night it might be a full circle. Later, on another night, it might be a thin crescent. Later still, the moon is full again. These changes in the moon's appearance are called the **phases of the moon.**

The phases you see are caused by reflected sunlight. The moon does not make light of its own. Instead, it shines by reflecting sunlight. The side of the

Positions of the Earth and Moon at Half and Full Phases

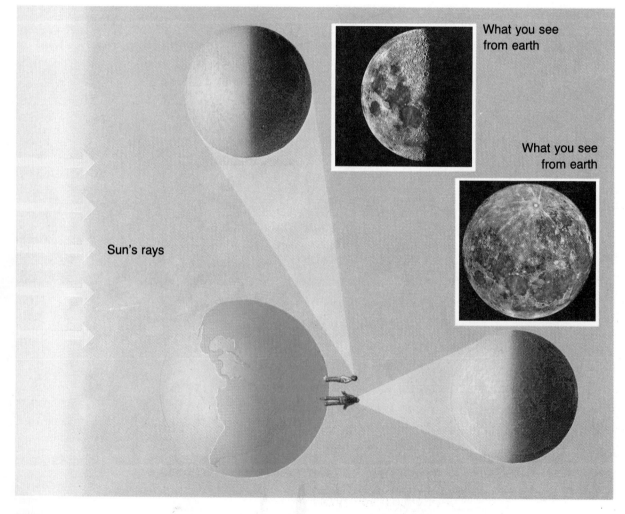

What you see
from earth

What you see
from earth

Sun's rays

moon facing the sun is always lighted. The side of the moon turned away from the sun is always dark. You only see a part of the moon that is reflecting sunlight.

Understanding the phases of the moon is not easy. But looking at the drawing below can help. First look at the new moon. The moon is between the sun and earth. In this position, the lighted side of the moon is facing away from the earth. From the earth, the moon shows no reflected sunlight. Therefore, you cannot see it. When do you see a full moon?

The Phases of the Moon

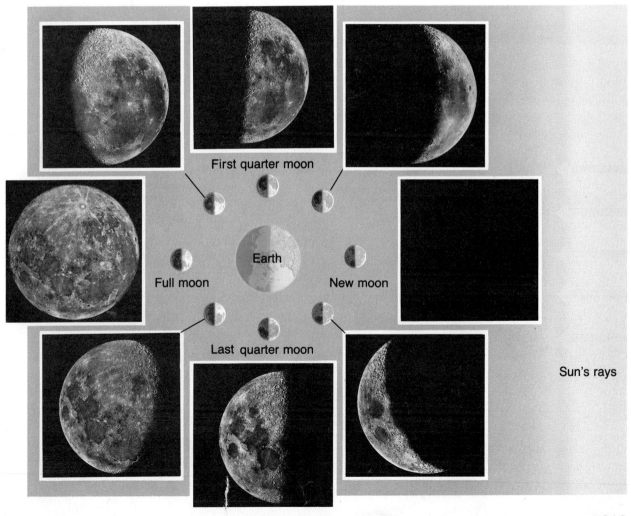

First quarter moon

Earth

Full moon

New moon

Last quarter moon

Sun's rays

Eclipses of the Moon   Place your hand between the classroom light and your desk. If your hand is really between the light source and the desk, a shadow falls on your desk. Sometimes the earth acts like your hand. As the earth revolves around the sun, it blocks sunlight and forms a shadow. This shadow falls into space.

Two to five times a year the earth, sun, and moon line up together. The earth gets between the sun and the moon. When this happens, the moon enters the earth's shadow. When the moon moves through the earth's shadow, a **lunar eclipse** (ih KLIHPS) occurs. You can see a lunar eclipse below.

Eclipses can be partial or full. If only part of the moon enters earth's shadow, there will be a partial eclipse. What makes a full eclipse?

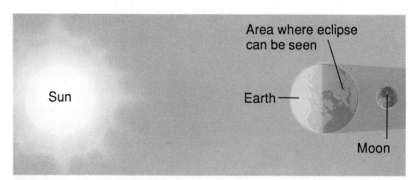

Positions of the Sun, Earth, and Moon During Lunar Eclipse

Different stages of a lunar eclipse

Eclipses of the Sun   Just as the earth's shadow can fall on the moon, the moon's shadow can fall on the earth. This happens when the moon gets between the earth and the sun. This is called a **solar eclipse.**

The moon's shadow does not cover the earth completely. It only falls on a small part of the earth. You can see this in the drawing below. Where the moon's shadow falls, the people on earth cannot see the sun. It is in these places that a solar eclipse can be seen.

Like a lunar eclipse, a solar eclipse can be partial or full. This means all or part of the sun is blocked by the moon. Usually, the sun is only partly blocked. Sometimes, however, the sun is completely hidden behind the moon. This is a total eclipse of the sun. During a total eclipse, day becomes like night. Stars can even be seen.

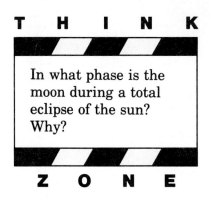

T H I N K

In what phase is the moon during a total eclipse of the sun? Why?

Z O N E

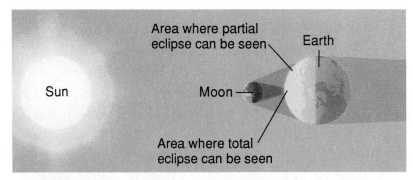

Positions of Sun, Earth, and Moon During Solar Eclipse

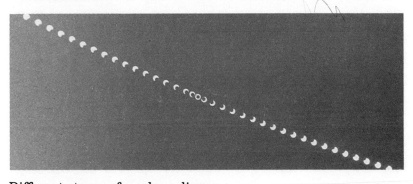

Different stages of a solar eclipse

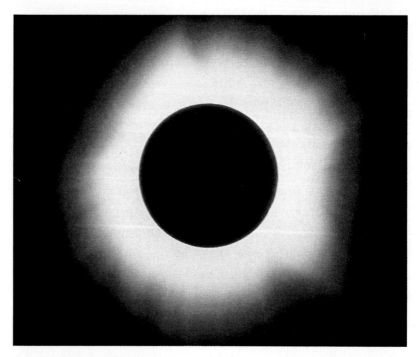

Total eclipse of the sun

Each month, the moon passes between the sun and the earth. But a total eclipse of the sun does not happen very often. The sun, moon, and earth must be in an exact line. This happens very rarely. The next total eclipse of the sun to be seen from North America will not happen until after the year 2000. The picture above shows a total eclipse of the sun.

A total eclipse lasts about eight minutes. During this time, scientists are able to study the sun's corona. The corona is the atmosphere of hot gas surrounding the sun. It cannot usually be seen because the sun's light is so bright. Look at the picture again. The white light around the edges of the sun is the corona.

Staring directly at the sun can cause serious eye damage. You should never look directly at the sun, especially during a solar eclipse. Scientists use special telescopes that reflect the sun's image to avoid hurting their eyes.

Building Skills: Predicting

What would a person on the moon see during a lunar eclipse?

Steps

Materials

flashlight
globe
rubber ball

1. Darken the room. Have someone shine the flashlight on the globe so that the light falls evenly on its surface.

2. Imagine you live on the moon. Predict what you would see on the moon during a lunar eclipse.

3. Move the rubber ball around the globe, like the moon orbits the earth. The rubber ball should be closer to the globe than to the flashlight. Observe the shadows that form on the globe and ball.

Questions

1. Where did the "moon" cast a shadow on the "earth"? What would someone in this area see?

2. What happened when the earth was between the "sun" and the moon? What is this called? What would someone on the moon see?

Step 3

✓ Lesson Checkup

1. Why do you only see one side of the moon?

2. What is the difference between a lunar eclipse and a solar eclipse?

3. **Think Critically!** If you were on the moon, the earth would have phases. When would you see a "full earth" and a "new earth"?

Technology Today

Artificial Moons

Today, you can see a live rock concert from London on television. You can even make a phone call from a flying airplane. These things are all possible because of communication satellites.

Like the moon, communication satellites revolve around the earth in orbits. A typical communication satellite travels 35,400 kilometers above the equator. It completes an orbit every 24 hours. The satellite's orbit matches earth's speed of rotation. Because of this, the satellite seems to hang above earth in a fixed spot. This lets antennas on earth point directly at the satellite without changing position. If you look at the night sky, this kind of satellite looks just like a shining star. It does not move across the skyline.

During orbit, the satellite receives signals from a ground station on earth. Then the satellite relays, or reflects, the signals toward a second ground station. From this station, the signals are sent as telephone calls and television programs.

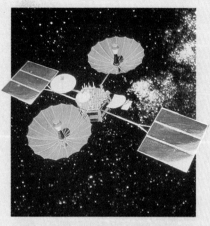

A satellite can relay phone calls and TV shows to earth.

Dish antennas receive signals from satellites.

Think About It

Almost 200 communication satellites have been sent into space. Many of these do not work. Yet they continue to orbit earth. These satellites will continue to do so for about 200 years, until gravity pulls them back to earth. Some people believe that space has become a junkyard for space vehicles. They think these broken satellites are a form of space pollution. What do you think? Think about this the next time you look at the night sky. How will the sky change as more and more satellites orbit the earth?

Exploring Science

Observing the Moon's Phases

Problem: What causes the phases of the moon?

Experimenting

1. Draw a circle on the cardboard. Divide the circle into 28 equal sections as shown.

2. Mold the clay into three round balls. Make the yellow clay represent the sun, the blue clay the earth, and the brown clay the moon.

3. Place the "earth" in the center of the circle and the "sun" outside the circle. Put the "moon" on the circle between the sun and earth as shown. This is your model of the moon's orbit.

4. Wait for a new moon. Draw what the moon looks like on a calendar like the one below.

5. On your model, write the date next to the clay moon. Then move the clay moon one section counterclockwise along the circle.

6. Watch and draw the moon each night. Repeat step 5 until the moon completes its orbit on the model.

Recording Data

Sun	M	T	W	Th	F	Sat
1	2	3	4	5	6	7
8	9	10	11	12	13	14

Drawing Conclusions

1. Why did you move the moon one section each night?

2. At what phases were the sun, moon, and earth in a straight line?

Materials

cardboard
yellow modeling clay
blue modeling clay
brown modeling clay
calendar

Step 3

✓ Chapter 13 Checkup

Summary

- The earth rotates on its axis once every 24 hours, causing day and night.

- The earth revolves around the sun in an orbit. One revolution is about 365 days, or one year.

- The tilt of the earth's axis as it orbits the sun causes the four seasons.

- The changing shapes of the moon are called phases.

- The moon's movement around the earth can cause solar and lunar eclipses.

Science Words

Draw pictures to represent each of the words below.

axis
ellipse
lunar eclipse
orbit
phases of the moon
revolution
rotation
satellite
solar eclipse

Science Ideas

1. Letter your paper from a to f. Write the cause and effect for each statement.

   a. The earth spins and day changes to night.

   b. As the earth orbits the sun, different stars are seen during different times of the year.

   c. The tilt of the earth's axis causes the seasons.

   d. When the earth gets between the sun and the moon, a lunar eclipse occurs.

   e. The same side of the moon always faces earth because the moon revolves at the same speed as it rotates.

   f. When the moon completely blocks the sun, a total eclipse of the sun occurs.

326

2. Letter your paper from a to d. Tell whether the drawings of the earth represent winter, spring, summer, or autumn in North America.

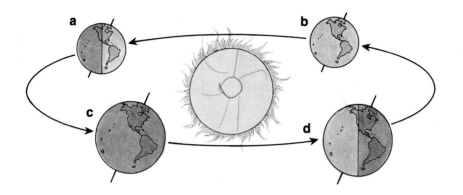

3. Look at the picture. Explain what causes a solar eclipse.

Data Bank

Use the map of the United States on page 385 to answer the following questions.

1. If it is 3:00 p.m. in Tucson, Arizona, what time is it in Atlanta, Georgia?

2. What is the difference in hours between Fairbanks, Alaska, and Atlanta, Georgia?

Science Ideas, Question 3

Problem Solving

An eclipse of the sun is coming and your class wants to view it. You know that you cannot look directly at the sun because it could damage your eyes. Go to the library and research ways in which you can safely see a solar eclipse. Write a report describing how this can be done. Make your own solar viewer.

Ask a Scientist

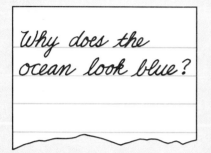

Why does the ocean look blue?

Mrs. Sharon Horner's class at Mary Evelyn Castle Elementary School in Indianapolis, Indiana

Dr. Mary Gaillard is a physicist at the University of California in Berkeley, California. You might think that all scientists spend lots of time in a laboratory doing experiments. Dr. Gaillard, however, spends much of her time doing math and trying to develop new theories in physics.

In her spare time, Dr. Gaillard often goes skiing or hiking. She enjoys the ocean and the mountain lakes of the western United States. As a physicist, Dr. Gaillard knows about things like light and color. Water is really clear. She says the "color" of water in oceans, lakes, rivers, and ponds can be caused by reflections of the sky. It can also be caused by the color of materials that are in the water.

The blue color of many lakes and ponds is mainly a reflection of the blue sky. The water acts as a mirror. If the water is very still and there are no waves, you can even see the reflection of trees and clouds.

Ocean water usually does not look as blue as the water in a lake. Even when there is a bright blue sky, ocean water can have a greenish-blue color. This is because salts and other substances in the water absorb much of the blue light. Therefore, not as much blue light is reflected.

Of course, substances that are in the water can also give it a certain color. If there is a lot of dirt and mud in the water, it will look dark. Chemicals may pollute the water and cause it to have different colors.

Sometimes plants called algae grow in the water and make it look green, purple, or red. The Red Sea got its name because of red-colored algae that grow in the water and make it look red.

Dr. Mary Gaillard

Weather Observer   At hundreds of weather stations across the country, readings are taken every three to six hours. People who take these readings are called weather observers. Some weather observers watch for changes in the sky. Others study instruments that record temperature, precipitation, and direction of the wind. They may also collect information from balloons that record the temperature and other weather conditions at high altitudes. To be a weather observer, you will have to learn to use computers and weather instruments in a trade school.

Mapmaker   Maps are often used in science. The people who plan maps are called mapmakers, or cartographers. Mapmakers use information provided by many people. They also study existing maps of an area and note any changes. A plan for the new map is given to a drafter, who draws the map according to the plan. If you like to plan projects, you may enjoy mapmaking. You can study cartography at a two-year or four-year college.

Paleontologist   Scientists who study fossils are known as paleontologists (pay lee ahn TAHL uh jihsts). Fossils help these scientists find out about organisms that lived millions of years ago. Paleontologists infer about the lifestyle of a prehistoric animal by studying its teeth, bones, footprints, and any other traces. They draw sketches of what the animal might have looked like. If you enjoy working out puzzles, you may want to be a paleontologist. Study geology in college. Then earn an advanced degree in paleontology.

💡 Thinking Critically

Generalizing

Suppose you move into a new neighborhood. If you find that the kids next door are friendly, you might think that all the kids in your neighborhood will be friendly. You are generalizing when you make a judgment about a large group from observations you have made about a part of that group. Generalizing is a thinking skill.

Whether or not your generalization is good depends on two things. First, a good generalization depends on how well you make your observations or get your information. If you are very careful, think about what you are observing, and perhaps write things down, then your observations may be very good. Second, a good generalization depends on the sample you study. If the sample is like the whole group, then your generalization is probably good.

1 | Practicing the Skill

Betty, Sandy, and Jim had to write a special report on space. To start the report Betty wrote, "All things in space revolve around something."

Sandy said, "That doesn't sound right. I've heard that some things in the universe don't move at all."

Jim said, "Well, the book says the moon orbits the earth. And the earth moves around the sun. The earth and moon are two different things that revolve. Those are two things to go by."

"Okay," said Sandy, "I guess we don't have to study every single thing in the sky to make a generalization about what happens."

Comet

Stars

Meteor shower

What was Betty, Sandy, and Jim's generalization? Did they make careful observations? Why or why not? What was their sample? Was the sample like everything in space? Do you think their generalization was a good one? Explain.

2 | Thinking About Thinking

Think about Betty, Sandy, and Jim. How did you decide whether their generalization was good? How did you know whether their sample was like the whole group? How did you know whether their observations were accurate?

3 | Using the Skill

We often generalize about people. Even though we make careful observations, we may make bad generalizations. Sometimes our generalizations are based on a sample that is not like the whole group. Tell about a time when you made a bad generalization because you met only one person from a group.

Unit Four
Health Science

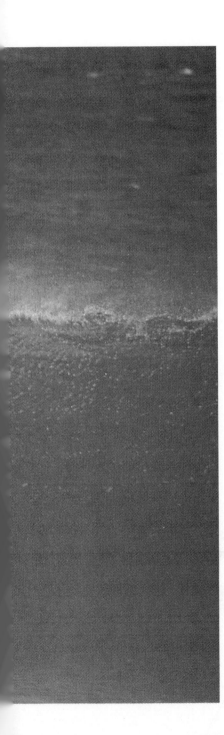

Chapter 14
Transport Systems

The body has systems to move gases, nutrients, and wastes from one part of the body to another. Good health habits can keep these transport systems healthy.

Chapter 15
Drugs and Your Health

Many drugs help prevent and cure sickness. But some types of drugs can cause harm. Learning to say no is the first step in avoiding drug abuse.

Chapter 14
Transport Systems

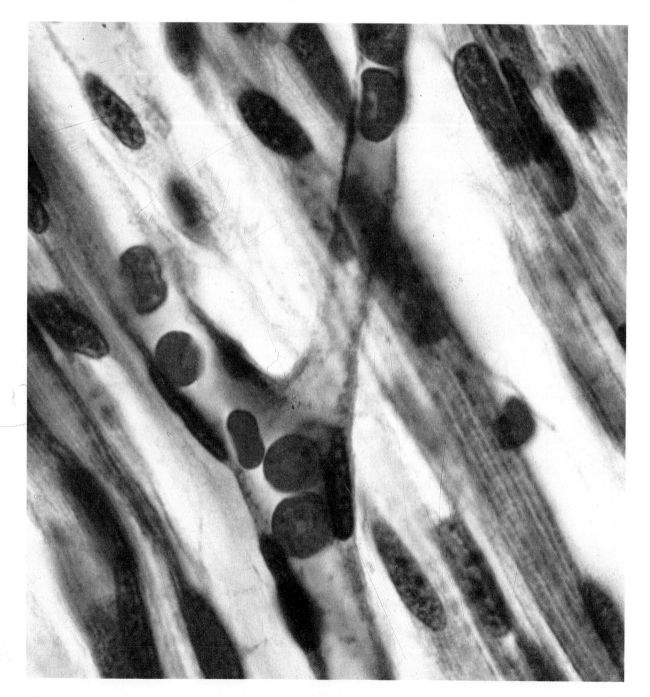

In this chapter, you will learn

■ how the circulatory system carries oxygen to the body

■ how the respiratory system brings oxygen to the lungs

■ how to keep the transport systems healthy

Marie was learning about the heart and blood in science. She was having a test next week and was worried. Carlos, her older brother, told Marie not to worry. He said he would help her study.

The next evening, Carlos and Marie sat down to study. Carlos said they were going to take a "field trip" to the heart. "Close your eyes," Carlos said. Marie did. "Now pretend we are very small," Carlos continued. "Imagine we are smaller than this book—even smaller than the dot over an 'i'."

Carlos said they were small enough to enter the blood. To reach the heart, Marie and Carlos traveled in the blood through tubes. The tubes looked like the picture on the left. Marie and Carlos traveled through the body to the heart. Carlos told Marie about everything they saw. And Marie told him some things she had learned from science class, too.

Carlos said to open her eyes. How did Carlos and Marie get to the heart? Marie knew the answer, now. Do you? You should know after reading this chapter.

Lesson 1   The Circulatory System

What are the three parts of the circulatory system?

Your body is made up of trillions of cells. The cells are organized so you can eat, breathe, play, work, and think.

Not all these cells are the same. One kind of cell is the heart muscle cell. Heart muscle cells work together to carry out certain jobs. Cells that are alike group together to form tissue. For example, heart muscle cells make up heart muscle tissue. Together, different kinds of tissues form organs.

Heart muscle tissue makes up most of an organ called the heart. Groups of organs that work together are called systems. The heart is an organ of the circulatory (SER kyuh luh TAWR ee) system.

The Organization of the Circulatory System

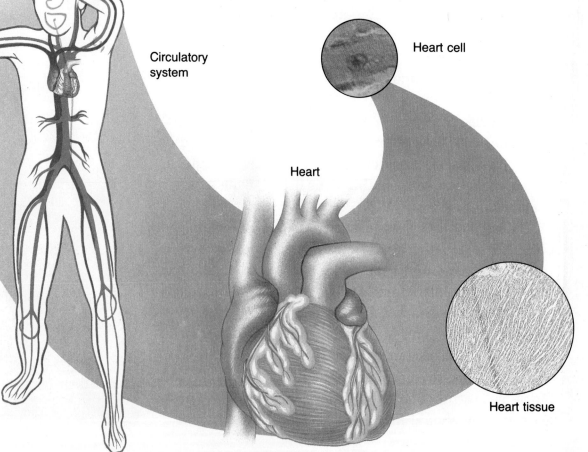

Circulatory system

Heart cell

Heart

Heart tissue

Several systems of the body are transport systems. These systems carry substances from one part of the body to another. The circulatory system is a transport system.

The **circulatory system** carries nutrients, oxygen, and other substances to all cells of the body. It also carries away wastes from the cells. The circulatory system is made up of the blood, the heart, and the blood vessels.

The Blood   Nutrients, oxygen, and body wastes are carried throughout your body by blood. Blood is the carrier of the circulatory system.

Blood is a mixture made up of a liquid part and solid parts. The liquid part of the blood is called **plasma** (PLAZ muh). Many people think that this part of the blood is red. As you can see in the picture, plasma is really the color of straw. Plasma is mostly water. Nutrients are dissolved in plasma. In this way, nutrients are carried around the body.

The solid part of blood is made up of red blood cells, white blood cells, and platelets. The solid part of blood is mostly red blood cells.

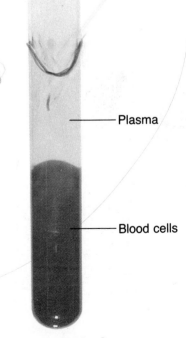

Plasma

Blood cells

Separated blood

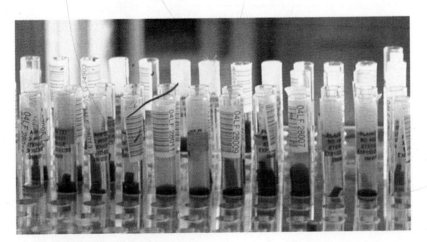

Samples of separated blood

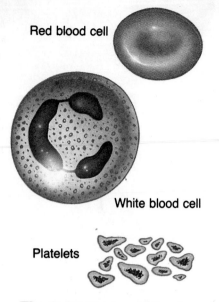

Red blood cell

White blood cell

Platelets

The Solid Parts of Blood

Red blood cells carry oxygen from the lungs to the body cells. When carrying oxygen, red blood cells turn bright red. They make the blood look red. Red blood cells are shaped like donuts. These "donuts" have thin middles instead of holes.

White blood cells are a second cell type. **White blood cells** help the body fight infection and disease. These cells surround and "eat" invaders in the blood and body cells. White blood cells are larger, but fewer, than red blood cells.

Last are platelets. **Platelets** help the blood to clot, or thicken. These tiny pieces of cells help the body stop bleeding. Without platelets, you could bleed to death from a small cut on your finger.

The Heart   In a single minute, a drop of blood can make a trip through your body. The heart pushes blood through your body 24 hours a day without rest. The heart is the pump of the circulatory system. Use the graph below to find how much blood the heart pumps in a day.

The Pumping Heart	
Time	**Volume of Blood Pumped**
1 Minute	5 L 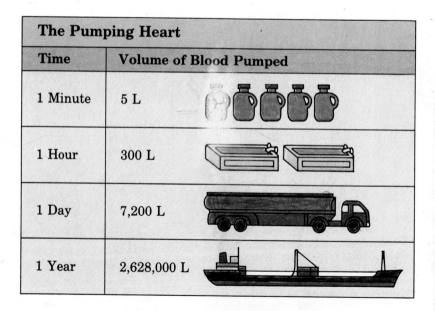
1 Hour	300 L
1 Day	7,200 L
1 Year	2,628,000 L

338

The heart is a hollow muscle. It is about the size of your fist. Place your fist slightly to the left of the center of your chest. Make sure your fist is level with your armpit. This is about the location of your heart within your chest.

The drawing below shows the inside of the heart. The hollow inside is divided into four sections. These sections are called chambers. Two of these chambers are on the right side of the heart. The top chamber receives blood from the body. The bottom chamber pumps blood to the lungs.

The other two chambers are on the left side of the heart. The top chamber receives blood from the lungs. The bottom pumps blood to the rest of the body.

In fact, the heart is really two pumps. The right side of the heart pumps blood to the lungs. The left side pumps blood to the rest of the body.

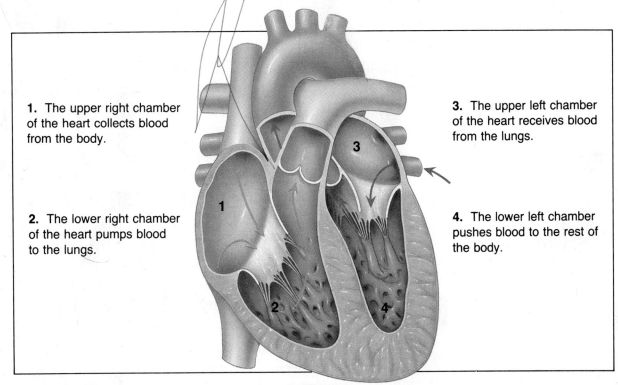

1. The upper right chamber of the heart collects blood from the body.

2. The lower right chamber of the heart pumps blood to the lungs.

3. The upper left chamber of the heart receives blood from the lungs.

4. The lower left chamber pushes blood to the rest of the body.

Inside the Heart

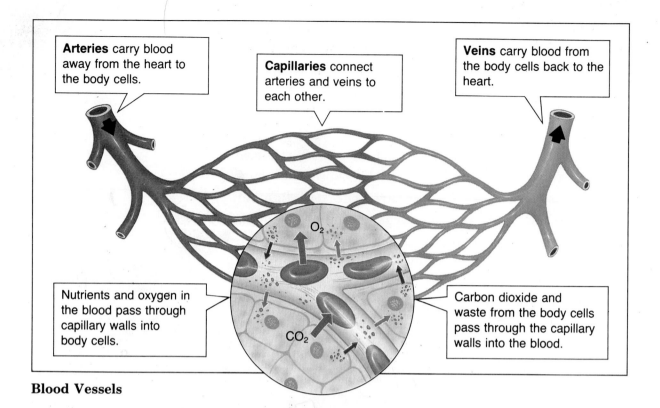

Arteries carry blood away from the heart to the body cells.

Capillaries connect arteries and veins to each other.

Veins carry blood from the body cells back to the heart.

Nutrients and oxygen in the blood pass through capillary walls into body cells.

Carbon dioxide and waste from the body cells pass through the capillary walls into the blood.

O_2

CO_2

Blood Vessels

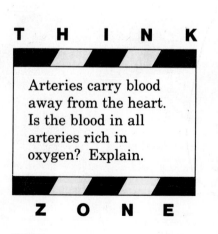

T H I N K

Arteries carry blood away from the heart. Is the blood in all arteries rich in oxygen? Explain.

Z O N E

Blood Vessels   You know that blood is pumped to and from the heart. But how does it get to all parts of the body? The body has a wonderful "plumbing" system to transport blood. Just as the plumbing system of your house transports water, hollow tubes called blood vessels transport blood in the circulatory system.

Your body has three kinds of blood vessels: **veins, arteries,** and **capillaries.** Read about these vessels in the drawing above.

As the heart pumps, it pushes blood into arteries. This stretches the arteries. When the heart relaxes, the arteries spring back. This pushes the blood along. This stretching out and springing back of an artery is called the pulse. You can feel the pulse of an artery where it lies near the skin and over a bone. Find the pulse in your wrist. Can you find a pulse anywhere else?

Blood travels a complete trip around the body in two "loops." Steps 1–2 below are the loop from the heart to the body. Steps 3–4 are the loop from the heart to the lungs. Follow the path of blood as it travels through the body.

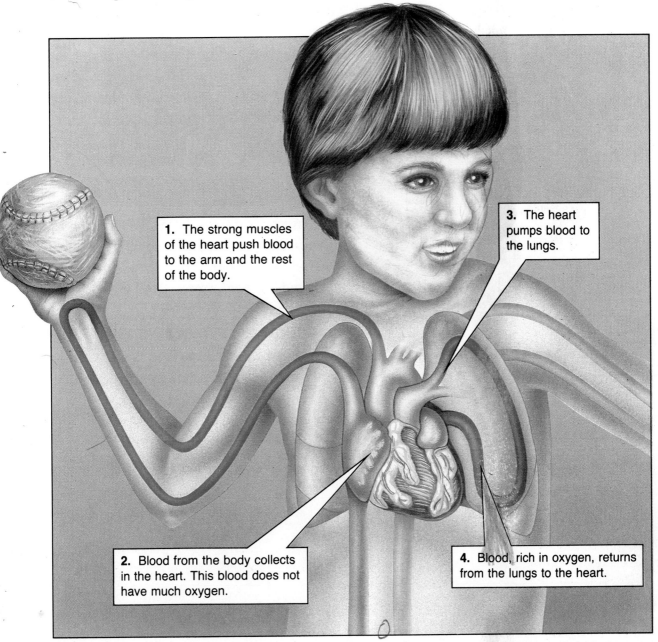

1. The strong muscles of the heart push blood to the arm and the rest of the body.

3. The heart pumps blood to the lungs.

2. Blood from the body collects in the heart. This blood does not have much oxygen.

4. Blood, rich in oxygen, returns from the lungs to the heart.

Path of Blood Through the Body

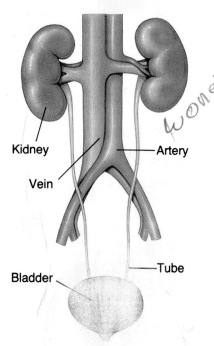

Kidneys and Bladder

Cleaning the Blood

Your body cells make two main wastes. These wastes are carbon dioxide gas and water. Carbon dioxide is carried to the lungs by blood. You get rid of this gas when you breathe out. The waste water is delivered by the blood to two places: the kidneys and the skin.

The **kidneys** remove most of the waste water from the blood. Look at the drawing on the left. A large artery enters each kidney. Within the kidneys, water and other dissolved wastes are removed from the blood. "Clean" blood leaves the kidneys through veins.

In the kidneys, the wastes are called urine. Urine leaves each kidney through a small tube. These two tubes connect to a hollow organ, the bladder. Urine collects in the bladder. A single tube leads from the bladder to an opening outside the body. When you go to the restroom, you empty your bladder.

Your skin also helps to "clean" the blood. Your skin has many sweat glands. Sweat from these glands carries wastes from the body.

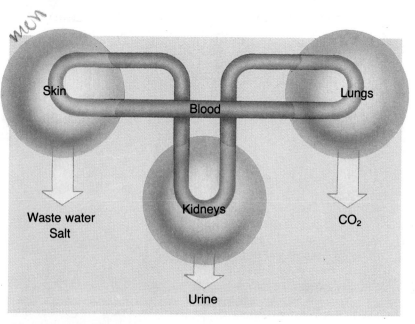

Cleaning the Blood

342

Building Skills: Observing

What can you identify in blood?

Steps

Materials

1. Place the slide on the stage of the microscope.

2. Using low power, look at the blood. Do the parts all look the same?

3. Using high power, look at the blood. Because of the stain, the red blood cells will look pink. The white blood cells will have blue centers. The platelets will look like small, blue specks.

4. Draw and label what you see. Count how many of each blood part are on the slide.

3 prepared blood
  smear slides
microscope
paper
pencil

Questions

1. Did your smear contain more red blood cells, white blood cells, or platelets?

2. Why did the center of the red blood cells look lighter than the edges?

3. Compare the shapes of each blood part. Describe what each does.

Step 4

✓ Lesson Checkup

1. What are the three main parts of the circulatory system? What are their jobs?

2. Why can the heart be described as two pumps?

3. **Think Critically!** Trace a drop of blood as it leaves your heart on a trip to and from your big toe.

Lesson 2 — The Respiratory System

How does the respiratory system work?

How long could you live without eating? A man from Scotland did not eat solid food for 382 days! He lived on liquids and vitamins. Could you live very long without sleeping? A woman in England did not sleep for more than 18 days. She stayed awake during a rocking chair marathon.

But how long could you live without breathing? Not very long. The cells of your body constantly need the oxygen found in the air you breathe. Most brain cells would die within three to five minutes without oxygen.

Oxygen is used by cells to unlock the energy in food. You have just learned how oxygen is carried to the cells by the blood. How does oxygen in the air get to the blood? Another transport system in the body does this.

Nutrients

Oxygen

Energy for swimming

Nutrients and oxygen provide energy for swimming.

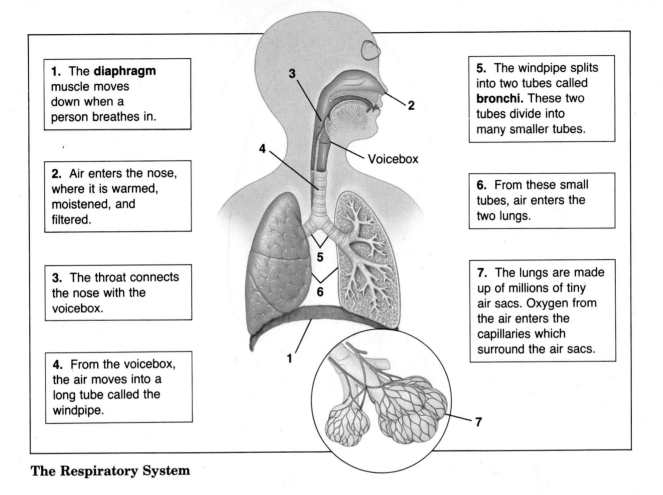

1. The **diaphragm** muscle moves down when a person breathes in.

2. Air enters the nose, where it is warmed, moistened, and filtered.

3. The throat connects the nose with the voicebox.

4. From the voicebox, the air moves into a long tube called the windpipe.

5. The windpipe splits into two tubes called **bronchi.** These two tubes divide into many smaller tubes.

6. From these small tubes, air enters the two lungs.

7. The lungs are made up of millions of tiny air sacs. Oxygen from the air enters the capillaries which surround the air sacs.

Voicebox

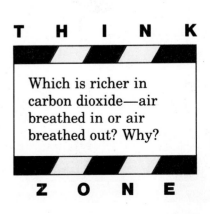

The Respiratory System

Delivering Oxygen to Blood

Oxygen is found in the air around us. The **respiratory system** (REHS puhr uh tawr ee SIHS tuhm) brings air into and out of the body. In the lungs, the circulatory system picks up the oxygen from the air. The circulatory system brings nutrients and oxygen to the body cells. Energy is released when the nutrients and oxygen combine in the cells. The body uses this energy to do "work," such as swimming, washing dishes, or thinking.

The organs of the respiratory system include the **diaphragm** (DY uh fram), **bronchi** (BRAHNG ky), lungs, and windpipe. The drawing above explains how oxygen in the air gets to the blood.

T H I N K

Which is richer in carbon dioxide—air breathed in or air breathed out? Why?

Z O N E

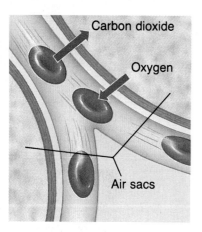

Gas Exchange in an Air Sac

Exchange of Gases

The walls of air sacs are only one cell thick. They are covered with capillaries. When you breathe in, air fills the air sacs. Oxygen in the air leaves the air sacs, passes through the capillary walls, and enters the blood. The red blood cells pick up the oxygen, and the heart pumps it to the body cells.

The respiratory system does more than bring oxygen to the blood. It also removes carbon dioxide from the blood. Blood carries carbon dioxide from the body cells. When blood reaches the lungs, carbon dioxide passes through the capillary walls into the air sacs.

Breathing

Air enters and leaves the lungs in a process called breathing. Breathing in is called inhaling. Breathing out is called exhaling. Your diaphragm helps you breathe.

Look at the drawing below. When you inhale, the diaphragm contracts, or tightens. This causes it to flatten. Other muscles pull your ribs upward. These two motions cause your chest cavity to get larger. Air rushes into the lungs to fill up this extra space.

When you exhale, the diaphragm relaxes. It becomes dome-shaped. The ribs go down. The chest cavity becomes smaller, pushing air out of the lungs.

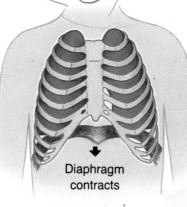

Diaphragm
contracts

Inhaling

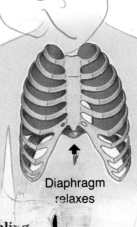

Diaphragm
relaxes

Exhaling

Building Skills: Making Models

Can you make a working model of a lung?

Steps

1. ◇ **SHARP!** Cut the plastic bottle in half as shown. Stretch the large balloon across the bottom of the bottle. Fasten the balloon with a rubber band. Be sure the balloon is tightly stretched.

2. Attach the small balloon to the straw with a rubber band.

3. Put the straw in the bottle opening. Press clay around the straw and bottle opening. This will keep air from coming in the bottle.

4. Pull down and push up on the bottom balloon. Observe the balloon inside the bottle.

Questions

1. Which part of your respiratory system acts like the bottom balloon? The balloon inside the bottle?

2. Push up on the bottom balloon. Is this like inhaling or exhaling? Explain.

Materials

large balloon
small balloon
soda straw
2 rubber bands
plastic liter bottle
scissors
modeling clay

Step 4

✓ Lesson Checkup

1. What are the organs of the respiratory system?

2. Make a list of steps that shows the path of oxygen from the air to the air sacs in the lungs.

3. **Think Critically!** At rest, you breathe about 15 times a minute. When you exercise, do you breathe faster or slower? Why?

Lesson 3   Care of Transport Systems

How can people keep their transport systems healthy?

Good health habits are important. A habit is something that you do regularly, like brushing your teeth. Did you brush your teeth this morning? Do you remember doing it? Often, you do not think about a habit—you just do it.

What are some other good health habits? Exercising regularly is one. Eating a good breakfast is another. Some good health habits help prevent problems with your body's systems. Many of these problems are caused by poor habits.

Transport System Problems   About 600,000 Americans die each year from heart attacks. During a heart attack, blood cannot reach some of the heart muscle cells. Without blood, the heart cells die. There are many causes of heart attacks. One cause is the clogging of arteries leading to heart cells.

Fat may clog these blood vessels. This fat is carried in the blood. Fat can stick to the inner walls of the arteries. A lot of fat on an artery's walls can make the artery very narrow. Then the flow of blood may be blocked. Through which of the arteries below could blood flow best?

Normal artery

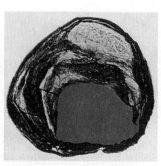
Partly clogged artery

Clogged artery

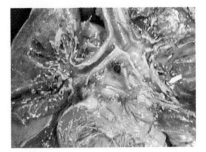
Nonsmoker's lung

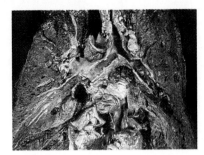
Smoker's lung

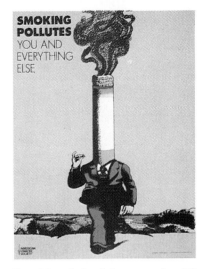

SMOKING POLLUTES YOU AND EVERYTHING ELSE

Smoking is bad for your health.

Cigarette smoke also harms the respiratory system. Smoke can cause the air sacs in the lungs to break apart. Therefore, there are fewer air sac walls through which oxygen can pass. The body cells, then, cannot get enough oxygen.

Smoking is also linked to lung cancer. Compare the two lungs shown above. Cancer cells destroyed the tissue in the smoker's lungs. Because it destroys tissue, lung cancer prevents people from getting the oxygen they need.

Healthy Transport Systems People can help their transport systems stay healthy. One way is to eat less fat. The fat in blood comes from fat in certain foods. Animal fat is an example. Dairy products and eggs also contain fat that can clog blood vessels.

People need some fat, but eating less fat may help reduce their chances of having a heart attack. Some doctors suggest that we drink skim milk instead of whole milk. Skim milk has less fat. Eating fruits and vegetables is also healthy for your heart.

Exercising and not smoking are two good health habits. Both help keep the respiratory system healthy. Exercise also helps lower the amount of fat in the blood. Exercise makes the heart stronger. A strong heart can pump more blood with each beat. Therefore, it can rest longer between beats.

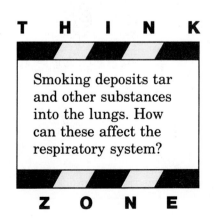

T H I N K

Smoking deposits tar and other substances into the lungs. How can these affect the respiratory system?

Z O N E

Treating Problems Sometimes the transport systems do not work properly. Sometimes, doctors can fix the parts that do not work. For example, they can usually replace damaged blood vessels. They can also help a heart with an uneven heartbeat. An artificial pacemaker can be placed inside a person's body. This device sends out electrical charges. These charges make the heart beat regularly.

Pacemaker

Pacemakers let many people have normal lives.

A person sometimes needs a new heart to stay alive. Surgeons can replace a patient's heart with a healthy heart from someone who has just died. This surgery is called a heart transplant. About 200 heart transplants are done every year in the United States. Eighty percent of heart transplant patients live for at least one year. Fifty percent live for at least five years.

Some people have kidney disease. Their kidneys do not function properly. These people use machines to filter wastes from their blood. The machines are really artificial kidneys. A person uses the machine a few times a week in a hospital. The artificial kidney cannot cure kidney disease. It is used until a kidney transplant can be done.

Building Skills: Inferring

How do clogged arteries affect blood flow?

Steps

1. Cover your desk with newspaper.

2. Using a dropper, drip some vegetable oil through a straw. Push the other straw into the animal fat. Remove the straw. Be sure some fat stays within the straw.

3. Holding a straw upright as shown in the picture, use the other dropper to drip ten drops of water through each straw. Record your observations.

4. Wash your hands when you are finished.

Questions

1. In what ways is the straw like an artery? In what ways is the water like blood?

2. What effect did each substance have on the "blood flow" through the arteries?

Materials

newspaper
2 soda straws
2 droppers
vegetable oil
uncooked animal fat

Step 3

✓ Lesson Checkup

1. How can doctors treat transport system problems?

2. How can exercise lower the risk of a heart attack?

3. **Think Critically!** Mary had some baked chicken, steamed beans, and buttered noodles for dinner. Suzanne had a hamburger with lettuce and tomato, french fries, and a glass of milk. Which meal is healthier for the heart and blood vessels? Why?

Artificial Hearts

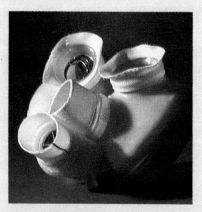

Jarvik-7 heart

An artificial heart is a machine that can replace a human heart. In 1957, the first artificial hearts were tested. They were put into dogs. One dog lived for 90 minutes. During the 1960s, these hearts were improved. One dog was kept alive for 50 hours.

In the 1970s, new types of artificial hearts were built. One was nuclear powered. Another was driven by an electric motor. Then in 1982, a retired dentist named Dr. Barney Clark became the first person in the United States to receive an artificial heart. This heart was called the Jarvik-7.

The Jarvik-7 heart is run by puffs of air. The air is supplied by a machine called a compressor. The air compressor is about the size of a grocery cart. This compressor is outside the body. It is connected to the body by two tubes. New Jarvik-7 hearts can run on a power system that fits in a shoulder bag.

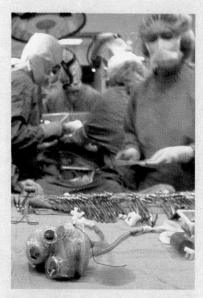

Heart surgery

Dr. Clark received the artificial heart because doctors could not fix his heart, and he was too old for a heart transplant. He lived with the Jarvik-7 heart for 112 days. Since 1982, other people have also received Jarvik-7s. William Schroeder received a Jarvik-7 heart in 1984. He lived for 620 days.

Think About It

Scientists do not agree on the use of the artificial heart. Some think that it is too risky for long term use. Others think that it should be used only until a donor heart is found for a transplant. Do you think the artificial heart should be used or not used? What more do you need to know to answer the question?

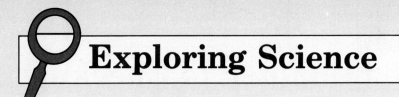

Exploring Science

Measuring Pulse

Problem: How does exercise affect your pulse?

Experimenting

1. Sit down.

2. Measure your pulse for one minute. To take your pulse, place two fingers (no thumbs) on your neck. Put your fingers under the jaw as shown in the picture. Make sure you can feel the pulse beat. Watch the second hand on the clock. Count the pulses for thirty seconds. Multiply this number by two. This is the number of heartbeats in one minute. Record the number of heartbeats on a data table like the one shown below.

3. Walk for three minutes.

4. Repeat step 2.

5. Run in place for three minutes.

6. Repeat step 2.

Recording Data

	Activity		
	Resting	**After walking**	**After running**
Heartbeats per minute			

Drawing Conclusions

1. What happened to your heartbeat after walking? After running?

2. How does exercise affect your pulse? How does your data show this?

Materials

clock to measure seconds

Step 2

Step 5

Chapter 14 Checkup

Summary

- The circulatory system delivers oxygen and nutrients to the body cells and removes wastes from these cells.

- The respiratory system brings oxygen to the blood and removes carbon dioxide from the blood.

- People can keep their transport systems healthy by eating less fat, exercising, and not smoking.

Science Words

Copy the word list. Find each word in the glossary and write its definition.

artery
bronchi
capillary
circulatory system
diaphragm
kidney
plasma
platelet
red blood cell
respiratory system
vein
white blood cell

Science Ideas

1. Number your paper from 1 to 7. Place the letter for each step of exhaling in the correct order.

   a. Air enters the throat.

   b. Carbon dioxide leaves the blood and enters the air sacs.

   c. The air moves into a long tube called the windpipe and passes through the voice box.

   d. Carbon dioxide leaves the body with the exhaled air through the nose.

   e. The diaphragm muscle relaxes when a person exhales, pushing air out of the lungs.

   f. Carbon dioxide mixes with the air in the two lungs.

   g. Air flows from the air sacs through small tubes into the bronchi.

2. Letter your paper from a to c. Write the correct term for each letter in the diagram.

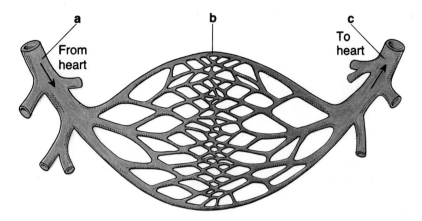

3. Look at the picture. Describe a field trip through the circulatory and respiratory systems.

Data Bank

Use the graph on page 385 to answer the following questions.

1. Which exercises are the best for improving the health of your heart and lungs?

2. What is the value of improving health by playing soccer or tennis?

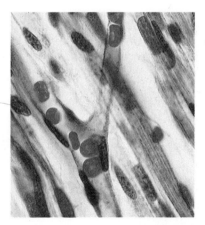

Science Ideas, Question 3

Problem Solving

When you run, your circulatory system works harder. Your respiratory system also works harder. Your breathing rate is a way to measure how hard your respiratory system works. Inhaling and exhaling count as one breath. How would you design an experiment to test if the two systems work together?

355

Chapter 15
Drugs and Your Health

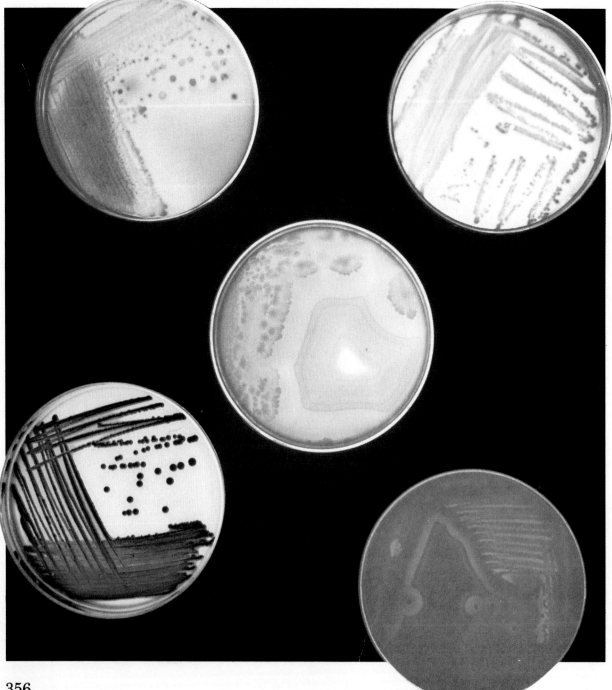

In this chapter, you will learn

- how drugs can help prevent and cure sickness

- how some types of drugs, including alcohol and tobacco, can cause harm

- how using caution and common sense about drugs can help people stay healthy

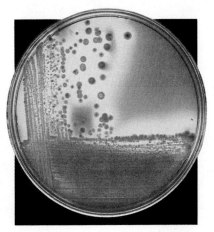

When Kelly saw mold on food, she threw the food away. She thought that since mold spoils food, it can only hurt you. While watching a television show about drugs one night, Kelly learned this is not always true.

Kelly knew germs make people sick. The program showed different germs, such as bacteria, growing in dishes. A special camera let her see the bacteria up close. The pictures show what Kelly saw.

In one dish, something kept the bacteria from spreading. The show explained that a substance made from a mold killed the bacteria.

Kelly was surprised to learn the substance could be used as a medicine. She learned that the same substance that kept bacteria from growing in the dish could stop the growth of bacteria in your body.

Kelly watched the rest of the program. She learned how drugs can be helpful and harmful. As you read this chapter, you will learn how drugs affect your health.

Lesson 1   Helpful Drugs

■ In what ways do helpful drugs differ from each other?

Long ago, people could not go to the drugstore to buy pills when they had a headache. Instead, they used substances that they found around them. For example, American Indians discovered that chewing willow bark eased pain.

Today we know that willow bark contains a substance that relieves pain. Any substance that has an effect on the way the human body works is a **drug.** Some drugs have helpful effects on the body. Others have harmful effects.

Some modern drugs are made from substances found in nature. Aspirin is a modern drug. The same pain-relieving substance found in willow bark is used in aspirin. You may have been given aspirin when you were not feeling well. In this lesson, you will learn about drugs that can help the body.

Long ago, most drugs came from plants.

Sorting pills

358

Medicines for Sickness   Exercise, a good diet, and rest are important to good health. A strong, well-nourished body can do an amazing job of staying well on its own. But sometimes even a healthy body needs help. A drug used for treating sickness, healing an injury, or easing pain is sometimes called a medicine. Some medicines must only be used with a doctor's permission. These drugs are called **prescription drugs.**

Other medicines, called **over-the-counter drugs,** do not require a doctor's prescription. These are the drugs people can buy off the shelves at supermarkets or drugstores. Some aspirins and cold medicines are over-the-counter drugs.

Effects of Drugs   Different types of drugs can help the body in different ways. The table below lists some of the ways each type of drug affects the body. These drugs can stop illness or make the body well.

Some drugs work with the body's immune system. The immune system fights infection by producing white blood cells that attack germs. These drugs are actually made from disease-causing germs. For example, **vaccines** (VAK SEENZ) are small amounts of dead or weakened germs. People take vaccines so that their immune systems will fight diseases.

Drugs That Help the Body		
Type	**Effect on body**	**Example**
Vaccine	Causes the body to produce substances that prevent disease	Polio vaccine
Antibiotic	Destroys harmful bacteria	Penicillin
Pain reliever, anesthetic	Relieves pain	Aspirin, Novocaine

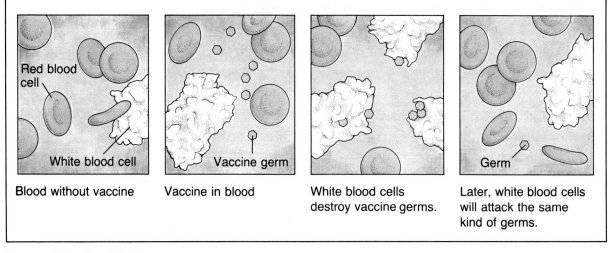

Red blood cell	Vaccine germ		Germ
White blood cell			
Blood without vaccine	Vaccine in blood	White blood cells destroy vaccine germs.	Later, white blood cells will attack the same kind of germs.

How a Vaccine Works

When a vaccine is taken, the immune system reacts to the germ. The body actually gets a mild infection. The immune system produces white blood cells that destroy the vaccine germ. Most people do not suffer from this infection because the amount of the germ is small and it is weak or dead.

Once exposed to the vaccine, the immune system "remembers" the germ. Later, if the same kind of germ enters the body, the immune system quickly produces white blood cells to destroy these germs. The person does not get sick. In this way, vaccines can prevent diseases such as measles, mumps, and polio.

Polio used to be a frightening disease. Each year it killed many people, especially children. During the 1950s, a polio vaccine was developed. Children who were given the vaccine did not get polio. You probably have taken a polio vaccine. All children entering school must take this vaccine.

When bacteria get into the body, antibiotics (AN tih by AHT ihks) may be used to fight the infection. An **antibiotic** is a drug that seeks out and destroys harmful bacteria. These drugs travel in the blood.

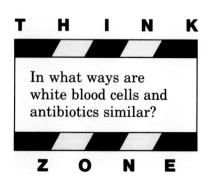

T H I N K

In what ways are white blood cells and antibiotics similar?

Z O N E

360

Penicillin is an antibiotic that kills bacteria. It is made by a mold. This mold is shown at the bottom of page 357. A doctor might prescribe penicillin when you have a sore throat caused by bacteria.

Pain relievers or **anesthetics** (AN uhs THET iks) are drugs that can reduce or remove the pain of injuries or illness. Anesthetics allow doctors to operate without the patient feeling pain. After the operation, pain relievers help prevent pain as the body heals.

Do you have fillings in your teeth? If so, you may have received an anesthetic at the dentist's office. Some dentists use Novocaine so you will not feel any pain when they are fixing your cavities.

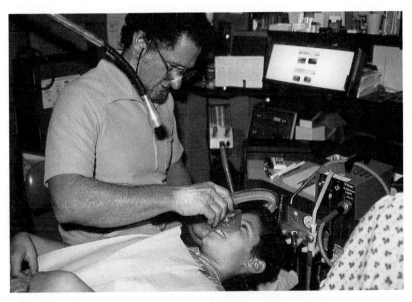

Nitrous oxide is an anesthetic used by some dentists.

Drugs: Handle With Care   Drugs, if used correctly, can help you get well and prevent illness. For a drug to help you, it is important to follow the directions on the label or from your doctor. If a label says to take a pill with meals, make sure you do. Taking that pill on an empty stomach may be harmful to you.

Warnings on labels tell you what to avoid while taking medicine. People using several medicines should be careful about taking more than one at a time. When different drugs get into the body, they may combine in harmful ways. Combining drugs with certain foods or alcohol can also be dangerous.

Drugs may act in unexpected ways. Many labels list unusual symptoms to watch for. If these symptoms occur, ask a doctor for advice. Each person reacts differently to drugs. Therefore, different people may need to take different amounts. Or, different people may need to take different drugs altogether. Because each person is different, no one should ever take a drug prescribed for someone else.

If you are not feeling well, always ask an adult to help you decide if you need medicine. The pills your parents use for headaches may be harmful to young people. Even children's aspirin can be dangerous. For this reason, all drugs should be kept in a safe place, out of reach of young children.

Care with Drugs

DO read the label.

DO NOT mix alcohol and drugs.

DO throw out old drugs.

DO NOT use a drug prescribed for someone else.

DO keep all drugs out of reach of young children.

DO NOT mix different drugs.

Building Skills: Classifying

What can you learn from the label on a drug container?

Steps

1. Read the labels of each drug container. You may have to use a dictionary to help you understand all the words.

2. Make a list of the kind of information found on all the labels. Group this information under the following headings: information about the medicine, directions for use, warnings, side effects.

Questions

1. Into what other groups could you put the information from a medicine's label? Why?

2. How do the labels on each container help you use the medicines correctly?

Materials

5 empty drug containers
dictionary

Step 1

✓ Lesson Checkup

1. What is the difference between prescription drugs and over-the-counter drugs?

2. How can a drug label protect a person taking the drug?

3. **Think Critically!** Suppose that you have a prescription for a sore throat. Your friend, Jackie, has a sore throat, too. He asks you for some pills. What would you do? Why?

Lesson 2   Harmful Drugs

■ How do the effects of harmful drugs on the body differ from each other?

In the hands of a young child, a bottle of children's aspirin can become a harmful drug. The child may think the aspirin is candy and eat enough to get dangerously sick.

Even though aspirin can do harm if it is misused, the substance is a useful medicine. But some drugs cause more harm than good. These drugs can make people sick. Harmful drugs can change the personalities of the people who use them. People using harmful drugs may hurt others and themselves.

The United States government considers most harmful drugs "controlled substances." That means it is against the law for people to use or sell the drugs. Still, some people use and sell harmful drugs. In this lesson, you will learn more about these harmful drugs.

Drugs Tried by Youths

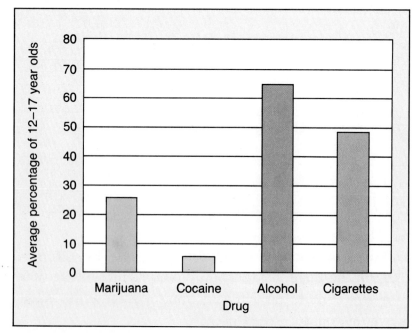

364

Would drug use change a dancer's performance?

Harmful Drugs in the Body Harmful drugs cause changes in the body. Most harmful drugs have an effect on the nervous system. Your nervous system is made up of your brain, spinal cord, and nerves. The nervous system allows you to react to your surroundings. It controls many of your body's activities.

Drugs can slow down or speed up activities controlled by the nervous system. For example, some drugs can increase the body's heart rate, breathing rate, and temperature. Other drugs can cause the nervous system to slow down these same body functions.

By affecting the nervous system, harmful drugs can change emotions. If drugs change your emotions, you may not be able to control how you act or feel.

Too much of some drugs can affect the heart so much that it stops beating. Each year many people die from drug overdoses. To take an overdose means to take too much of a drug.

Harmful drugs affect different people in different ways, just as helpful drugs do. A certain amount of a drug may have little effect on one person while causing an overdose in another.

Misused Drugs   The table on this page lists four types of misused drugs. It tells what the drugs do to the way the body works. By affecting the nervous system, harmful drugs may dull physical and emotional feelings. Or these drugs may make a person seem stronger. People who misuse drugs often become dependent on these effects.

Narcotics (nahr KOT ihks) are powerful painkillers. They numb feelings by acting on the nervous system. Narcotics can sometimes be useful in medicine. Doctors sometimes prescribe these painkilling drugs after surgery.

Morphine (MAWR FEEN) and heroin (HEHR oh uhn) are two narcotic drugs. Narcotics can slow a person's breathing rate. Users may stop breathing if they take too much of these drugs.

Another type of drug, called a **depressant,** slows down the action of the nervous system. Sleeping pills and alcohol are two common forms of depressant drugs. Depressants can cause sleepiness, slurred speech, dizziness, and poor vision.

Misused Drugs		
Type	Effect on nervous system	Example
Narcotic	Numbs feelings	Morphine, heroin
Depressant	Slows down nervous system	Alcohol, sleeping pills
Stimulant	Speeds up nervous system	Cocaine, caffeine
Hallucinogen	Causes a user to see, hear, or sense something that exists only in the mind	PCP, marijuana, LSD

A third group of misused drugs is **stimulants.**
These drugs speed up the nervous system. Two stimulants are found in common substances. **Nicotine** (NIK uh TEEN) is a stimulant found in tobacco smoke. People who use tobacco may cough or suffer from shortness of breath. Nicotine, tar, and other substances in cigarettes may cause cancer and lung diseases.

Caffeine (KAF EEN) is another stimulant. It is found in coffee, tea, chocolate, and other foods. Caffeine can cause nervousness, sleep problems, and loss of appetite.

Normal spider web

After spider given caffeine

The fourth group of harmful drugs changes the way users understand the world around them. These drugs are called **hallucinogens** (huh LOO sn uh jenz). LSD and marijuana (MAR uh WAH nuh) are hallucinogens.

When using a hallucinogen, a user may not be able to tell the difference between what is real and what is imaginary. People who use hallucinogens may have trouble remembering things. They may feel anxious and unhappy. Some hallucinogens cause changes in behavior, such as violent rages, long after the drug has been taken.

T H I N K

Some people always drink a cup of tea or coffee in the morning. Why do you think they have this habit?

Z O N E

What is Addiction?   People who misuse or abuse drugs often become dependent on the drugs' effects. In other words, the person may feel he or she must take the drug often. People who misuse harmful drugs can become dependent on them quickly.

The more a drug is used, the less effect the drug has on the body. The effect lasts for a shorter and shorter length of time. As a result, users take more of the drug each day. This dependency can become an addiction.

A person addicted to a drug needs to use the drug over and over again. Once a user is addicted to or dependent on drugs, it is very hard to stop. If he or she does not get the drug, chills or fever may make the person feel very sick. The user may need help to stop the habit.

Drug users often lose interest in normal relationships and activities. The desire to use drugs may become more important to the user than family or friends. To pay for the drugs, some users steal from their family and friends. Rather than join family activities, some users prefer to be alone.

Cigarettes contain nicotine, an addictive drug.

How much money do smokers spend on their habit?

Steps

1. Find out how much a pack of cigarettes costs.

2. Estimate how much a smoker spends each year on cigarettes if he or she smokes one pack a week.

3. Repeat step 2 for five and ten pack a week habits.

4. Using a catalog, list some things each smoker could have bought with the money he or she spent on the cigarettes.

Questions

1. How much did each person spend? How much did the three smokers spend altogether?

2. What are some items that each person could have bought from the catalogs? What items could the three smokers have bought together?

Materials

department store catalog

Step 4

✓ Lesson Checkup

1. Why do some laws control the sale and use of certain drugs?

2. Describe the physical effects of narcotics, depressants, stimulants, and hallucinogens.

3. **Think Critically!** Some people drink alcohol and smoke cigarettes at the same time. Why might the combined effects of these substances be harmful to the body?

Lesson 3   Drug Choice and Health

■ How can you prevent drug abuse?

When you read about the harmful effects of drugs, you probably say, "I'll never try that stuff." But it takes strength not to try drugs, tobacco, and alcohol—especially when other people your age are doing it. They may tell you that it is exciting or it makes them feel grown up.

Still, it is much easier for people to avoid drugs than it is to overcome an addiction to drugs. In this lesson, you will learn some ways to say no to drugs.

Why People Start   Every year people in America spend millions of dollars on drugs, alcohol, and tobacco. Look at the graph below. In 1982, Americans spent more than $75 billion on these products. Each year these numbers grow.

Increase in Drug, Alcohol, and Tobacco Sales

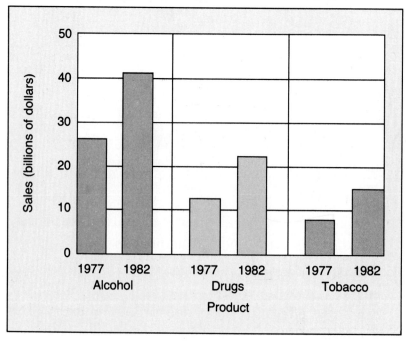

It is not easy to explain why people use harmful substances. Curiosity may make some people start. Friends can influence drug use, too. When someone sees that other people are trying something, he or she may feel left out. "If everyone else is doing it, why not me?" that person may ask.

In our society, alcohol, tobacco, and some drugs are easy to get. Advertisements may suggest that using them will make us feel happier, look "cool," or feel more relaxed. This advertising is hard to ignore.

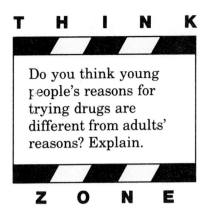

T H I N K

Do you think young people's reasons for trying drugs are different from adults' reasons? Explain.

Z O N E

Learning to Say No   The first step in avoiding drug abuse is not to start. You must want to say no. But saying no can be difficult. You need to prepare yourself for dealing with people who might ask you to try drugs. The steps that follow may help you say no.

1. *List* reasons not to use drugs.

2. *Plan* what you will say ahead of time. Have a reason to refuse. Understand how the body works and how drug use can interfere with health.

Student learning to avoid drug abuse

371

3. *Think* of situations where you might find drugs. How will you handle these situations? If someone invites you to a party where you think people will be using drugs, you can refuse to go. Remember, your real friends will like you even if you do not try drugs.

4. *Consider* other things to do instead of using drugs. Be ready to suggest these alternatives. Check the drawings on this page for some ideas.

5. *Practice* your answers to people who offer you drugs, alcohol, or tobacco. You can learn to say no. Say that you know the substance is bad for you. Say that you have something else you would rather do right then. Say no. Try changing the subject or suggesting another activity. If the person insists, say no again. Your refusal might make the person think twice about using the substance.

Other Things to Do Instead of Using Drugs

Play

Hike

Dance

Talk

Listen to music

Nothing

Building Skills: Inferring

How does advertising influence people?

Steps

1. Collect drug, tobacco, and alcohol advertisements from magazines.

2. Discuss the methods the ads use to sell their products. Look for happy faces, slogans, and movie stars in the ads. Check if the ads tell what the product is, how it works, or how it was made. Think about how the ads influence your feelings.

3. Pretend you are an advertising genius. Design an anti-smoking, anti-drug, or anti-alcohol campaign. Create slogans, jingles, and posters.

Questions

1. What do the advertisers suggest will happen if you use their products? Do you think the claims are true? Why or why not?

2. Compare your ads to the magazine ads.

Materials

magazines
markers or paints
poster board
cassette recorder
cassette tape
scissors

Step 3

✓ Lesson Checkup

1. Explain the reasons why people begin using drugs, alcohol, and tobacco.

2. What is the first step in avoiding drug abuse?

3. **Think Critically!** If the most popular person in school asked you to drink a beer, smoke a cigarette, or take some pills, how would you say no?

New Ways to Make Drugs

A new technology changes bacteria into "factories" for making useful drugs. To do this, the technology changes a cell's genes.

All living creatures have cells that contain genes. Genes control the many traits, or features, of an organism. The information in a gene determines what an organism will be like. For example, genes determine if a baby will have red hair or black hair.

In this new technology, scientists transfer genes from one cell to another. This process is called genetic engineering. In the pictures at the left, a gene from a firefly was transferred to a plant. The plant now can "glow" in the dark.

Genetic engineering is an effective way to make useful substances, such as human growth hormone. Human growth hormone, or HGH, controls growth during childhood. Some people's bodies make too little of this substance. A supply of HGH can help children with this disorder. But HGH is difficult to get.

Some scientists can now join a human gene for making HGH with genes from bacteria. When the bacteria reproduce, the new bacteria can produce HGH. These new bacteria could increase the HGH supply and help children with HGH disorders.

Think About It

With genetic engineering, many people fear scientists might create new forms of life. Others feel the technology is exciting and useful. Do you think genetic engineering is dangerous? Why? If you needed HGH, would you feel differently about genetic engineering?

Scientists gave this plant firefly genes.

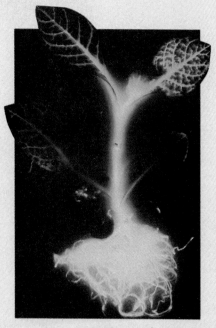

Same plant showing the effects of its firefly genes

374

Exploring Science

Comparing the Spread of Germs

Problem: How can you stop germs from spreading?

Experimenting

1. Label four self-lock bags 1 through 4.

2. ◇ **SHARP!** Cut the fresh apple into four parts. Put one apple section in bag 1.

3. Rub the decaying apple over the three remaining apple sections. Throw away the bad apple. Wash your hands with soap and water.

4. Wash one apple section with soap and water. Dry this apple well and put it in bag 2.

5. Rub another apple section with alcohol. Put it in bag 3.

6. Do nothing more to the last apple section. Place it in bag 4.

7. Store all the bags in a dark place for one week.

8. After a week, look at the apples. Compare apples 1 through 4. Record your observations.

Recording Data

Bag	Observations
1	
2	

Materials

4 self-lock bags
labels
decaying apple
fresh apple
plastic knife
soap
water
alcohol
paper towels

Step 4

Drawing Conclusions

1. What caused the changes you saw?

2. Based on this activity, why do you think it is important to wash your hands before eating?

375

Chapter 15 Checkup

Summary

- Drugs can help prevent and cure sickness by working with the body's immune system, destroying harmful bacteria, or relieving pain.

- Some drugs, including alcohol and tobacco, can cause harm to users by affecting the nervous system or changing the way the users understand the world around them.

- By learning to say no, people can avoid the physical and emotional problems caused by harmful drugs.

Science Words

Copy the words. Define each word in a sentence.

anesthetic
antibiotic
caffeine
depressant
drug
hallucinogen
narcotic
nicotine
over-the-counter drug
prescription drug
stimulant
vaccine

Science Ideas

1. Letter your paper from a to f. Write the cause and effect for each statement.

   a. Antibiotics fight infection by traveling in the blood, seeking out harmful bacteria, and destroying them.

   b. When you use helpful drugs correctly, you can prevent illness or get well.

   c. People who use or sell controlled substances break the law.

   d. Your nervous system can be harmed if you use harmful drugs.

   e. Use of harmful drugs can become more important than other needs.

   f. You can avoid drug abuse by not starting.

2. Letter your paper from a to c. Use the label below to answer the following questions.

   a. What is the correct dose for children?

   b. What cautions are listed?

   c. For what is this drug used?

ASPIRIN
ANALGESIC
For relief from headache, colds, and muscle aches.
DOSE: Adults and children over 12 years, 1 or 2 tablets with water. Children under 12, see doctor.
WARNING: Contact a doctor before giving to children with chicken pox or flu.

3. Look at the picture. What kind of drug attacks harmful bacteria? Name three other helpful drugs.

Data Bank

Use the table on page 385 to answer the following questions.

1. How many milligrams of caffeine are in a cola drink?

2. If you ate two chocolate bars, how many milligrams of caffeine would you eat?

3. Which substance listed contains the most caffeine? The least?

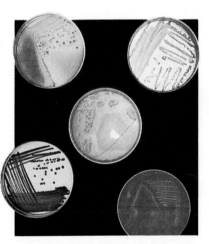

Science Ideas, Question 3

Problem Solving

Millions of dollars are spent trying to stop the use of harmful drugs and the crime that is associated with illegal drugs. In what ways can our society slow or stop the use of harmful drugs? What plan do you think would work the best? Give your reasons.

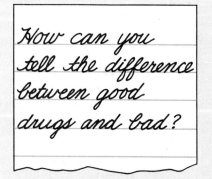

How can you tell the difference between good drugs and bad?

Dr. Cynthia F. Tricou's class at Southeastern University Lab School in Hammond, Louisiana

Dr. John Gavin is a scientist who works for a research company in Germantown, Maryland. Dr. Gavin has a Ph.D. degree in microbiology. For many years, he worked for a drug company. He helped discover and make many different kinds of drugs.

Dr. Gavin is deaf and uses a wheelchair. As you might expect, this often causes problems for him. But Dr. Gavin has not let his disability stop him from being a success in life. He has done important research, has written many scientific articles, and has helped write several books.

Dr. Gavin says good drugs are those that make sick people feel better and help them get well. Bad drugs are those that cause harm to people who take them.

Sometimes, however, there is no easy way to tell a good drug from a bad one. Good drugs can become bad drugs if they are used incorrectly. A good drug can have a bad effect if a person takes too much of it. Also, a drug that may be good for one person may be bad for another. Drugs that are usually considered good drugs can cause bad effects in certain people.

Drugs can be very helpful. However, they can also be very dangerous and harmful. It is important that we make sure to take only the good drugs and stay away from the bad ones. Illegal drugs that are sold by drug dealers are bad drugs. Using these kinds of drugs can be very dangerous. Using these drugs can make a person develop a need for more and more drugs. These drugs can even kill someone who uses them. Never take drugs given to you by another student or someone you do not know. Only take drugs that your parents, a doctor, or a nurse gives you.

Dr. John Gavin

Careers & Science

Emergency Medical Technician   You may have seen a team of workers helping at the scene of an accident. These are emergency medical technicians, also called EMTs. They give first aid to injured people and help transport them to hospitals. They keep radio contact with doctors at the hospital for instructions on how best to help the victims. To become an EMT, you need on-the-job training after high school.

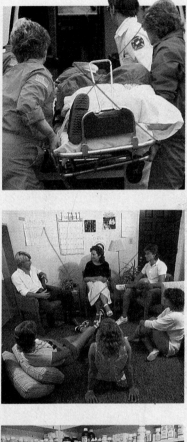

Drug Rehabilitation Counselor   People trying to break a drug habit may be helped by drug rehabilitation counselors. These counselors help people after the people leave the care of a doctor. The counselors listen to their personal problems and give help and support. They also help the people learn new jobs. Later, the counselors help them find jobs. The work of a rehabilitation counselor is difficult but can be rewarding. Many states require a college degree in counseling or social work for this career.

Pharmacist   Prescriptions from a doctor or a dentist are taken to a pharmacy. Pharmacists (FAHR muh sihsts) fill the prescriptions for the medicine requested by the doctor. They are careful to measure and prepare the correct amount. Pharmacists write labels with instructions on how often and when to take the medicine. On the label, they record the date, the number of the prescription, the name of the person taking it, and the name of the doctor. This record is kept on file to protect the person's health. To become a pharmacist, you must receive a degree from a four-year college of pharmacology.

Thinking Critically

Predicting

Before you decide to do something, it is always important to think about the consequences, or results, of what you are considering. You might want to go to a movie tonight. But you realize that if you do, you will not have enough time to do your homework. So you decide not to go to the movie till the weekend. This is because you thought about some of the consequences of going to the movie. When you did this, you tried to predict what would happen if you went. Predicting is a thinking skill.

Good prediction is not just guessing what will happen. You should always try to have good reasons for your predictions. When your reasons are good, you can say that the things you predict are likely to happen. If your reasons are not good, you could make a bad prediction. That could lead you to make a bad decision about what to do.

1 | Practicing the Skill

After studying about safety in class, Sally went home and talked to her parents about cleaning out the medicine cabinet. They said they would do it when they got a chance.

Sally wanted to convince her parents that it was important to clean out the medicine cabinet. So she made a chart of things that might happen if they did not clean it. Look at the chart on page 381. Sally wrote two possible consequences of not cleaning the cabinet.

What other consequences can you predict that could be added to Sally's chart? Pick one of these possible consequences. If you were Sally, what reasons would you give your parents to convince them that this consequence is likely to happen? What might make them feel that this consequence is unlikely to happen?

Suppose you have a younger brother who likes to get into cabinets and chew on things. What do you predict is likely to happen if:

a. Something in the medicine cabinet says "For External Use Only"?

b. There are just bandages and empty bottles in the medicine cabinet?

List your reasons for each prediction you gave above.

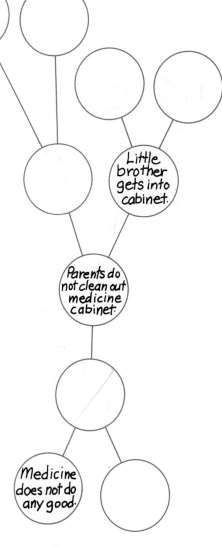

2 | Thinking About Thinking

When you made the list, what did you think about to predict what might happen? There are things you did not list because you thought that they probably would not happen. Pick one thing that you left out and tell why you left it out. What would you tell Sally to do to make sure that she was not just guessing about her predictions?

3 | Using the Skill

Think of something that you want to do this weekend. Predict what might happen if you do it. Do you have any reason for thinking that any of these possible consequences is likely to happen? What are your reasons?

Data Bank

Chapter 4
Wetlands of the World

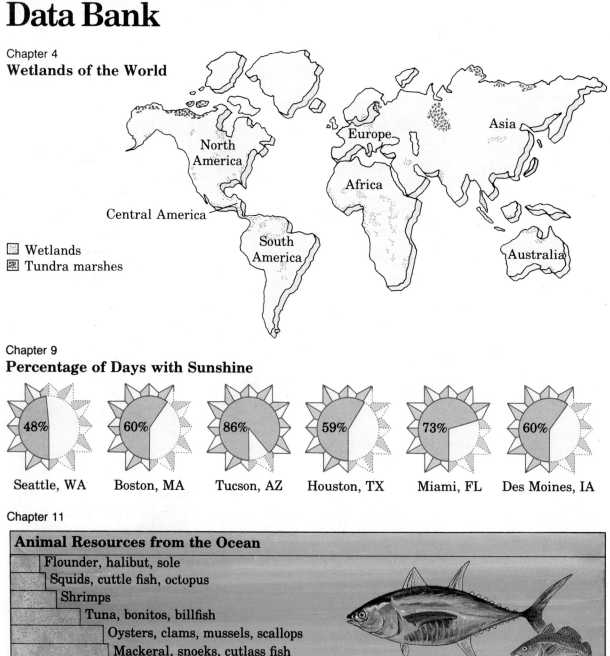

North America

Europe

Asia

Africa

Central America

South America

Australia

☐ Wetlands
☒ Tundra marshes

Chapter 9
Percentage of Days with Sunshine

48%	60%	86%	59%	73%	60%
Seattle, WA	Boston, MA	Tucson, AZ	Houston, TX	Miami, FL	Des Moines, IA

Chapter 11

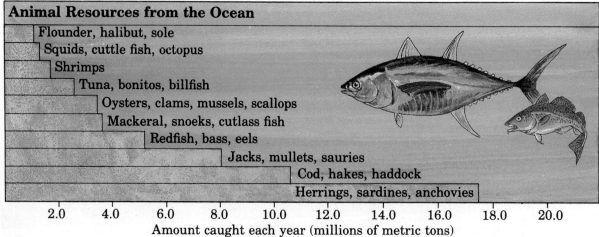

Animal Resources from the Ocean

- Flounder, halibut, sole
- Squids, cuttle fish, octopus
- Shrimps
- Tuna, bonitos, billfish
- Oysters, clams, mussels, scallops
- Mackeral, snoeks, cutlass fish
- Redfish, bass, eels
- Jacks, mullets, sauries
- Cod, hakes, haddock
- Herrings, sardines, anchovies

2.0 4.0 6.0 8.0 10.0 12.0 14.0 16.0 18.0 20.0

Amount caught each year (millions of metric tons)

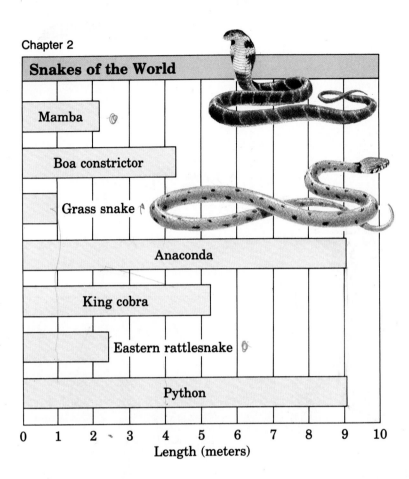

Chapter 2
Snakes of the World

Snake	Length (meters)
Mamba	
Boa constrictor	
Grass snake	
Anaconda	
King cobra	
Eastern rattlesnake	
Python	

0 1 2 3 4 5 6 7 8 9 10
Length (meters)

Chapter 5
Spices from Tropical Plants

Spice	Place grown
Allspice	Mexico, Central America
Cinnamon	Southeast Asia, India
Clove	Malagasy Republic, Zanzibar, Indonesia
Nutmeg	Indonesia, Grenada, Sri Lanka
Pepper	India, all tropical regions
Vanilla	Mexico, Indonesia, Malagasy Republic

Chapter 1
The Animal Kingdom

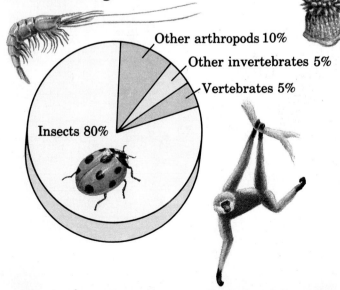

Other arthropods 10%
Other invertebrates 5%
Vertebrates 5%
Insects 80%

Chapter 10
Time Clock of Animal Life
(Millions of years)

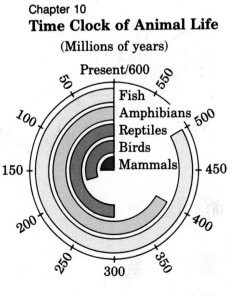

Present/600
Fish
Amphibians
Reptiles
Birds
Mammals

50 100 150 200 250 300 350 400 450 500 550

Chapter 12

Diameters from Different Types of Weather

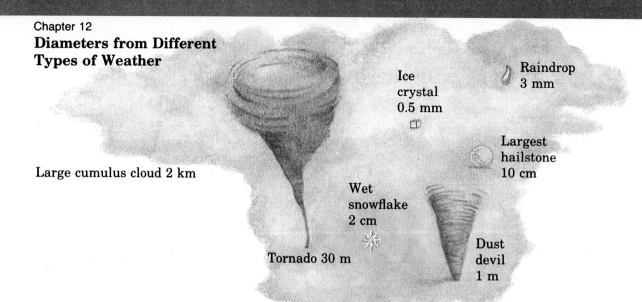

Large cumulus cloud 2 km

Ice crystal 0.5 mm

Raindrop 3 mm

Largest hailstone 10 cm

Wet snowflake 2 cm

Tornado 30 m

Dust devil 1 m

Chapter 8

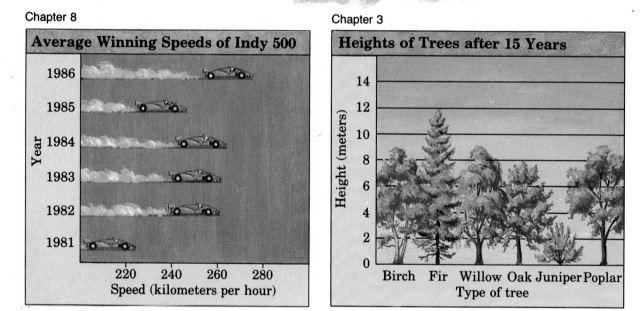

Average Winning Speeds of Indy 500

Year

1986
1985
1984
1983
1982
1981

220 240 260 280
Speed (kilometers per hour)

Chapter 3

Heights of Trees after 15 Years

Height (meters)

14
12
10
8
6
4
2
0

Birch Fir Willow Oak Juniper Poplar
Type of tree

Chapter 6

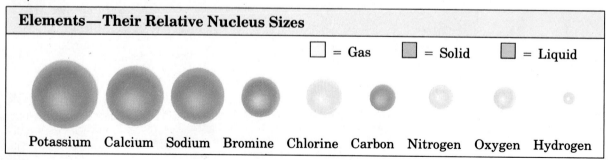

Elements—Their Relative Nucleus Sizes

□ = Gas   ■ = Solid   ▨ = Liquid

Potassium Calcium Sodium Bromine Chlorine Carbon Nitrogen Oxygen Hydrogen

Hearing Ranges of Animals

Animal	Sound frequency ranges (cycles per second)
Crocodile	20–6,000
Human	20–20,000
Cat	20–60,000
Lizard	70–8,000
Wood Turtle	100–5,000
Finch	100–8,000
Katydid	100–100,000

Caffeine in Commonly-Used Substances

Substance	Number of milligrams
Coffee	64–124
Tea	30–48
Cocoa	5–40
Cola drink	32–65
Chocolate bar	5–25
Stay-awake pill	100
Cold medicine	16–32
Headache tablet	65
Diet pill	50

Value of Exercise for the Heart and Lungs

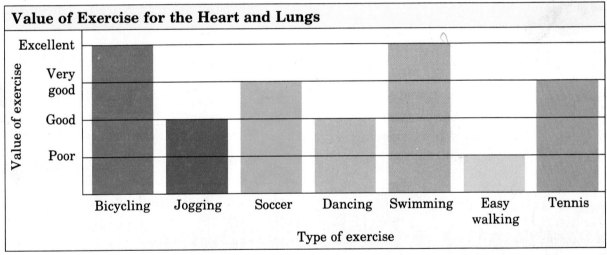

Value of exercise: Excellent, Very good, Good, Poor

Type of exercise: Bicycling, Jogging, Soccer, Dancing, Swimming, Easy walking, Tennis

Chapter 13

Standard Time Zones

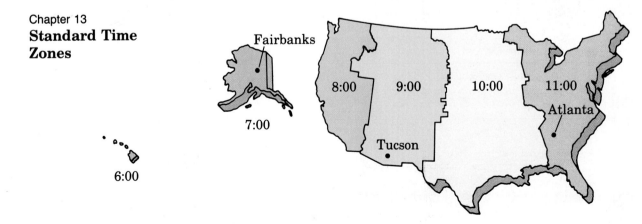

Fairbanks
7:00
6:00
8:00   9:00   10:00   11:00
Tucson
Atlanta

Science Fair

"How did you gather your data in this experiment?" asked Ms. Stewart, a science fair judge.

"I was playing with my toy race car," Paul said. "I wondered if the car was heavier, would it go farther?" Paul described his hypothesis and how he gathered his data. When Paul finished, Ms. Stewart moved to the next science fair project.

"Tell me about your project," she said as she studied the exhibit.

"I want to be a pilot someday," Linda said, "so I made a model of a jet engine." Then she explained how it worked. Linda tried to answer all of Ms. Stewart's questions.

Ms. Stewart approached Karen next. Karen was surrounded by colorful posters she had made. "What did you learn from this project?" Ms. Stewart asked.

"I did research about different kinds of exercise," Karen said. She pointed to the posters as she began to explain.

Ms. Stewart told Karen, "I need to get more exercise myself," before moving on to Ted's project. There was an assortment of soda cans on the table. "What is your project?" Ms. Stewart asked.

"I invented a way to close soda cans after they are opened, so the soda doesn't lose its fizz." Ted explained his invention, then gave Ms. Stewart a sample of soda from a can that was opened the day before.

After the science fair, Ms. Stewart told one of the teachers, "Your students had some great projects. Where did they get their ideas?"

"Well, I told them to look for ideas in the world around them," the teacher said, "—at the zoo, on TV, in books and magazines, or at home for example. The main thing was to choose a project they were really interested in."

You may have a chance to do a science fair project. Maybe you, like Paul, have a question that an **experiment** could answer. You may want to know how something works, like Linda, so you could **make a model.** Perhaps, like Karen, there is an activity you enjoy that you can **research.** Maybe you know of a problem, like Ted, that an **invention** could solve. Or you may have an idea for a different kind of project.

Whatever project you choose, follow these steps.

1. Think of something you want to know more about. Or think of a problem to solve. Make that the purpose of your project.

2. Plan your project. Make a list of the steps you will follow. List all the materials you will need.

3. Collect the materials and begin. Follow your plan. Record any information you collect.

4. Make your display. Show what you did and what you learned. Include these things in the display: purpose, plan, information.

Chapter 1 Double Check

Lesson 1 Review

1. Are people invertebrates or vertebrates? How can you tell? (p. 18)

2. How are hollow-bodied animals and sponges similar? Different? (p. 19)

3. What does it mean to say that segmented worms are more complex than flatworms and roundworms? (p. 21)

Lesson 2 Review

1. Look at the drawings below. How do the mantles and feet of the three mollusks differ? (p. 25)

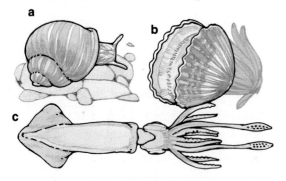

2. How are mollusks and spiny-skinned animals similar? Different? (p. 25)

3. What body parts of a starfish let it pull open a scallop to eat the soft meat inside? (p. 26)

Lesson 3 Review

1. Why must arthropods molt? (p. 29)

2. Look at the drawings below. Classify each animal into one of the five arthropod groups. (p. 34)

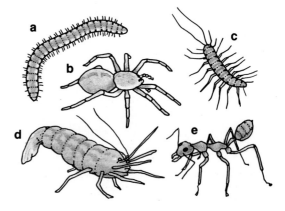

3. Suppose you found an animal in your back yard that had three body segments, two antennas, six legs, and four wings. How would you classify this animal? Why? (p. 34)

Science Projects

1. Working in a group, draw a mural that shows the different kinds of invertebrates and how they are classified.

2. Nervous systems control body senses such as seeing and feeling. Design an experiment to show that a snail has a simple nervous system.

Chapter 2 Double Check

Lesson 1 Review

1. How does an endoskeleton differ from an exoskeleton? Which do you have? (p. 42)

2. If the water temperature in a fishbowl increases, what happens to the body temperatures of the fish in the water? (p. 43)

3. Which main group of fish have air bladders? Why? (p. 44)

Lesson 2 Review

1. In what ways do salamanders and toads differ? (p. 47, p. 48)

2. Classify each animal below into one of the four reptile groups. How does one group differ from the other? (p. 49)

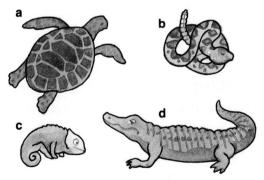

3. If a lizard's body temperature gets too cold, how can the lizard warm itself? If it gets too hot, how can the lizard cool itself? (p. 49)

Lesson 3 Review

1. How do the bones of a bird differ from the bones of a mammal? How does this help the bird? (p. 53)

2. What are three main groups of mammals, based on how their young develop? (p. 56)

3. Which drawing shows the teeth of a carnivore? Of a herbivore? (p. 57)

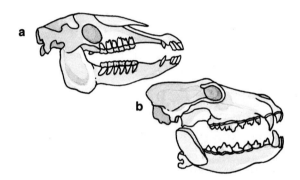

Science Projects

1. There are interesting stories about the egg laying and hatchings of turtles, alligators, and crocodiles. See what stories you can find. Share your findings in class.

2. Investigate an area of the world where it is very hot or very cold. What kinds of animals live there? What do they eat? Present your findings in a way that your classmates will enjoy.

Chapter 3 Double Check

Lesson 1 Review

1. Why can all the food that you eat be traced back to plants? (p. 66)

2. To make sugar, what three things do plants need from their environment? (p. 66)

3. What two functions do a plant's roots perform? (p. 67)

4. How are the xylem and phloem of a plant similar? Different? (p. 68)

5. Look at the drawing below. Label the parts of the leaf. (p. 70)

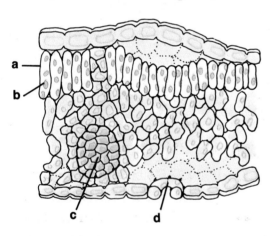

6. What are the products of photosynthesis? (p. 71)

Lesson 2 Review

1. How is the energy in food released so that it can be used by living things? (p. 74)

2. What are the waste products of respiration? (p. 75)

3. Which one of the following drawings represents photosynthesis? Which drawing represents respiration? (p. 75)

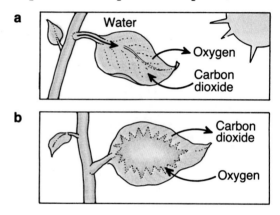

4. Draw a picture that shows how oxygen and carbon dioxide recycle in nature. (p. 76)

Science Projects

1. Make a list of foods from plants that you ate yesterday. In each case, tell the plant part in which the food energy was stored.

2. Make believe you receive seeds but you do not know what kind of plant they are from. Design an experiment to find out what conditions are best for that kind of plant.

Chapter 4 Double Check

Lesson 1 Review

1. What nonliving things limit the size and number of populations in a community? (p. 86)

2. Identify the following organisms as producers, consumers, predators, or prey. (p. 87)

3. Draw and label an energy pyramid that includes third-level consumers. (p. 88)

Lesson 2 Review

1. Draw a picture that shows how water recycles in nature. (p. 90)

2. How does nitrogen get from the air into plants and animals? (p. 92)

3. In the drawing below, which letter stands for oxygen? Carbon dioxide? (p. 91)

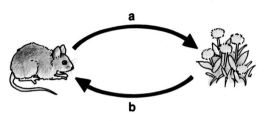

Lesson 3 Review

1. Name four things that can change an ecosystem. (p. 94)

2. What is a climax community? (p. 95)

3. Give an example of a slow succession. (p. 96)

Science Projects

1. Find at least one ecosystem near your home. What kinds of things live there? What conditions cause those things to live there? Draw this ecosystem. Label the living and nonliving things in it.

2. List conditions for a make-believe ecosystem. Exchange your list with a partner. Fill in the names of plants and animals that would live in each ecosystem.

Chapter 5 Double Check

Lesson 1 Review

1. What are the six major biomes on the earth? (p. 105)

2. Which two biomes receive the least rainfall in a year? (p. 107)

3. How does climate affect the plants and animals in a biome? (p. 108)

Lesson 2 Review

1. What nonliving condition causes cone-bearing trees to be common to the taiga but not the tundra? (p. 107, p. 112)

2. Classify the leaf and cone below as belonging to the taiga or the temperate forest. (p. 112, p. 113)

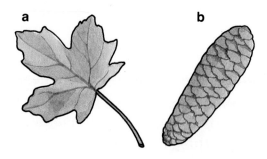

3. What must desert plants and animals be able to do in order to survive? (p. 116)

4. How can red foxes and weasels live in the grasslands if they do not eat grass? (p. 118)

Lesson 3 Review

1. What affects the plants and animals of a water ecosystem more—temperature or light? (p. 121)

2. Where in a pond would you expect to find more plants—near the surface or the bottom? Why? (p. 122)

3. Write the letter of the organism drawn below that does not belong to a tide pool ecosystem. (p. 123)

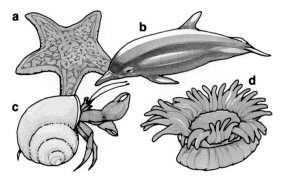

Science Projects

1. Bring some house plants to school. For each plant, tell what growing conditions are best for it. Based on that information, in what biome would you expect to find each plant? Make an exhibit of this.

2. Collect pictures of animals from different biomes. Compare the body coverings, body shapes, and other features that help each animal survive in its biome.

Chapter 6 Double Check

Lesson 1 Review

1. Compare the properties of metals and nonmetals. (p. 140)

2. Why is there more than one model of the atom? (p. 141)

3. If an atom has six electrons, six protons, and six neutrons, is the atom positive, negative, or neutral? (p. 141, p. 142)

Lesson 2 Review

1. Are more elements or compounds found in nature? Explain. (p. 144)

2. What are two ways in which atoms may form chemical bonds? Give an example of each. (p. 146)

3. Write the chemical formula for each molecule or ion drawn below. (p. 148)

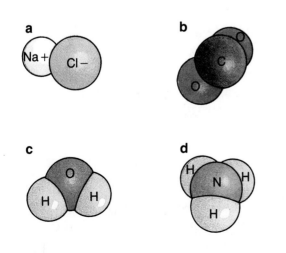

Lesson 3 Review

1. Compare the properties of mixtures and compounds. (p. 145, p. 151)

2. Give an example of a liquid solution, a solid solution, and a gas solution. (p. 153)

3. Which drawing below shows a solution? A suspension? (p. 152, p. 154)

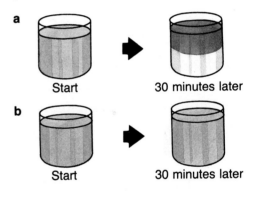

Science Projects

1. Look at a table that lists the elements. Choose several elements from the table that interest you. For each symbol, find out the word it stands for and what that word means.

2. Pick an element or substance to research. Where is it found? How is it obtained? What is it used for? Present your findings to the class.

Chapter 7 Double Check

Lesson 1 Review

1. How is the sound of a drum produced? (p. 163)

2. Why can sound travel only through matter? (p. 164)

3. How could you cut down the amount of echo in a room? (p. 166)

4. How can sound be used to determine the location of objects? (p. 166)

Lesson 2 Review

1. The human ear can distinguish among 400,000 different sounds. How can there be so many? (p. 168)

2. What are three features of every sound wave? (p. 168)

3. What feature of a sound wave is marked below? (p. 168)

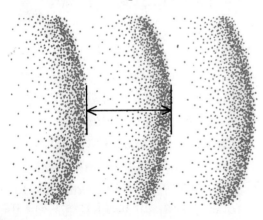

4. What are decibels? (p. 171)

Lesson 3 Review

1. How are the sounds of the human voice produced? (p. 174)

2. Put the letters in the correct order to trace the sound of a bell from the bell to your brain. (p. 176)

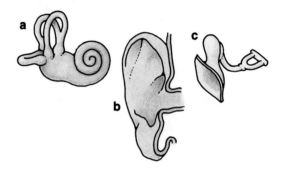

3. How do ear plugs prevent ear injury? (p. 178)

Science Projects

1. Visit a library and research the sounds you often hear. List the sounds and their decibel values from softest to loudest. Indicate which sounds can be harmful to your ears. Share this information with your classmates.

2. Compare the major groups of musical instruments in a band or orchestra. How do the woodwinds produce sound? The strings? The brass? The percussion instruments?

Chapter 8 Double Check

Lesson 1 Review

1. Write the letter of the reference object in the drawing below. (p. 186)

2. Suppose you visited your grandparents who live 200 kilometers from your home. If it took you two hours to get there, what was your speed? (p. 187)

3. Give three examples of acceleration in a car. (p. 188)

Lesson 2 Review

1. According to Newton's first law of motion, what is needed in order to make something move? (p. 191)

2. According to Newton's second law, what happens to the speed of an object if its mass increases but the force causing the motion remains constant? (p. 192)

3. Look at the drawing below. How is the motion of the balloon like the motion of a rocket? (p. 194)

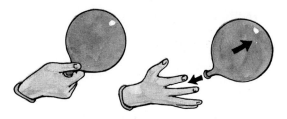

Lesson 3 Review

1. If all objects are drawn toward each other, why do objects move toward the earth's center rather than toward each other? (p. 197)

2. What would happen to a person's weight if the force of gravity were to change? What would happen to the person's mass? (p. 198)

3. How is friction helpful? How is it not helpful? (p. 199, p. 200)

Science Projects

1. Design an experiment that shows someone what Newton's second law of motion means.

2. Choose something that interests you such as animals, athletes, planes, or cars. Find the fastest speeds that different members in your category have reached.

Chapter 9 Double Check

Lesson 1 Review

1. Which drawing below shows the correct way energy in food can be traced from the sun? (p. 209)

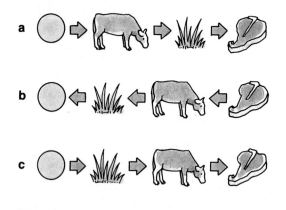

2. Why is oil a nonrenewable source of energy? (p. 210)

3. Why are coal, oil, and natural gas called fossil fuels? (p. 211)

4. What is nuclear fission? (p. 214)

Lesson 2 Review

1. How is water used in solar heating? (p. 217)

2. What are some advantages of using geothermal heat as a source of energy? (p. 218)

3. How can the tides be used as a source of energy? (p. 219)

4. How can biomass be used as a source of energy? (p. 219)

Lesson 3 Review

1. How much of the energy used in homes is spent in heating and cooling? (p. 223)

2. Write the letter of the drawing below that does not show a way to save energy. (p. 223)

3. How can using trains and buses save energy? (p. 224)

4. How can recycling aluminum cans save energy? (p. 224)

Science Projects

1. Make posters that show how people can save energy at home and at school. Display these posters in your school.

2. Suppose that a nuclear power plant will be built near your town. Present reasons for and against such a plant.

Chapter 10 Double Check

Lesson 1 Review

1. How are sandstone, shale, and limestone similar? How are they different? (p. 239)

2. In sedimentary rock, would you expect to find the oldest layers at the top or bottom? Explain. (p. 240)

3. Which drawing below is a fossil cast? A fossil mold? (p. 241)

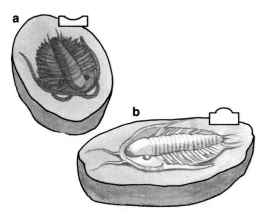

4. Describe several kinds of fossils that would indicate that a rabbit once lived in a certain place. (p. 242, p. 243)

5. Is a petrified tree made of wood or rock? (p. 242)

6. Why are fossils of trilobites useful to scientists? (p. 243)

7. How can a seashell fossil found on land be a clue of changes in the earth's surface? (p. 244)

Lesson 2 Review

1. List the four geologic eras from oldest to most recent. (p. 246)

2. Why are fossils from the Precambrian Era hard to find? (p. 247)

3. Look at the drawings. Write the letter of the living thing that does not belong to the Mesozoic Era. (p. 248, p. 249, p. 250)

Science Projects

1. Make a model that shows how rock layers can be used to determine comparative ages of rocks as well as the ages of plant and animal fossils.

2. Find out about the place where you live. What kind of rock is under your town or city? How old is this rock? What kinds of fossils does it contain? What can you infer about the conditions there long ago?

Chapter 11 Double Check

Lesson 1 Review

1. Where did the salt in sea water come from? How might this have happened? (p. 261)

2. Compare the causes of surface currents and deep water currents. (p. 264, p. 265)

3. If you are at a beach, how can you tell whether the tide is coming in or going out? (p. 266)

Lesson 2 Review

1. How have scientists been able to use sound and light to learn about the ocean bottom? (p. 269)

2. Why does the continental shelf provide some of the best fishing areas in the world? (p. 270)

3. In the drawing below, which letter labels a seamount? A trench? (p. 272, p. 273)

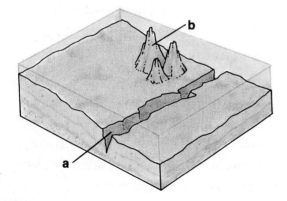

Lesson 3 Review

1. What is table salt and how do some people obtain it? (p. 276)

2. Which drawing below is not an ocean resource? (p. 277, p. 278)

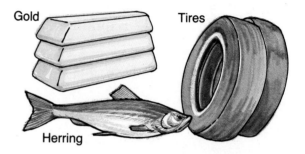

Gold   Tires

Herring

3. How can pollution of sea water affect the world's food supply? (p. 278)

Science Projects

1. Make a model or diorama of the ocean floor. Try to show a variety of features. Add some of your favorite kinds of underwater plants and animals.

2. Put an object in the bottom of a container of cloudy, murky water. Make sure no one knows what the object is or can see it through the water. Using a weighted string and measuring depths at various locations, have your classmates try to guess what the object is.

Chapter 12 Double Check

Lesson 1 Review

1. How does air get warm? (p. 287)

2. How do winds form? (p. 287)

3. Which is usually more humid, warm air or cold air? Why? (p. 288)

4. What are the three main types of clouds? (p. 289)

5. Look at the maps below. Which one is correct? (p. 290)

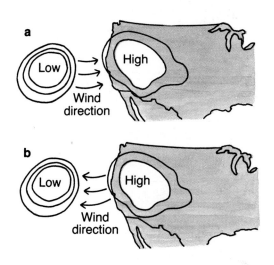

Lesson 2 Review

1. What is an air mass? (p. 292)

2. How would you describe an air mass that forms over the Sahara Desert? (p. 292)

3. What kind of weather would you expect with a cold front? A warm front? (p. 295, p. 296)

4. What kind of front does each drawing show? (p. 295, p. 296)

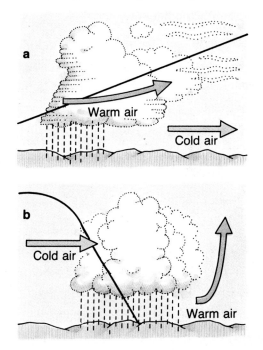

5. How are hurricanes different from tornadoes? (p. 298, p. 300)

Science Projects

1. Find out storm safety rules for your region. Present the rules to your family and make a storm safety plan for your home.

2. Make a weather station. Use instruments to measure wind speed and direction, temperature, humidity, and air pressure. Make observations every day.

Chapter 13 Double Check

Lesson 1 Review

1. What causes day and night on earth? (p. 309)

2. Suppose you live in New York and you want to telephone your friend in California. Should you call before you leave for school or wait until you get home? Why? (p. 310)

3. Which drawing shows the shape of the earth's orbit around the sun? (p. 311)

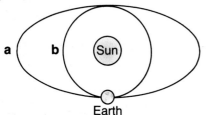

4. If you look at the night sky in March, why will you see different stars than those that shine in October? (p. 311)

5. Why is it winter in New York when it is summer in Australia? (p. 313)

Lesson 2 Review

1. Why are moon days longer than earth days? (p. 317)

2. Do people in China see a different side of the moon than you do? Explain. (p. 317)

3. Put these phases of the moon in the correct order. Start with the full moon at the top of the circle. (p. 319)

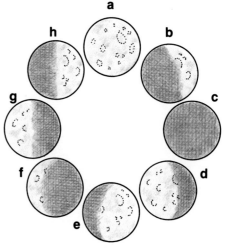

4. Draw the positions of the earth, moon, and sun in a lunar eclipse and a solar eclipse. (p. 320)

5. Why should you never look directly at the sun? (p. 322)

Science Projects

1. Make models of the earth and moon. Use your models to demonstrate to the class what happens during lunar and solar eclipses.

2. Get monthly star charts at a library. Use them to see how the night sky changes.

Chapter 14 Double Check

Lesson 1 Review

1. Name the four parts of blood. (p. 337)

2. Put the letters in the correct order to show how blood flows through the heart. (p. 339)

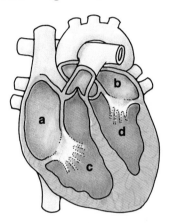

3. Which kind of blood vessel carries nutrients to your cells? (p. 340)

4. How are wastes removed from your body? (p. 342)

Lesson 2 Review

1. What does the respiratory system transport? (p. 346)

2. What are the parts of the respiratory system? Tell what each part does. (p. 345)

3. Does the diaphragm contract during inhaling or exhaling? (p. 346)

Lesson 3 Review

1. What are three good health habits? Tell how they can help keep you healthy. (p. 348)

2. Which blood vessel below probably belongs to someone who ate a diet high in fat? (p. 348)

3. How does cigarette smoking affect the respiratory system? (p. 349)

4. Tell what doctors may do to treat these transport system problems. (p. 350)
   a. Uneven heartbeat
   b. Kidney disease
   c. Damaged blood vessels

Science Projects

1. Make anti-smoking posters to display in your school.

2. Visit a blood bank. Find out how blood is obtained, stored, and used. Report to your class.

3. Tell your family what you have learned about transport systems. Make a family plan to keep your transport systems healthy. Discuss the plan with your family doctor.

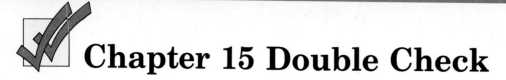

Chapter 15 Double Check

Lesson 1 Review

1. Why does a healthy person sometimes need drugs? (p. 359)

2. What kinds of drugs can you buy at a supermarket without a doctor's permission? (p. 359)

3. Tell how each of these drugs affect the body. (p. 359)
   a. Aspirin
   b. Measles vaccine
   c. Penicillin

4. Why should you read the label of any drug before you take it? (p. 361)

5. What are these people doing wrong? Explain. (p. 362)

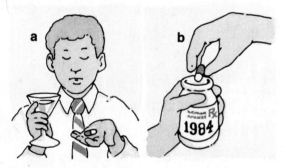

Lesson 2 Review

1. How can a drug be both helpful and harmful? (p. 364)

2. If a person drinks too much alcohol, why should he or she not drive a car? (p. 366)

3. What kind of drug does each substance drawn below contain? (p. 366)

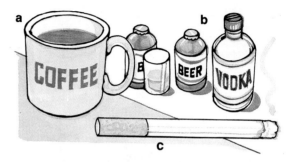

Lesson 3 Review

1. What is the best way to avoid drug abuse? (p. 371)

2. List three reasons not to use drugs. (p. 371)

3. Draw ten things you like to do instead of using drugs. (p. 372)

Science Projects

1. Ask your parents to help you make a drug survey of your home. Make sure all drugs are out of the reach of children.

2. Find out what vaccines you have been given. Make a chart to show when you received them and what diseases they prevent.

3. Make a "How to Say No to Drugs" poster to display in your school.

Glossary

Pronunciation Key					
Respelling	**Example**	**Respelling**	**Example**	**Respelling**	**Example**
a	hat (HAT)	eh	let (LEHT)	oy	voice (VOYS)
ah	hot (HAHT)	eye	ice (EYES)	u	put (PUT)
ai	care (KAIR)	ih	pin (PIHN)	uh	cup (KUHP)
aw	all (AWL)	oh	grow (GROH)	ur	term (TURM)
ay	age (AYJ)	oo	rule (ROOL)	y	five (FYV)
ee	leaf (LEEF)	ow	house (HOWS)		

Adapted from *The World Book Encyclopedia*, © 1988. Used by permission.

acceleration any change in the speed or direction of an object (p. 188)

air mass a large body of air with the same temperature and amount of moisture throughout (p. 292)

amphibian a cold-blooded vertebrate that can live in water or on land (p. 46)

amplitude the amount of energy in a sound wave (p. 169)

anesthetic (AN uhs THEHT ihk) a drug that can reduce or remove the pain of injury or illness (p. 361)

antenna a feelerlike sense organ common to arthropods (p. 29)

antibiotic a drug that seeks out and destroys harmful bacteria (p. 360)

artery a blood vessel carrying blood from the heart to body cells (p. 340)

arthropod (AHR thruh pahd) a joint-legged animal with a segmented body, exoskeleton, and antennas (p. 28)

atom the smallest particle of an element that can exist and keep the element's chemical properties (p. 141)

axis an imaginary line, passing through the North and South Poles, around which the earth spins (p. 309)

biomass the remains or wastes of plants and animals (p. 220)

biome a large region of the earth with similar temperature, rainfall, and kinds of organisms (p. 104)

blizzard a blinding snowstorm with very strong winds (p. 299)

breaker a wave that breaks along the shore (p. 263)

bronchi (BRAHNG ky) the two tubes through which air enters the lungs (p. 345)

caffeine (KAF EEN) a stimulant found in coffee, tea, chocolate, and other foods (p. 367)

capillary a blood vessel that connects an artery and a vein (p. 340)

carnivore (KAHR nuh vawr) an animal that eats only animals (p. 57)

cast a fossil that has the same shape as the original organism (p. 241)

chlorophyll (KLAWR uh fihl) the green-colored substance in plants that absorbs energy from sunlight (p. 71)

chloroplast (KLAWR uh plast) plant cell part that contains chlorophyll; where photosynthesis occurs in a plant (p. 71)

circulatory system (SER kyuh luh TAWR ee SIHS tuhm) the group of organs that carries nutrients, oxygen, and other substances to all cells of the body (p. 337)

cirrus cloud a thin, wispy cloud mostly made of ice crystals (p. 289)

climate the average weather in one place over a long time (p. 106)

climax community a community with stable plant populations (p. 95)

cochlea (KAHK lee uh) the snail-shaped, fluid-filled part of the inner ear (p. 177)

cold front a boundary formed when cold air pushes into a mass of warm air; violent weather usually occurs along a cold front (p. 294)

cold-blooded having a body temperature that changes with the surrounding temperature (p. 43)

community all the different populations in a given area (p. 85)

compound a substance formed when two or more elements chemically combine (p. 144)

continental shelf the ocean bottom closest to the shoreline (p. 270)

continental slope the steep region of the ocean that drops from the continental shelf to the deep ocean floor (p. 271)

crest highest part of a wave (p. 262)

crustacean (KRUHS TAY shuhn) a hard-covered arthropod with two main body parts, four or more pairs of legs, and two pairs of antennas (p. 31)

cumulus cloud a puffy cloud that forms at almost any altitude (p. 289)

decibel the unit of measure for the loudness of a sound (p. 171)

404

depressant a drug that slows down actions of the nervous system (p. 366)

desert a biome with high daytime temperatures and very little rainfall (p. 116)

diaphragm (DY uh fram) a muscle that contracts and moves down when a person breathes in (p. 345)

drug any substance that has an effect on the way the human body works (p. 358)

echo a sound that you hear repeated many times as the sound reflects off hard objects (p. 166)

ecosystem a community and its non-living things (p. 85)

electron a particle with a negative electric charge that moves around the nucleus of an atom (p. 142)

element a substance that cannot be changed to a simpler substance (p. 139)

ellipse a flattened circle; the shape of the earth's orbit (p. 311)

endoskeleton (EHN doh SKEHL uh tuhn) a skeleton inside the body of a vertebrate (p. 42)

energy the ability to do work (p. 208)

energy pyramid a model of the way energy flows in an ecosystem (p. 88)

environment the surroundings of a living thing (p. 84)

era one of four large units of time dividing the earth's past (p. 246)

exoskeleton (EHK soh SKEHL uh tuhn) a hard outer covering that protects the bodies of arthropods (p. 29)

first law of motion Newton's observation that objects at rest stay at rest and objects in motion stay in motion unless acted upon by a force (p. 191)

fission (FIHSH uhn) the splitting of an atom's nucleus (p. 214)

fossil the remains or print of a dead organism that is usually found in rock layers (p. 241)

fossil fuel an energy source that formed from organisms that died long ago; oil, coal, or natural gas (p. 211)

frequency the measure of the number of times a sound source vibrates in one second (p. 169)

friction a force that resists motion between two objects in contact (p. 199)

front a boundary formed where two different air masses meet (p. 294)

geothermal energy energy from heat trapped inside the earth (p. 218)

gill a featherlike stucture that fish use to take in oxygen (p. 43)

grassland a grassy biome with little rainfall and great changes in daily temperature (p. 118)

gravity a force that pulls all things toward each other (p. 197)

hallucinogen (huh LOO sn uh jen) a drug that changes the way users understand the world (p. 367)

herbivore (HER buh vawr) an animal that eats only plants (p. 57)

humidity the amount of water vapor in the air (p. 288)

hurricane a storm with circular high winds and heavy rains that forms over an ocean (p. 300)

hydroelectric power electricity produced by capturing the energy of flowing water (p. 213)

hydrosphere all of the earth's water (p. 260)

index fossil a fossil that helps scientists date rock layers (p. 243)

invertebrate (ihn VER tuh briht) an animal without a backbone (p. 18)

ion (EYE uhn) an atom that has lost or gained at least one electron and has a positive or negative charge (p. 146)

kidney an organ that removes waste water from blood (p. 342)

lunar eclipse the movement of the moon through earth's shadow (p. 320)

mammal a warm-blooded vertebrate that has milk glands and hair (p. 55)

mantle a tough outer covering that protects the bodies of mollusks (p. 25)

mid-ocean ridge a large underwater mountain range (p. 273)

mixture a combination of two or more substances that are not chemically joined (p. 150)

mold a fossil that is a hollow space in rock left by a dead organism (p. 241)

molecule a group of atoms linked together by shared electrons (p. 147)

mollusk an invertebrate with a soft body usually covered by a shell (p. 24)

molt to shed (p. 29)

motion a change of position (p. 186)

narcotic a powerful painkilling drug (p. 366)

neutron (NOO trahn) a particle with no electric charge that is found in the nucleus of an atom (p. 142)

newton a unit of measure for the force of gravity, or weight (p. 198)

nicotine (NIK uh TEEN) stimulant found in tobacco (p. 367)

nitrogen cycle the movement of nitrogen in the environment (p. 92)

nonrenewable resource a source of energy not replaceable within a person's lifetime (p. 210)

nuclear energy the energy locked up in the nucleus of an atom (p. 214)

nucleus (NOO klee uhs) the central core of an atom made of protons and neutrons (p. 141)

omnivore (AHM nih vawr) an animal that eats plants and animals (p. 57)

orbit the path of the earth around the sun (p. 311)

over-the-counter drug a medicine that may be used without a doctor's permission (p. 359)

oxygen–carbon dioxide cycle the recycling of oxygen and carbon dioxide in the environment (p. 76, p. 91)

parasite an organism that feeds and lives on another organism (p. 21)

phases of the moon the changes in the moon's appearance (p. 318)

phloem (FLOH ehm) tubes that carry sugar from the leaves to all parts of a plant (p. 68)

photosynthesis (foh toh SIHN thuh sihs) the process by which a plant makes sugar from carbon dioxide and water in sunlight (p. 70)

pitch the highness or lowness of a sound (p. 170)

plains large flat areas at the ocean bottom (p. 272)

plankton tiny organisms that drift about in bodies of water (p. 122)

plasma (PLAZ muh) the liquid part of the blood (p. 337)

platelet a piece of a cell that helps the blood to clot (p. 338)

population all of the same type of organisms living in a place (p. 84)

precipitation any form of moisture that falls to the earth (p. 107)

prescription drug a medicine that must be used only with a doctor's permission (p. 359)

proton a particle with a positive electric charge that is found in the nucleus of an atom (p. 142)

recycle to use again (p. 224)

red blood cell a blood cell that carries oxygen to the body cells (p. 338)

reference object an object used to give clues to the motion of another object (p. 186)

renewable resource a source of energy that can be easily replaced (p. 210)

reptile a cold-blooded vertebrate with scaly skin that lives on land (p. 46)

respiration (REHS puh RAY shuhn) the process by which living things use oxygen to release energy in food (p. 75)

respiratory system (REHS puhr uh tawr ee SIHS tuhm) the group of organs that brings air into and out of the body (p. 345)

revolution the motion of the earth around the sun (p. 311)

rift valley a valley that runs the length of a mid-ocean ridge (p. 274)

root hair part of a plant that absorbs water; grows from the tip of the root into the soil (p. 67)

rotation the daily turning of the earth on its axis (p. 309)

satellite an object that revolves around a larger object (p. 316)

seamount a large underwater mountain (p. 272)

second law of motion Newton's observation that an object's acceleration depends on its mass and the size and direction of the force acting on it (p. 193)

solar eclipse movement of the earth through the moon's shadow; the partial or full blocking of the sun by the moon (p. 321)

solar energy energy from the sun (p. 217)

solute the subtance of lesser quantity in a solution (p. 153)

solution a mixture of substances that are evenly mixed and do not easily separate (p. 152)

solvent the substance of greater quantity in a solution (p. 153)

sound wavelength the distance a sound wave travels between two bunches of molecules (p. 168)

speed the distance an object moves in a certain amount of time (p. 187)

stationary front a weather front that does not move (p. 295)

stimulant a drug that speeds up the nervous system (p. 367)

stomata (STOH muh tuh) holes on the underside of leaves through which gases enter and exit (p. 68)

stratus cloud a cloud forming a wide sheet across the sky with its base near the earth's surface (p. 289)

succession a change in the kind of organisms that live in a place (p. 95)

taiga a biome with long, cold winters, short, cool summers, and trees that make cones (p. 112)

temperate forest a biome with cold winters, warm summers, plenty of rain, and trees that lose their leaves in winter (p. 113)

tentacle (TEHN tuh kuhl) a movable, fingerlike body part (p. 20)

third law of motion Newton's observation that every force has an equal and opposite force (p. 194)

tidal energy the energy from rising and falling sea water (p. 219)

tide the slow change in an ocean's water level (p. 266)

tornado a small, violent windstorm in the form of a rotating column of air (p. 298)

trace fossil a fossil that shows an animal's activity (p. 242)

trench a deep ocean valley (p. 273)

tropical rain forest a biome with heavy rains, strong sunlight, and a year-round growing season (p. 114)

trough (TRAWF) the lowest part of a wave (p. 262)

true form fossil the unchanged remains of an organism or part of an organism (p. 242)

tuber the underground stem of a plant, where starch is stored (p. 72)

tundra a treeless biome in which the layer of soil beneath the surface is always frozen (p. 110)

vaccine (VAK SEEN) a small amount of a dead or weakened germs taken so that the immune system will fight a disease (p. 359)

vacuum a space empty of all matter (p. 165)

vein a blood vessel that carries blood from body cells to the heart (p. 340)

vertebrate (VER tuh briht) an animal with a backbone (p. 18)

vibration a rapid back-and-forth movement (p. 162)

vocal cords thin, elastic bands of body tissue that vibrate to produce sound (p. 175)

warm-blooded being able to keep a steady body temperature (p. 52)

warm front a boundary formed when a warm air mass pushes into a cold air mass; light rain usually falls along a warm front (p. 294)

wave height the vertical distance from the crest to the trough of a wave (p. 262)

wavelength the distance from one wave crest to the next, or one wave trough to the next (p. 262)

weather the condition of the air at a given time and place (p. 286)

weight the pull of gravity on an object (p. 198)

white blood cell a blood cell that helps the body fight infection and disease (p. 338)

xylem (ZY luhm) tubes in plant stems through which water moves from the roots to the leaves (p. 68)

Index

A

Acceleration, 188
Addiction, 368
Agronomist, 131
Air, water in, 288–289
Air masses, 292–295
Air pressure, 290
    storms and, 297
Amphibians, 46–48, 58,
    248
Amplitude, 169
Anesthetics, 361
Animals
    cold-blooded, 43
    hollow-bodied, 20, 30
    joint-legged, 28–34
    shell, 24–25
    simple, 18–22
    spiny-skinned, 26, 30
    warm-blooded, 52, 55
Antennas, 29, 31, 32
Antibiotics, 360–361
Aquarium guide, 131
Arteries, 340
Arthropods, 28–34
Artificial hearts, 352
Artificial reefs, 98
Atoms, 141–142, 146–
    147
    energy from, 214
    microscrope scanning,
        156
Axis of earth, 309

B

Biomass, 220
Biomes, 104–106, 110–
    118
    plant and animal life
        in, 108
Biosphere II, 126
Birds, 53–54, 58
Blizzards, 297, 299
Blood, 337–338
    cleaning, 342
    delivering oxygen to,
        345
Blood vessels, 340–341
    fat clogging, 348
    replacing, 350
Breakers, 263
Breathing, 346
Bronchi, 345

C

Caffeine, 367
Capillaries, 340, 346
Carbon dating, 254
Carbon dioxide, 247
    photosynthesis and,
        71, 91
    respiration and, 75–
        76
    levels in air, 78
Carnivores, 57
Cartilage, 44
Casts, 241

Cenozoic Era, 251–252
Centipedes, 34
Chemical bonds, 145–
    147
Chemical engineer, 231
Chemical formulas, 148
Chlorophyll, 71
Chloroplasts, 71
Circulatory system,
    336–342
Cirrus clouds, 289
Climate, 106–107
Climax plants, 105, 113
Clouds, 289, 295–298
Cochlea, 177
Cold-blooded, 43, 46, 49
Cold fronts, 294
Color of the oceans, 328
Communication
    satellites, 324
Community, 85
    climax, 95
Compounds, 144–147
    formulas of, 148
Continental shelf, 270
Continental slope, 271,
    273
Control, 10
Crest, 262
Crustaceans, 31
Cumulonimbus clouds,
    289, 298
Cumulus clouds, 288

D

Day and night, 309–310
Decibels, 171, 178
Depressants, 366
Desert habitat, 86
Deserts, 105–107, 116–117
Diaphragm, 345–346
Dinosaurs, 249–250
Dissolving, 152–153
Doppler radar, 302
Drafter, 231
Drug rehabilitation counselor, 379
Drugs, 378
  effects of, 358–362
  harmful, 364–368
  helpful, 358–362
  misused, 366–368
  new ways to make, 374
  precautions for, 361–362
  saying no to, 371–372
  why people take, 370–371

E

Ear, 176–177
Eardrum, 176, 178
Earth
  movement of, 308–314
  revolution of, 311
Echo sounding, 269
Echoes, 166

Eclipses
  lunar, 320
  solar, 321–322
Ecosystems, 84–88
  cycles in, 90–92
  freshwater, 120–122
  saltwater, 123–124
  succession in, 94–96
Electron cloud atom, 141–142
Electrons, 141–142, 146–147
Elements, 139–141
Ellipses, 311
Emergency medical technician, 379
Endoskeleton, 42
Energy
  biomass, 220
  food, 74–75
  geothermal, 218
  nuclear, 214, 230
  pathways of, 209
  plants and, 68–69
  solar, 208–209, 217
  sound as, 163
  tidal, 219
  wind, 219
Energy conservation, 222–224
  community, 224
  home, 223
Energy pyramid, 88
Energy resources, 208–214
  future, 216–220

Environment, 84–88
Eras, 246–252
Exercising, transport systems and, 349
Exoskeleton, 29

F

Fat, 348–349
Feeding relationships, 87
First law of motion, 190–191
Fish, 42–44, 58, 122, 124, 248
Fission, 214
Flatworms, 21, 30
Food
  getting energy from, 74–75
  from the ocean, 278
Foodmaking in plants, 66–72
Force, 191
  acceleration and, 192–194
Forest ranger, 131
Fossil fuels, 211–212
Fossils, 241–244, 252
  carbon dating, 254
  cast, 241
  index, 243
  mold, 241
  petrified wood, 242
  trace, 242
  true form, 242
Frequency, 169

Freshwater ecosystems, 120–122
Friction, 196, 199–200
Fronts, 294–296
  cold, 294, 296
  stationary, 295
  warm, 294–295
Fusion, 226

G
Gasohol, 220
Genetic engineering, 374
Geologic eras, 246–252
Geothermal energy, 218
Gills, 43, 46–47
Grasslands, 105, 118
Gravity, 196–198

H
Hallucinogens, 366, 367
Hearing, 176–178
Heart, 338–339
  artificial, 352
  artificial pacemaker for, 350
Heart transplant, 350
Herbivores, 57
High tides, 266
Human growth hormone, 374
Humidity, 288
Hurricanes, 297, 300
Hydroelectric power, 213
Hydrosphere, 260

I
Immune system, drugs and, 359–360
Index fossils, 243
Inner ear, 176
Insects, 32–34, 114, 117, 118, 122, 248
Invertebrates, 18–22, 24–26, 28–34, 42
Ions, 146

J
Jarvik-7 heart, 352
Jellyfish, 20, 30, 247

K
Kelp, 278
Kidneys, 341
  artificial, 350
Krill, 60

L
Leaves
  foodmaking in, 70–71
  plant, 68–69
Limiting factors, 86
Low tides, 266
Lunar eclipse, 320
Lungs, 47, 48, 53, 55, 345–346

M
Mammals, 55–58, 250, 251
Mantles, 25
Mapmaker, 329

Mass, 198
  acceleration and, 192–193
Matter, 138–142
Mesozoic Era, 249–250
Metals, 140
Microgravity, 202
Microscope, scanning atoms, 156
Middle ear, 176–177
Mid-ocean ridges, 273–274
Millipedes, 34, 248
Mixtures, 150–154
Molds, 241
Molecules, 147
Mollusks, 24–25, 30
Molting, 29
Moon
  eclipses of, 320
  movements of, 316–322
  phases of, 318–319
  tides and, 266
Motion, 186
  laws of, 190–194

N
Narcotics, 366
Neutrons, 141–142
Nicotine, 367
Night and day, 309–310
Nitrogen cycle, 92
Nonrenewable resources, 210
Nuclear energy, 214

Nuclear power plant
accidents, 230
Nuclear reactors, 214
Nucleus, 141–142

O
Ocean bottom, 268–274
Ocean currents, 264–265
Ocean resources, 276–278
Ocean water, 260–266
Oceans, color of, 328
Omnivores, 57
Orbits, 311
Outer ear, 176
Over-the-counter drugs, 359
Oxygen, 145, 247
delivering to blood, 345
photosynthesis and, 91
Oxygen–carbon dioxide cycle, 76, 91

P
Pain relievers, 361
Paleozoic Era, 248
Parasites, 21
Penicillin, 361
Pesticides, 36
Petrified wood, 242
Pharmacist, 379
Phases of the moon, 318–319

Phloem, 68
Photosynthesis, 70–71, 91
respiration compared, 75
Pitch, 170
Plains, 272
Plankton, 122–124
Plants, climax, 105, 113
Plasma, 337
Platelets, 337–338
Polio, 360
Populations, 84–85
Precambrian Era, 247
Precipitation, 107
Predators, 87
Prescription drugs, 359
Prey, 87
Protons, 141–142

R
Radar, Doppler, 302
Rain, 107, 296, 298
Rain forests, 78, 105, 114–115
Recycling, 224
Red blood cells, 337–338, 346
Reefs, artificial, 98
Reference objects, 186
Renewable resources, 210
Reptiles, 46, 48–50, 58
Respiration, 74–75, 91
photosynthesis compared, 75

Respiratory system, 344–346
smoking and, 349
Revolution of earth, 311
Rift valleys, 274
Robot submarines, 280
Rock layers, 239–240
Root hairs, 67
Roots, plant, 67
Rotation of earth, 309
Roundworms, 21, 30

S
Saltwater ecosystems, 84–85, 123–124
Satellites, 316
communications, 324
Science fairs, 386
Sea water, 260–261
energy from, 226
minerals in, 260–261, 276–277
Seamounts, 272
Seasons, 312–313
Second law of motion. 192–193
Segmented worms, 22, 30
Senses, 130
Smoking, respiratory system and, 349
Solar eclipse, 321–322
Solar energy, 217
Solutes, 153
Solutions, 152–153
Solvents, 153

Sonic booms, 180
Sounds
    hearing, 176–178
    loudness of, 171
    making, 174–175
    pitch of, 170
    quality of, 172
    reflection and
        absorption of, 166
    source of, 162–163
    transmission of, 164–
        165
Sound wavelength, 168
Sound waves, 168–169
Speed, 187
Speed of sound, 180
Spiders, 30–32, 118
Sponges, 19, 30, 247
Starch storage in
    plants, 72
Stationary fronts, 295
Stems, plant, 68–69
Stimulants, 366, 367
Stomata, 68, 70, 75
Storm fronts, 294–300
Storms, 292–300
Stratus clouds, 289
Submarines, robot, 280
Succession, 94–96
Sugar storage in plants,
    72
Sun
    eclipse of, 321–322
    energy from, 208–
        209, 217
Suspensions, 154

T
Tiaga, 104, 112
Telephone-line installer,
    231
Temperate forests, 105,
    113
Temperature, air
    pressure and, 290
Tentacles, 20, 25
Third law of motion,
    193–194
Thunderstorms, 297
Tidal energy, 219
Tide pools, 123
Tides, 266
Tokamak, 226
Tornadoes, 297–299
Trace fossils, 242
Trenches, 273
Tropical rain forests,
    104, 114–115
Troughs, 262
True form fossils, 242
Tubers, 72
Tundra, 104, 105, 110–
    111

V
Vaccines, 359–360
Vacuum, 165
Variables, 10
Veins, 340
    root, 67
Vertebrates, 18, 42, 58
Vibrations, 162
Vocal cords, 175

W
Warm-blooded, 52, 55
Warm fronts, 294
Water, 145, 247
    in air, 288–289
    energy from, 213
    ocean, 260–266
    photosynthesis and,
        71
    plants and, 68–69
    sea, 260–261
Water cycle, 90
Wave height, 262
Wavelength, 262
Waves, 262–265
Weather
    causes of, 286–290
    predicting changes in,
        302
Weather fronts, 295–
    297
Weather observer, 329
Weight, 198
Wheels, friction and, 200
White blood cells, 337–
    338
Wind, air temperature
    and, 287
Wind energy, 219
Worms, 247
    flatworms, 21, 30
    roundworms, 21, 30
    segmented, 22, 30

X
Xylem, 68

Acknowledgements

Illustration Acknowledgements

Barbara Hoopes Ambler p. 22, 25, 26, 31, 43, 47, 53, 55
Barbara Barnett p. 382TM, 383BR, 355B
Sherry Balestra p. 362, 372
Cynthia Brodie p. 197
Carl Dennis Buell p. 246, 247, 248, 249, 250, 251, 252
Kirk Caldwell p. 384T
Polly Christensen p. 385M
Wayne Clark p. 382B, 384M, L, R
Cyndie Clark-Huegel p. 42, 45, 63, 81, 101, 129, 159, 183, 205, 229, 257, 283, 305, 327, 355, 360, 377
Leslie Dunlap p. 388B, 390A/B, 391B, 394A/B, 396A, 398A, 399B, 400A/B, 401A/B
Susan Jaekel p. 387
Jean Helmer p. 19, 20, 30, 58, 67, 68, 69, 70, 71, 74
Marilyn Hill p. 384B, 385TL/TR
Intergraphics p. 261, 262, 263, 265, 266, 268, 269, 271, 272, 288, 289, 295, 296, 297, 299, 300
JAK Graphics p. 106, 111, 112, 113, 114, 116, 118, 264, 270, 293
Kathie Kelleher p. 389A/B, 392A, 393A/B, 397A, 399A
Craig Marshall p. 107, 164R, 168, 171, 209, 232
Masami Miyamoto p. 156, 213, 214, 217, 218, 240, 243, 338, 360
Deborah Morse p. 141, 142, 146, 147, 157, 164L, 168, 169, 170, 290
Susan Nelson p. 223
Mel Petersen & Associates/Michael Courtney p. 175, 176, 177, 338T, 339, 340, 342T, 345, 346/**Michael Woods** p. 44, 54, 166
Pronk & Associates p. 273, 309, 310, 311, 312, 313, 314, 317, 318, 319, 320, 321
   P&A/Steve Pilcher p. 84, 85, 88, 91, 92, 96, 115,
   P&A/Greg Ruhl p. 192
Phyllis Rockne p. 383TL/TR/BL
Carla Simmons p. 33
Joel Snyder p. 388A, 391A, 392B, 395A/B, 396B, 397B, 398B, 402A/B
Kate Sweeney p. 336, 341

Photo Acknowledgements

4B Kirk Aeder/Focus West; 4CB Gary Withey/Bruce Coleman Inc.; 4CT Vic Huber/West Light; 4T James Balog/Black Star; 8 Runk-Schoenberger/Grant Heilman Photography

Unit 1: 14–15 James Balog/Black Star; **Chapter 1:** 16 © W. Gregory Brown/Animals, Animals; 17BR Barry E. Parker/Bruce Coleman Inc.; 17L Brian Parker/Tom Stack & Associates; 17TC Neil G. McDaniel/Tom Stack & Associates; 17TR Neil G. McDaniel/Tom Stack & Associates; 18 © Chris Newbert/Bruce Coleman Inc.; 19 Breck P. Kent/Animals, Animals; 20BR Runk-Schoenberger/Grant Heilman Photography; 20TL Rod Bonand/Bruce Coleman Inc.; 21L E.J. Cable/Tom Stack & Associates; 21R Runk-Schoenberger/Grant Heilman Photography; 22 OSF/Animals, Animals; 24C Runk-Schoenberger/Grant Heilman Photography; 24L © Robert Maier/Animals, Animals; 24R © Ralph Oberlander/Stock, Boston; 26 Gary Milburn/Tom Stack & Associates; 28L Ron Goor/Bruce Coleman Inc.; 28R E.R. Degginger/Animals, Animals; 29BL Robert P. Carr/Bruce Coleman Inc.; 29R Dr. E.R. Degginger; 29TR Paul Skeicher/Rainbow; 31 Newbert/Bruce Coleman Inc.; 32 Dr. E.R. Degginger; 33C © James H. Carmichael/Bruce Coleman Inc.; 33L OSF/Animals, Animals; 33R D.R. Specker/Animals, Animals; 34L © Jack Dermid/Bruce Coleman Inc.; 34R Dwight R. Kuhn; 36B E.R. Degginger/Animals, Animals; 36T Dwight R. Kuhn; 39 W. Gregory Brown/Animals, Animals

Chapter 2: 40 Kim Taylor/Bruce Coleman Inc.; 41BR Zig Leszczynski/Animals, Animals; 41L Breck P. Kent/Animals, Animals; 41T Grant Heilman Photography; 42 Ed Robinson/Tom Stack & Associates; 44 Brian Parker/Tom Stack & Associates; 46BL Zig Leszczynski/Animals, Animals; 46R Dwight R. Kuhn; 46TL Jane Burton/Bruce Coleman Inc.; 47L Dwight R. Kuhn; 47R Dwight R. Kuhn; 48BL Dwight R. Kuhn; 48BR Kerry T. Givens/Tom Stack & Associates; 48T J. Cancalos/Tom Stack & Associates; 49 Bob McKeever/Tom Stack & Associates; 50C © 1983 Frans Lanting; 50L John Cancalosi/Tom Stack & Associates; 50R Sharon Gerig/Tom Stack & Associates; 52 E. A. O'Connell/Animals, Animals; 53R Dr. E. R. Degginger; 55 P. J. Heller; 56 John Cancalosi/Tom Stack & Associates; 56C Hans & Judy Beste/Animals, Animals; 56R F. Erize/Bruce Coleman Inc.; 57C Runk-Schoenberger/Grant Heilman Photography; 57L Grant Heilman Photography; 57R Anup Shah/Animals, Animals; 60B Jeff Foott/Tom Stack & Associates; 60T OSF/Animals, Animals; 63 Kim Taylor/Bruce Coleman Inc.

Chapter 3: 64 Gerard Murrell/Bruce Coleman Inc.; 65BR Barry L. Runk/Grant Heilman Photography; 66 Grant Heilman Photography; 67 Barry L. Runk/Grant Heilman Photography; 68B Terry Ashley/Tom Stack & Associates; 68TL E.R. Degginger/Bruce Coleman Inc.; 72C John Colwell/Grant Heilman Photography; 72L Dwight R. Kuhn; 72R Norman Owen Tomalin/Bruce Coleman Inc.; 74 L.L.T. Rhodes/Earth Scenes; 75 John Chellman/Earth Scenes; 76 Patti Murray/Animals, Animals; 78B Claus Meyer/Black Star; 78T Gerald Corsi/Tom Stack & Associates; 81 Gerard Murrell/Bruce Coleman Inc.

Chapter 4: 82 Martin W. Grosnick/Bruce Coleman Inc.; 83BR Phil Degginger; 83TR Jeff Foott/Bruce Coleman Inc.; 86C Dave Millert/Tom Stack & Associates; 86L Dr. E.R. Degginger; 86R Peter Ward/Bruce Coleman Inc.; 87B Jen & Des Bartlett/Bruce Coleman Inc.; 87T Marc & Evelyn Bernstein/Woodfin Camp & Associates; 90 Grant Heilman Photography; 94 Dr. E.R. Degginger; 95C Bob & Ira Spring; 95TL Bob & Ira Spring; 95TR Bob & Ira Spring; 98 Tim Rock/Animals, Animals; 101 Martin W. Grosnick/Bruce Coleman Inc.

Chapter 5: 102 John Shaw/Bruce Coleman Inc.; 103 Dr. E.R. Degginger; 103L Brian Parker/Tom Stack & Associates; 103TR Thomas Kitchin/Tom Stack & Associates; 104C Jack Covffer/Bruce Coleman Inc.; 104L Tom Leigh/Rainbow; 104R Dr. E.R. Degginger; 105C Stephenie S. Ferguson; 105L Breck P. Kent/Earth Scenes; 105R John Shaw/Tom Stack & Associates; 108L Dr. E.R. Degginger; 108R Eric Crichton/Bruce Coleman Inc; 110L David C. Fritts/Animals, Animals; 110R Johnny Johnson/Animals, Animals; 111BR Caron Pepper/Tom Stack & Associates; 111C Dale Johnson/Tom Stack & Associates; 111L Breck P. Kent/Earth Scenes; 111TR Bob & Clara Calhoun/Bruce Coleman Inc.; 112BL E.R. Degginger/Animals, Animals; 112C Brian Parker/Tom Stack & Associates; 112R Runk-Schoenberger/Grant Heilman Photography; 112TL Dwight R. Kuhn/Bruce Coleman Inc.; 113BR L. L. Rue/Bruce Coleman Inc.; 113C Dr. E.R. Degginger; 113L John Shaw/Bruce Coleman Inc.; 113TR Joseph Van Wormer/Bruce Coleman Inc.; 114C © 1984 Frans Lanting; 114L Wardene Weisser/Bruce Coleman Inc.; 114R Sydney Thomson/Earth Scenes; 116BR Zig Lesczynski/Animals, Animals; 116C Jim Brandenburg/Woodfin Camp & Associates; 116L M.P.L. Fogden/Bruce Coleman Inc.; 116TR Zig Leszczynski/Animals, Animals; 117BL Lois & George Cox/Bruce Coleman Inc.; 117C Dr. E.R. Degginger; 117R Patti Murray/Earth Scenes; 118BL Jim P. Garrison/Rainbow; 118C Thomas Kitchin/Tom Stack & Associates; 118R Jim Brandenberg/Woodfin Camp & Associates; 118TL Roger & Donna Aitkenhead/Animals, Animals; 120 Tom Walker/Stock, Boston; 121L Dr. E.R. Degginger; 121R Millard H. Sharp/Black Star; 122BL Breck P. Kent/Animals, Animals; 122C Michael Fogden/Earth Scenes; 122TL Mary Clay/Tom Stack & Associates; 122TR John Gerlach/Tom Stack & Associates; 123BR Dr. E.R. Degginger; 123C Alfred Owczarzak/Taurus Photos; 123L John Gerlach/Animals, Animals; 123TR L.L.T. Rhodes/Animals, Animals; 124BL Erich Simmons/Stock, Boston; 124C E.R. Degginger/Animals, Animals; 124TL Jeff Foott/Bruce Coleman Inc.; 124TR Brian Parker/Tom Stack & Associates; 126B Ed Robinson/Tom Stack & Associates; 126T D. Wilder/Tom Stack & Associates; 129 John Shaw/Bruce Coleman Inc.; 130 Dr. Sheila Stiles; 131B Mike Andrews/Earth Scenes; 131C Julie Habel/West Light; 131T Hank Morgan/Rainbow; 132 Bonnie Rauch/The Image Bank West; 133C John Colwell/Grant Heilman Photography; 133L G.I. Bernard/Earth Scenes; 133R Runk-Schoenberger/Grant Heilman Photography

Unit 2: 134–135 Vic Huber/West Light; **Chapter 6:** 138 Grant Heilman Photography; 139C Dr. E.R. Degginger; 140B F. Stuart Westmorland/Tom Stack & Associates; 144 The Bettmann Archive, Inc.; 145L © Fundamental Photographs; 145R Richard Megna/Fundamental Photographs; 147 D. Wilder/Tom Stack & Associates; 148C Ann Duncan/Tom Stack & Associates; 148C (inset) John Shaw/Tom Stack & Associates; 148L Zig Leszczynski/Earth Scenes; 148L (inset) OSF/Earth Scenes; 148R Ralph A. Reinhold/Earth Scenes; 154B Jerry Howard/Stock, Boston

Chapter 7: 160 David Madison/Bruce Coleman Inc.; 162 Hans Pfletschinger/Peter Arnold Inc.; 163C Dan McCoy/Rainbow; 163L Ron Goor/Bruce Coleman Inc.; 163R Bruce Curtis/Peter Arnold Inc.; 165C Brian Parker/Tom Stack & Associates; 165L Robert McKenzie/Tom Stack & Associates; 165R Dr. E.R. Degginger; 172 Debra Hershkowitz/Bruce Coleman Inc.; 180B Charles Palek/Tom Stack & Associates; 180T Charles Palek/Tom Stack & Associates; 183 David Madison/Bruce Coleman Inc.

Chapter 8: 184 Ottmar Bierwagen/Black Star; 186 Unique Technic's/Peter Arnold Inc.; 187 Focus on Sports; 188C Focus on Sports; 188L Focus on Sports; 188R Focus on Sports; 190 Peter Menzel/Stock, Boston; 193 Ralph A. Reinhold/Animals, Animals; 194B Focus on Sports; 194T NASA; 196 Tim Carlson/Stock, Boston; 197T NASA; 198 Walker Bros/Black Star; 199B Arthur Grace/Stock, Boston; 202B NASA; 202T NASA; 205 Ottmar Bierwagen/Black Star

Chapter 9: 206 Keith Gunnar/Bruce Coleman Inc.; 208 Bill Gallery/Stock, Boston; 210B Ron Watts/Black Star; 210C Stewart M. Green/Tom Stack & Associates; 210L Jim McNee/Tom Stack & Associates; 210R Peter Menzel/Stock, Boston; 211 Brian Payne/Black Star; 211R OSF/Animals, Animals; 212B Pat Lanzafield/Bruce Coleman Inc.; 212R Cameron Davidson/Bruce Coleman Inc.; 213 Richard Kolar/Earth Scenes; 214 Mike Andrews/Earth Scenes; 218 Bill Gillette/Stock, Boston; 219 Peter Menzel/Stock, Boston; 222 Bill Gillette/Stock, Boston; 226B Mark Sherman/Bruce Coleman Inc.; 226T Tom Stack/Tom Stack & Associates; 229 Keith Gunnar/Bruce Coleman Inc.; 230 Dr. Fred Begay; 231B Bruce Davidson/Magnum Photos; 231C Miriam Caravella/The Image Bank West; 231T Jay Freis/The Image Bank West

Unit 3: 234–235 Gary Withey/Bruce Coleman Inc.; **Chapter 10:** 236 T. A. Wiewandt/DRK Photo; 237BR Runk-Schoenberger/Grant Heilman Photography; 237L Grant Heilman Photography; 237TR Runk-Schoenberger/Grant Heilman Photography; 238BL Don & Pat Valenti/DRK Photo; 238R Mike Mazzaschi/Stock, Boston; 238TL T.A. Wiewandt/DRK Photo; 239 David Smart/DRK Photo; 240B W. Klek/BPS; 240T A. Nelson/Tom Stack & Associates; 241L John Pawloski/Tom Stack & Associates; 241R John Cancalosi/Peter Arnold Inc.; 242C James Blank/Stock, Boston; 242L Spencer Swanger/Tom Stack & Associates; 242R Dr. E.R. Degginger; 244 Painting by Doug Henderson; 244 (inset) Jack Horner; 254B Ronald Thomas/Bruce Coleman Inc.; 254T Malcolm S. Kirk/Peter Arnold Inc.; 257 T.A. Wiewandt/DRK Photo

Chapter 11: 258 Steve Lissau/Rainbow; 260 NASA; 261B Norman Tomalin/Bruce Coleman Inc.; 261L NASA; 261R Woods Hole Oceanographic Institution; 266L Alan Pitcairn/Grant Heilman Photography; 266R Alan Pitcairn/Grant Heilman Photography; 270B © 1984 Frans Lanting; 270T W. B. Finch/Stock, Boston; 274 Jet Propulsion Lab; 276 Eric Kroll/Taurus Photos; 277 Ron Sherman/Bruce Coleman Inc.; 278 Stephen Frisch; 280B Woods Hole Oceanographic Institution; 280T Woods Hole Oceanographic Institution; 283 Steve Lissau/Rainbow

Chapter 12: 284 Thomas Kitchin/Tom Stack & Associates; 285TR Paul Skelcher/Rainbow; 286 John Shaw/Tom Stack & Associates; 287 Glenn Short/Bruce Coleman Inc.; 290L Spencer Swanger/Tom Stack & Associates; 290R Dr. E.R. Degginger; 292 Bill Gallery/Stock, Boston; 294 John Zoiner/Peter Arnold Inc.; 297 Dan McCoy/Rainbow; 297B R.P. Kingston/Stock, Boston; 297T Dr. E.R. Degginger; 298 Dr. E.R. Degginger; 300 NASA; 302 Dr. E.R. Degginger; 305 Thomas Kitchin/Tom Stack & Associates

Chapter 13: 306 NASA; 307BR NASA; 307C NASA; 307L Jet Propulsion Lab; 307T NASA; 309L John Stern/Earth Scenes; 309R John Stern/Earth Scenes; 310CL David Overcash/Bruce Coleman Inc.; 310CR Dan McCoy/Rainbow; 310TL David Overcash/Bruce Coleman Inc.; 310TR Dan McCoy/Rainbow; 314T NASA; 316 Dr. E.R. Degginger; 317 NASA; 318 Lick Observatory; 319 Lick Observatory; 320 NASA; 321 © 1979 Hans Vehrenberg/Hansen Planetarium; 322 Kitt Peak National Observatory; 324B NASA; 324T NASA; 327 NASA; 328 Dr. Mary Gaillard; 329B Yoram Kahana/Peter Arnold Inc.; 329C Camilla Smith/Rainbow; 329T Keith Gunnar/Bruce Coleman Inc.; 330 Don & Pat Valenti/DRK Photo; 331C Hansen Planetarium/Celestron International; 331L © Hans Vehrenberg/Hansen Planetarium; 331R © 1974 Charles Capen/Hansen Planetarium

Unit 4: 332–333 Kirk Aeder/Focus West; **Chapter 14:** 334 © Lennart Nilsson from BEHOLD MAN, Little, Brown & Co., Boston; 335BR Warren Rosenberg-Iona College/BPS; 335L Makio Murayama/BPS; 335TR Jeff Persons/Stock, Boston; 336 Bob Gossington/Bruce Coleman Inc.; 336T Runk-Schoenberger/Grant Heilman Photography; 337L Richard Pasley/Stock, Boston; 337R Martin Rotker/Taurus Photos; 348 American Heart Association; 349TC Martin Rotker/Taurus Photos; 349TL Martin Rotker/Taurus Photos; 350L Martin Rotker/Taurus Photos; 350R Tom Stack/Tom Stack & Associates; 352B William Strode/Black Star; 352T Tim Kelly/Black Star; 355 © Lennart Nilsson from BEHOLD MAN, Little, Brown & Co., Boston

Chapter 15: 358L The Bettmann Archive, Inc.; 358R Patrick L. Pfister/Stock, Boston; 361 Dian Duchin/Bruce Coleman Inc.; 365 Bruce Curtis/Peter Arnold Inc.; 367 Dr. Witt/Courtesy Ann Moreton, The Spider Museum, Powhatan, Virginia; 374 Keith V. Wood/University of California, San Diego; 378 Dr. John Gavin; 379B Dan McCoy/Rainbow; 379C Rick Brown/Stock, Boston; 379T Barry L. Runk/Grant Heilman Photography; 380 Dean Abramson/Stock, Boston

Wayland Lee*/Addison-Wesley Publishing Company: 65L, 65TR, 83L, 137, 140 (except B), 145C, 146, 152, 153, 154T, 161BR, 161TR, 200T, 207BR, 207L, 207TR, 212L, 259L, 349.

All other photographs taken expressly for the publisher by Janice Sheldon.

Front Cover: E. P. I. Nancy Adams/Tom Stack & Associates
Back Cover: Kenneth W. Fink/Bruce Coleman Inc.

*Photographs taken expressly for the publisher

Special thanks to California Academy of Sciences, Department of Birds and Mammals; Bill Graham & Shoreline Amphitheater; College of Marin, Department of Chemistry; Douglas M. Green, Goldsmith, Kensington, California; East Bay Regional Park, Oakland, California; Jesuit High School, Sacramento, California; Sweet Dreams Toy Store, Berkeley, California; Arvin Elementary School, Arvin, California; California School for the Deaf, Fremont, California; Chabot Elementary School, Oakland, California; Del Dayo Elementary School, Sacramento; Ecole Bilingue French American School, Berkeley, California; Green Acres Elementary School, Bakersfield, California; Hawthorne Elementary School, Oakland, California; University of California, Department of Medical Microbiology, Berkeley, California; Washington Elementary School, Berkeley, California; Whitton Elementary School, Oakland, California; Fruitvale Junior High School, Oakland, California.